THE BASEBALL SCRAPBOOK

BREWERS
Angels
BLUE JAYS
Orioles
Athletics
RED SOX
INDIANS
Royals
Twins

Dodgers

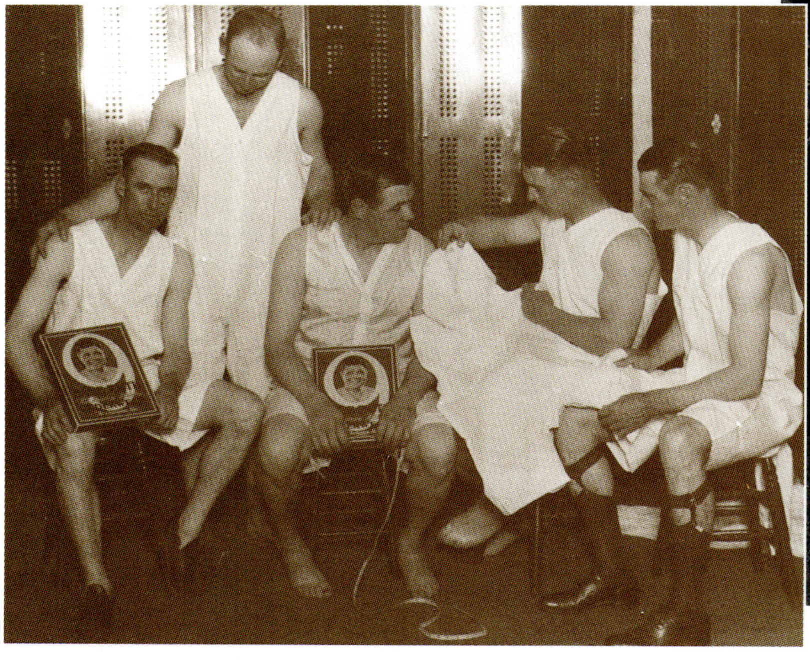

THE BASEBALL SCRAPBOOK

PETER C. BJARKMAN

JG PRESS

Published by World Publications Group, Inc.
140 Laurel Street
East Bridgewater, MA 02333
www.wrldpub.net

Copyright © 2008 World Publications Group, Inc.

All rights reserved. No part of this publication may be reproduced, stored in a retrieval system or transmitted in any form by any means, electronic, mechanical, photocopying or otherwise, without first obtaining the written permission of the copyright owner.

ISBN 1-57215-326-1
978-1-57215-326-4

Printed and bound in China by SNP Leefung Printers Limited.

2 3 4 5   06 05 03 02

This book is for John S. Bowman,
my own favorite baseball writer and
Literary Baseball's number one birddog!

Page 3:
CENTER: Boston Red Sox Cy Young Award winner Roger Clemens (left) limbers up as teammate Oil Can Boyd (center) and manager John McNamara watch other members of the team during their opening day of spring training in Winter Haven, Florida in 1987; **BOTTOM RIGHT:** World Series 1988's Most Valuable Player Orel Hershiser of the Los Angeles Dodgers winds up in the second inning of the October 20 game.

Page 2:
TOP: The 1987 American League All-Stars pose for a "team" photo;
CENTER LEFT: Darryl Strawberry of the Mets gives his autograph;
BOTTOM LEFT: Babe Ruth (third from left), Lou Gehrig (fourth from left), and teammates model new Babe Ruth Underwear in the Yankees locker room; **BOTTOM RIGHT:** Gil Hodges of the Brooklyn Dodgers carries the world's biggest stick in this 1950 publicity photo.

CONTENTS

Author's Foreword	7
The Magic of Baseball	8
The Art of Baseball	124
The Baseball Family	194
Take Me Out to the Ballgame	250
Index	321

These pages:
OPPOSITE LEFT: Those were the days! Souvenir programs for the 1947 World Series went for a mere 50 cents; **LEFT:** Big bats line up for a photo before the start of the 1937 All-Star Game at Griffith Stadium in Washington, DC; **ABOVE:** The three Ritz Brothers (left) cut up at home plate during a mock baseball game for the benefit of Mount Sinai Hospital in 1938.

LIFE

DEVOTED TO

BASE BALL, TRAP SHOOTING AND GENERAL SPORTS.

5¢

Volume 44—No. 8.   Philadelphia, November 5, 1904.   Price, Five Cents.

LUNDGREN, P. | WEIMER, P. | BROWN, P. | WICKER, P. | BRIGGS, P.
J. J. O'NEILL, C. | KLING, C. | EVERS, 2ND B. | CHANCE, 1ST B.
CASEY, 3RD B. | TINKER, S.S. | O. WILLIAMS, SUB. | McCARTHY, O.F.
D. JONES, O.F. | J. BARRY, O.F. | McCHESNEY, O.F. | SCHULTE, O.F. | SLAGEL, O.F.

CHICAGO BASE BALL CLUB
NATIONAL LEAGUE
FRANK SELEE, M'G'R
1904

Sporting Life
Phila

AUTHOR'S FOREWORD

Baseball's long history has been chronicled in loving detail, especially during recent decades. The past two decades, in particular, have witnessed a kind of explosion in literary accounts of the nation's favorite game, and increasing attention has also been paid by both professional historians and enthusiastic amateur sleuths to cataloguing the impact of America's ballgame upon our nation's folkways. But the recent spate of books, novels, articles and movies is only one indication of baseball's hold on the American imagination. Television, in a manner hardly imaginable a few years ago, now brings the games to millions of viewers in the comfort of their living rooms. After a prolonged slide during the 1950s and 1960s, attendance at big league games today stands at all-time levels: minor league turnstiles are humming and even big-league numbers have soared beyond disastrous 1995 post-strike levels.

How do we explain this national passion for baseball? In some ways it defies explanation. As big-league catcher Wes Westrum once remarked, "Baseball is like church – many attend and few understand." But a few hypotheses are nevertheless possible.

First, there is baseball's inescapable link to childhood memories and our nostalgia for our lost youth. In a sense, the nation seeks its collective childhood in this exciting game which so perfectly mirrors – both in symbol and style – a more innocent and pastoral age. Each fan enters a magical world in any big-league ballpark – one where fading childhood heroes remain forever miraculously alive.

Second, baseball is living folklore, its legends transformed into an American mythology. Ruth, Gehrig, DiMaggio and Mays are as much today's national folk heroes as they were in their own times. Indeed, the lives of such heroes as Ruth and DiMaggio were from the first more appropriately the stuff of fiction than of history. Ruth's feat of 60 homers in a single season took place in the same year as Lindbergh's solo flight across the Atlantic, parallel events and parallel expressions of the nation's sense of limitless possibility. DiMaggio's own marvelous hitting streak of 56 consecutive games (to many fans the game's most unapproachable record) was like a beacon in the darkness of that summer of 1941 when the nation was sliding inexorably toward global war. Both men were legends in their own day; now they have been translated from the realm of legend into that of myth.

Third, baseball, above all other bat and ball games yet invented by man, is deeply dramatic. The players seem the most human of our sporting heroes, normal in physical stature, eminently subject to failure and defeat. Each diamond position presents an identifiable human type: small-framed speedy infielders are distinct from lead-footed bulky catchers, who in turn contrast with strong-armed and power-laden flychasers in the outfield positions. An entire baseball culture has grown up around the "flaky character" and antic deeds of the southpaw hurler – baseball's most renowned comic character type. Furthermore, the game's rules and exhaustive record-keeping stress basic human accountability. No successful base hit, crucial putout or fielding miscue goes unrecorded or unremembered. The box score records each player's failures as well as his triumphs. For every hard-earned credit in one man's batting average there is an equal debit for another's pitching record. To paraphrase Casey Stengel, in baseball, you could always look it up.

The subject of statistics brings us to a final point. To the uninitiated, the baseball fan's notorious addiction to statistics might seem a passion for bloodless abstraction, a penchant for mere accountancy. Nothing could be farther from the truth. In fact, it speaks of a sense of history unique in sport. Thanks to the stats, baseball's past and present seem always to coexist in a timeless "now". No baseball game is ever solely a matter of two teams competing between themselves for victory. Both are always competing with the past as well. They are in competition not just with records set by great teams and players of former days but also with the memories of individual fans, for each fan carries in his or her heart a personal set of stats composed of hundreds of treasured performances – recollections that can reach back half a century. Thus every game resonates with history, and the stats are the shorthand of that history.

The scrapbook that follows is not a formal history of baseball but, rather, an attempt to recreate baseball history as it lives in our imaginations. It is a treasure trove of information, but it is not an encyclopedia, both because it makes no pretense of being all-inclusive and because many of the facts it contains are of a kind you could probably never find in an encyclopedia. But though factual, it is also sentimental in that it revels unabashedly in baseball mythology. By the same token, it does not turn a blind eye to the fads, follies and occasional evils that are also a part of baseball's history and a part of our collective memory of baseball as well.

What this book aims to do is not to present the orderly decade-by-decade recital found in usual baseball histories but to concentrate on the game's thematic dimensions, from its most heroic legends to its most engaging trivia, from its winning onfield techniques and strategies to the smell of its ballparks and the look of its scoreboards. Our intention is to explore as fully as possible that "stadium of the mind" in which we are never surprised to find a Ruth or a Gehrig trotting on to the same field where a Clemens or a Canseco are playing. And if we cannot fully explain it, we nevertheless want to affirm again, as powerfully as we can, that central mystery that Jim Bouton was thinking about when he wrote: "You see, you spend a good piece of your life gripping a baseball, and in the end it turns out that it was the other way around all the time."

THE MAGIC OF BASEBALL

Every baseball fan savors his own private, almost endless list of near mythical baseball heroes, legendary events and action-filled images: Wee Willie Keeler "hittin' them where they ain't" in the game's infant days; the bow-legged yet agile Honus Wagner gobbling up countless grounders in the Pittsburgh infield at the close of the century's first decade; Tinker to Evers to Chance; John McGraw glowering at the opposition from the Giants' dugout; Grover Cleveland Alexander, with his ever ungainly and shambling walk, almost comical in his undersized cap and oversized uniform, striking down Tony Lazzeri in the crucial game of the 1926 World Series; Pepper Martin running wild across the Gas House summers of St. Louis; Daffiness Dodgers stumbling into memorable traffic jams along the basepaths; slight Carl Hubbell of the Giants mowing down an All-Star lineup in New York's Polo Grounds; barrel-chested Hack Wilson exploiting his blacksmith arms to drive home another Chicago run; Joltin' Joe DiMaggio legging out one more hit during his miraculous streak in 1941; the sweet swing and not so sweet disposition of "Teddy Ballgame" Williams; the towering home run blasts of Adonis-like Mickey Mantle; the pitching mastery of diminutive Whitey Ford; the high-leg mound actions of Boston's Warren Spahn and of Frisco's Juan Marichal; the unhittable fall-away delivery of the Cardinals' Bob Gibson; Willie Mays, cap flying, catching up to a towering Vic Wertz drive; the Amazin' Mets led by Gil Hodges and the still more amazing Whiz Kids inspired by Eddie Sawyer; the last-minute long-ball heroics of Bobby Thomson and Bill Mazeroski; Johnny Bench and Pudge Rodriguez redefining the position of catcher, and Hank Aaron redefining the standards for power-hitting excellence; Pete Rose dropping hit number 4192 into the Cincinnati outfield, then fumbling away the dreams of millions of fans. ...The list could be multiplied almost indefinitely.

Such images both give form to the decades of baseball history and capture for all of us that aura of heroism that is baseball's greatest charm. It is our baseball champions who have become the twentieth-century Paul Bunyans, the Lord Nelsons and the Robin Hoods of our national folk mythology.

And with memories of legendary ballplayers there arise also fond memories of legendary hometown teams. First perhaps, would come the "Murderers' Row" Yankees of Ruth, Gehrig and Lazzeri, almost rendering helpless the rest of the American League throughout the late twenties and early thirties. This was surely the greatest juggernaut in diamond history, a freeswinging gang providing the yardstick by which all future champions in our summer sport would be measured.

Next come the incomparable Bronx Bombers of the Casey Stengel era, winners of an unprecedented five straight World Titles and a Series participant every year but one across an entire decade, ironically falling short only in the very season in which they actually captured the most games of any Stengel-led club. No team made winning so easy or so inevitable as those outfits wearing the Yankee pinstripes under "the Old Professor," Casey Stengel, between 1949 and 1960. No team – neither the Celtics of professional basketball nor the glory-era Notre Dame footballers under Knute Rockne – holds a better claim to the title of greatest dynasty in American sports history. However, in a game where balanced competition and noble defeat reign so supreme (where the losing Brooklyn Dodgers, and not the victorious New York Giants, were most immortalized by Bobby Thomson's "shot heard round the world"), Yankee domination and business-like efficiency at winning has succeeded only in stamping these Stengel-era Yankees as America's favorite object of envy and derision – as those insufferable "damned Yankees."

But the Yankees under Miller Huggins and Casey Stengel have not been summertime's only unstoppable winners. No discussion of dynasty teams excludes the Big Red Machine of Johnny Bench and Pete Rose which so stirred passions in baseball's original hometown of Cincinnati. There were also Philadelphia's Athletics during Connie Mack's early glory years, a ballclub outstanding enough to derail the Gotham Murderers' Row Boys for three consecutive campaigns spliced between the end of Miller Huggins' reign and the beginning of Joe McCarthy's legendary tenure in the Bronx. Behind the bold slugging of Jimmie Foxx and Al Simmons and the true mound mastery of Robert "Lefty" Grove and George Earnshaw, the Mackmen of 1929-1931 came within but a single dramatic World Series game in 1931 of preceding McCarthy's potent Yankees powerhouse as history's very first three-straight-Series winners.

Eventually there arose the distant descendants of those bold Mackmen, Oakland teams built by charismatic rebel owner Charlie Finley in the early 1970s, and later those directed by law-school-educated skipper Tony LaRussa in the final seasons of the 1980s. The former Oakland outfit was a colorful bunch of brawlers who battled with each other equally as much as they did with the remainder of an outclassed league, yet who were thrice inspired toward Series glories by their universal hatred for tightwad owner Finley. The latter was an immensely talented and truly formidable winning machine embarked upon a mission to recapture pride as the early-1990s' most invincible team.

And if baseball offers us such a fine legacy of predictable winners, it also provides a rare gallery of surprise victors. Recall the Miracle Boston Braves in 1914, stunning seven National League opponents by recklessly charging all the way from their nest in the cellar in mid-July to a World Championship by mid-October. Or the equally shocking 1969 Miracle New York Mets, casting off a doleful seven-year expansion past that had never seen them rise above ninth place, and suddenly rocketing toward the zenith of the sporting world with a Series flag in their first-ever winning baseball season. Earlier, there were the underdog World Champion Cincinnati Reds of 1919, catching the nation and Comiskey's White Stockings napping in what would turn out to be baseball's most infamous Fall Classic. And perhaps most cherished of all hopeless underdogs are those "Whiz Kid" Phillies of manager Eddie Sawyer, a spirited no-name outfit stealing a pennant from Burt Shotton's Dodgers with Sisler's dramatic 10th-inning shot on Brooklyn's most breathtaking season-final day.

There are, to boot, legendary teams burned into baseball's inexhaustible collective memory as much for laughable high jinks as for their consistent winning ways. First to come to mind are those Gas House Gang Cardinals who ran wild with insufferable tomfoolery (plus three league pennants) across that glorious decade graced by Dizzy Dean, Ducky Medwick and Pepper Martin. Whether ensconced in the safe shadows of clubhouse and dugout or basking in the limelight of the playing field, Dean and Martin were almost always up to some outrageous prank – that is, when they weren't preoccupied with beating the rest of the league silly. Equally vivid are images of Wilbert Robinson's "Daffiness Dodgers" from the same epoch, that stumblebum bunch of diamond cut-ups who once featured baseball's most infamous basepath bungle – Babe Herman alongside a pair of his astonished mates, all simultaneously hugging third.

To be sure, our diamond sport draws its lasting appeal as much from tears as from laughter, and some of its most cherished teams are those that have mixed truckloads of heart-wrenching seasonal collapse with noble near-moments of foiled victory. The Chicago Cubs have built a hometown legacy of unmitigated woes for over three generations of loyal fans. To live as a diehard Cubs fan is to wear a countenance of stoic gloom, one seemingly surgically implanted on the occasion of a first outing to the pennant-race coffin known fondly as Wrigley Field. Boston's Red Sox stand beside the Cubs as our other best-loved and most inevitable seasonal losers, a ballclub that has battled gamely during the two most gripping World Series epics of the past 25 autumns, yet which searches still for its first championship since American troops marched wearily home from the trenches of World War I.

And when it comes to baseball's most charmed and loveable teams, no ballclub has ever tugged a nation's imagination more than those "Boys of Summer" Dodgers immortalized by author Roger Kahn. These Brooklyn "Bums" who occupied tiny Ebbets Field throughout most of the fifties were hardly stumblebums by any stretch of the imagination, though today they are relegated to a spot in sporting legend as one of America's most inveterate losers – victims of Bobby Thomson's shattering homer, sufferers of Dick Sisler's pennant-snatching blow and perennial foils to the invincible Stengel Yankees who many a year tantalized them in Subway Series play. The truth is that these Dodgers were in fact the most dominant team in any one decade in National League history, a ballclub that came within a mere handful of late-season victories (nine over a decade, to be exact) of collecting an unheard-of eleven straight National League crowns. Yet these Brooklyn Bums were baseball's darlings precisely because they taught us time and again life's rude lesson about instructive failure. And they taught as well how to cope with failure. "Wait until next year!" How could any true baseball fan survive without that refrain?

The chapter unfolding here is a collage of some of baseball's most legendary teams and players. Not every great hometown team or revered star is automatically included, for we have tried to save some space for rogues and clowns as well as saints – the warts as well as the wonderment of a lengthy baseball past. Beside Gehrig's 1938 Yankees – a true dynasty team boasting four straight champion's flags – sit those infamous Black Sox who authored the diamond sport's worst post-season fiasco. Spliced between the noble DiMaggio and cherubic Ruth are the ruthless Ty Cobb and ignoble John McGraw. Together they provide but a pastiche of baseball's colorful past – yet enough to fuel nostalgia and whet appetite anew for yet another season of baseball memories.

GREAT TEAM LEGENDS OF THE PAST

Fans cherish favored teams from baseball's rich past, legendary teams featuring invincible lineups or unmatched championship victories. Yet some clubs are equally remembered for their gaudy, sometimes calamitous failures.

Some of baseball's truly memorable teams have been distinguished for imposing individual stars, others for dramatic come-from-behind victories in post-season play, still others for some mythic moment unique to diamond legend. Durocher's 1951 Giants will live for us always by virtue of Bobby Thomson's "shot-heard-round the world" alone, while the 1954 Polo Grounders survive today through living images of a truly incomparable World Series catch by Willie Mays. Yet others are etched in our memories for deeds less glorious. Despite an imposing lineup of strong-armed hurlers (Ed Cicotte and Lefty Williams) and adept batsmen (Shoeless Joe Jackson and Eddie Collins), the American League champion 1919 White Sox (**OPPOSITE TOP**) will stand always in our collective memories as little more than the scandalous "Black Sox," alleged to have dumped a regrettable World Series to their less talented Cincinnati opponents. As the first winner of four consecutive World Championships, the 1936-1939 New York Yankees under Joe McCarthy were baseball's first true dynasty team. Yet the 1938 New Yorkers (**OPPOSITE BOTTOM**) are remembered less as a club which dominated both circuits in long-ball production (174 homers) and slugging proficiency (.446 team SA), or even as a team which swept the Cubs in four straight during one of the most lopsided Fall Classics ever, but more for the swan song of incomparable Lou Gehrig, playing out his last season before being struck down by disease. Another great Yankee team, that of the Casey Stengel era, would soon replace the McCarthy-epoch Bronx Bombers as baseball's greatest dynasty, achieving five consecutive World Titles (1949-1953). Featuring such dependable role players as Gil McDougald, Phil Rizzuto, Billy Martin, Joe Collins and Yogi Berra (**RIGHT TOP**), the 1953 Yankees ballclub supplanted the star-dominated lineups of the Ruth-Gehrig-led "Murderer's Row" Yankee teams with one of the most balanced lineups ever. While true sluggers like the young Mantle and the seasoned Berra paced regular-season onslaughts, it was the less heralded regulars like Martin (.500 BA with 12 hits in 1953) and McDougald (with a crucial 1951 grand slam) who came to the fore in Series play. It was not until Cincinnati's vaunted "Big Red Machine" ballclubs led by Johnny Bench and Sparky Anderson (**RIGHT BOTTOM**) in the mid-1970s that another team would feature such awesome balanced power in its starting lineup.

MEN BEHIND THE LEGENDARY TEAMS

A few special ballclubs are linked for all time with a handful of unforgettable baseball names and faces – men giving both personality and color to the home team cities they represented and the uniforms they proudly wore.

The Magic of Baseball

Some ballclubs are inseparable from the rare personalities of the few great stars which led them. The Yankees of the Ruth era in the Roaring Twenties will always be known by the epithet "Murderer's Row" – an apt moniker first attached to an imposing lineup of (l to r) Wally Pipp, Babe Ruth, Roger Peckinpaugh, Bob Meusel and Frank "Home Run" Baker (**OPPOSITE TOP**) which pioneered the long ball at the outset of the "Big Stick" era. The Cardinals of the early 1930s are forever branded baseball's lovable "Gashouse Gang" (**OPPOSITE BOTTOM**) for the antics of Pepper Martin, Dizzy and Daffy Dean, and the irrepressible Leo Durocher. Here Martin (l) and slugger Joe "Ducky" Medwick (r) enjoy a spring training cut-up session. No group of youngsters more successfully captured the imagination of fans than did the slugging Philadelphia Phillies lineup of 1950 Whiz Kids (**ABOVE LEFT**) featuring (l to r) Willie "Puddin' Head" Jones, Del Ennis, Andy Seminick and Dick Sisler. And Roger Kahn's immortal "Boys of Summer" Dodgers (**PAGES 14-15**) are linked forever with the keystone combination of shortstop Peewee Reese and second baseman Jackie Robinson (**BELOW**).

14 THE BASEBALL SCRAPBOOK

The Magic of Baseball 15

"ERNIE, LET'S PLAY TWO TODAY!"

Some players made a career of being in the right place at the right time – like Dusty Rhodes in the 1954 World Series. Others, like Ernie Banks, never seemed to get a break from baseball's true patron saint: Lady Luck.

The Magic of Baseball 19

Ernie Banks might very well have been best remembered by future generations for his sunny personality and the truly joyous enthusiasm that marked every day of his 19-year career. It was just that unbounded joy which the eternally youthful Banks displayed (**OPPOSITE TOP**) here outside Wrigley Field in January 1977, when word first arrived that he had become the eighth man in big league history to be elected to the Hall at Cooperstown in his first year of eligibility. Banks might also have been best recalled as the most popular player in Chicago Cubs history. Whether as a power-laden 22-year-old rookie shortstop (**LEFT**) in the early 1950s or a seasoned slugger (**BELOW**) of the mid and late 1960s, Banks was heart and soul of the otherwise lackluster Cubs lineups that paraded through Wrigley Field for two full decades. Finally, he might have earned immortality as one of the most honored players of his era – league MVP in 1958 and 1959, frequent league pacesetter in numerous offensive and defensive categories and the first player to win two simultaneous awards from Chicago's baseball writers when he copped dual honors in 1958 as "Chicago Player of the Year" and the Will Harridge Award for "Baseball Achievement of the Year" (**OPPOSITE BOTTOM**). Yet the misfortune of Banks is that he will in all likelihood be remembered best as one of a rare handful of unlucky Hall of Famers never to enjoy the thrills of baseball's postseason play.

THE MAN WHO REVAMPED CATCHING

Once Johnny Bench pioneered his flashy style of one-hand receiving there was no turning back for young catchers anywhere in baseball. A whole generation of receivers grew up emulating this Picasso among backstops.

The Magic of Baseball   21

No one would dare argue today that Johnny Bench – backstop anchor of the awesome "Big Red Machine" Cincinnati Reds teams of the 1970s – was anything but a bona fide Hall of Famer and one of the most talented receivers ever to don the "tools of ignorance" during baseball's modern age. Bench's power-hitting (second in career homers among catchers) and throwing skills leave him almost without peer among the game's greatest backstops. Yet there are those – such as ex-catcher and keen observer of the game, Bill Starr – who would now contend that Johnny Bench's pioneering one-handed catching style (**BOTTOM LEFT**) is perhaps a barometer of unwelcomed change from the more proficient (in Starr's view) style of play popular in the twenties and thirties to the much flashier, yet less fundamentally sound, playing techniques of the modern age. While protecting catchers from injury, Bench's pioneering one-handed style also reduced the pitcher's strike zone, since two-handed catchers can often fool umpires with imperceptible movements to guide errant pitches into the approved strike area. Bench's style and new hinged glove did prove to have other advantages, however, like his ability to stand away from a sliding runner and make a sweeping tag more like that practiced by shortstops or second basemen (**TOP LEFT**). And if his catching style was sometimes slightly controversial, his consistent clutch hitting was always a trademark during the Reds' string of championship years. After suffering his worst regular season in 1976, Bench outhit the American League's stellar catcher Thurman Munson .533 to .529 to win that year's Series MVP. The World Series was, in fact, Johnny Bench's special showcase, whether blasting a game-winning homer in the 1976 Series (**OPPOSITE TOP**) or celebrating with skipper Sparky Anderson (**OPPOSITE BOTTOM**) the dramatic 1975 Series victory over the Boston Red Sox, the Reds' first World Title in 35 long years.

BARRY BONDS

Overnight San Francisco's Barry Bonds catapulted from his already impressive status as one of baseball's top all-around players of the nineties to a more rarified air as the diamond's greatest power basher of all-time. With the launching of a new century it didn't take long for McGwire and Sosa to be swept from the record books and for Bonds to seize the fast lane toward becoming the most celebrated of all long-ball sluggers.

The Magic of Baseball 23

Few ballplayers have ever boasted such a pedigree—son of 1960s star Bobby Bonds (**BOTTOM**), a long-term all-star outfielder with 332 career dingers of his own, godson of immortal Willie Mays (third on the all-time homer list with 660), and cousin to Reggie Jackson (seventh on the career list at 563). Fewer still have ever lived up so thoroughly to the gifts implied by such a gene pool. Simply put, Barry Bonds (at least the Barry Bonds of recent seasons in San Francisco) is easily the most fearsome home run slugger the game has ever produced. His single-year performance of 2001 arguably leaves Babe Ruth's legendary 1927 and 1921 seasons far in the dust for overall brilliance, total domination with the lumber, and statistical singleness. Stroking homer number 71 in Pac Bell Park on October 5 Bonds obliterated the Mark McGwire record that stood for only three years (**CENTER**). The eventual total of 73 was combined with a .328 average and 137 RBIs. Without parallel, however, were the record 177 walks and .863 slugging percentage, both topping the Babe's earlier standards. A .515 on-base percentage added to the mix was the first above .500 since Mickey Mantle and Ted Williams both turned the same trick way back in 1957. So great was the respect for Bonds that he rarely received hittable pitches and was intentionally walked nearly every time he came to the plate with runners in scoring position. It was a sudden turnaround, but only one of degree. Bonds was five years into his career in Pittsburgh before he topped 30 round trippers for the first time; only four times before 2001 had he reached the 40-homer plateau. Yet Bonds was always deemed a brilliant player, both offensively and defensively. In 1990 he became only the second athlete in history to pilfer 50 bases and slug 30-plus homers. He won MVP honors that year and again in 1992. This view of overall excellence sometimes came grudgingly from a press and fans who also saw him as sullen and selfish, and teammates who occasionally groused that he was a clubhouse distraction. One could hardly have guessed when looking at the slim young Bonds who donned a Pirates uniform in the early 1990s (**TOP**) that a decade later he would be transformed by rigid conditioning and diet into a muscle-bound paragon of raw power. He had started slowly (the Pirates tried to unload him several times when productivity did not match growing salary demands), but only by standards he himself would later set. With several years left, Bonds will certainly surpass Mays in lifetime home runs, he will likely overhaul the iconic Babe when he soars above 700, and he may even outstrip Aaron. The final incomparable legacy is not yet entirely written.

A LEFTY FOR ALL-TIME

The second winningest lefty in baseball history, behind Warren Spahn, is also second on the all-time list of strikeout pitchers, trailing only Nolan Ryan. Yet when it comes to colorful personalities this recent Hall of Famer – Steve Carlton – deserves second billing to no one.

Steve Carlton made a 24-year career out of shutting down opposition batters and shutting out opposing teams. His 55 whitewashings stand 14th on the all-time list. But no one was shut out more often by the incomparable lefty than the baseball press. Beginning in 1978 Carlton imposed an eight-year silence on a media which he disdained and distrusted. When he has spoken out publicly in post-retirement years the newly elected Hall of Famer has frequently been controversial and quixotic on topics ranging from politics to world history to his own alternative lifestyle. Carlton's reputation as a lefty flake during his playing days came not only from his strained relationships with press and fans but also from his dedication to a strict regimen of yoga exercises (**BOTTOM LEFT**), which extended his career by improving his concentration and fine-tuning his body. As an intense competitor and fiercely private person, Carlton was often painted as moody and sullen, an image which probably increased his effectiveness against enemy batters. As a four-time winner of the Cy Young Award, owner of 329 career victories and six 20-win seasons, and author of 4,136 strikeouts, Steve Carlton has few peers among even the game's greatest hurlers. His numbers alone are enough to dismiss any personality idiosyncracies. And Carlton was not always inscrutable and aloof from his admiring fans, as is demonstrated by the smiling pitcher (**TOP LEFT**) who addressed Philadelphia faithful alongside his wife Bev at Steve Carlton Night, held in Veterans Stadium late in his 27-10 Cy Young season of 1972. While the ninth-winningest pitcher in baseball history spent the first 21 years of his long career with the Cardinals and Phillies of the National League, he would play his final years in the junior circuit with the Chicago White Sox (**OPPOSITE**), Cleveland Indians and Minnesota Twins. Whatever uniform or persona he chose to put on, however, he never changed his posture as one of the greatest lefty hurlers that baseball has ever known.

The Magic of Baseball 25

SILENT PIONEER

Campy, with his quiet style and booming bat, did as much for acceptance of blacks in the big leagues as Jackie Robinson did with his ceaseless competitive spirit.

The Dodgers seem dogged by a special vulnerability to career-ending injuries. Pete Reiser was a sure-fire Hall of Famer until his rare talent for crashing headlong into outfield fences overcame his talent for hitting the baseball. Sandy Koufax stood unquestioned as the greatest pitcher of the modern era until a tired arm cut off his brilliant career at its very zenith. But perhaps no Dodger was ever treated more cruelly by the unpredictable hand of fate than Roy Campanella. A solid fireplug of a man (**OPPOSITE BOTTOM RIGHT**), Campy's graceful fielding belied his stumpy physique, and as baseball's first black big-league catcher his skillful handling of Brooklyn's nearly all-white pitching staff justified Branch Rickey's noble experiment equally as much as did Jackie Robinson's flamboyant style of offensive play. Campy reaching the dugout after another titanic home run was a familiar sight in Brooklyn throughout the 1950s (**RIGHT**), as he spearheaded a potent Dodgers offense with three MVP seasons in five years and major league records for catchers in home runs (41) and RBIs (142) during his brilliant 1953 campaign. Yet like many catchers, Campy's brief career was punctuated by injury, and in January 1958 that career was cut off after only 10 big-league seasons by an automobile accident that left him confined as a quadriplegic (**BELOW**). Whether sliding home with another vital tally (**OPPOSITE TOP**) or enjoying some spring training fishing with his teammates (**OPPOSITE BOTTOM LEFT**), Campy was the rock-solid inspirational leader of the teams Roger Kahn called "The Boys of Summer."

THE LATIN HERO

The very sight of Clemente tearing around the bases, legging out extra base hits, was as thrilling an image as any in all of baseball's long and exciting history.

Simply stated, he may well have been the most exciting baseball player who ever lived. Young Clemente played the outfield with recklessness, yet also with incomparable grace and style (**TOP RIGHT**). His cannon-like throwing arm – the very arm that had first attracted legions of big league scouts to his native Puerto Rico when he was but a youngster of 17 first starring in the Caribbean winter leagues (**OPPOSITE TOP**) – was unmatched anywhere in the game's history. Only Jackie Robinson could compare with the daring Clemente on the basepaths; and perhaps only Willie Mays played the outfield with quite the same flair. Yet neither of these two immortal black superstars of the same baseball era was as mysterious or as transfixing a figure as Roberto Clemente Walker, the first Latin American player ever enshrined in Cooperstown. Like Campanella, however, Clemente was to fall victim of senseless tragedy, killed in a plane crash while he was on a mercy mission to earthquake victims of Nicaragua on Christmas eve of 1972. A national hero in his native island of Puerto Rico, Roberto always loved the poverty-stricken children of his homeland as much as he loved the game of baseball (**BELOW**). Today the Roberto Clemente Sports City, a community center for disadvantaged youth located on the outskirts of his native San Juan, provides as fitting a tribute to Clemente's heroic stature as does the handsome bronze plaque in Cooperstown that records his four league batting titles and numerous other remarkable baseball milestones.

GEORGIA PEACH

Cobb was baseball's most hated competitor. For later generations he was the game's most celebrated batsman, outpolling even Ruth in Cooperstown's first election.

The Magic of Baseball 31

It seems almost incomprehensible that Tyrus Cobb's long-lasting baseball reputation could be based on anything but his unmatched hitting talent. This is the man who still holds the highest lifetime career batting average (.367) in baseball history. This is the singular owner of twelve career batting titles, nine in a row. Upon his retirement in 1928 the incomparable Cobb held no fewer than 90 major league records for hitting and baserunning, and his standards for lifetime hits (eventually chased down by Pete Rose), career stolen bases and single-season stolen bases were for decades considered unreachable milestones, fixed in the game's mythology alongside Ruth's home run records. Yet as remarkable as it may seem, Cobb's legacy (like that of his later alter ego Pete Rose) was not destined to be that of exemplary hitter alone. For Ty Cobb's skill with the bat has long been overshadowed, for historians and fans alike, by his lack of skill in human relations, as well as by his indelible reputation as the fiercest competitor ever to don a glove and a pair of baseball spikes. It was his flashing spikes, in fact, rather than his talented bat, which became Cobb's most remembered emblem throughout his 24-year big-league career. The standard portrait of the fearless Cobb is that of the daring baserunner sliding recklessly into third base (**BOTTOM CENTER**), infield dust flying, spiked shoes lashing at the third base bag as well as at the defending third sacker who is usually defending his own limbs more than the base itself. The almost cherubic face (**OPPOSITE TOP**) that the young Cobb displayed in some of his posed portraits belied his status as one of the game's most hated and feared combatants. So infamous was Cobb's reputation that the Tiger outfielder often arranged his own security guards at the ballpark, such as Boston Police Inspector O'Neill, pictured here (**TOP LEFT**) chatting with the irascible Cobb at the Boston ballyard during pre-game activities in 1915. But Cobb's league-wide reputation for mean-spirited play was one he fostered from the first, often picking out a prominent location on the dugout steps during pre-game warmups and proceeding to sharpen his lethal spikes in full view of nervous opposing infielders huddled in the neighboring dugout.

32 THE BASEBALL SCRAPBOOK

Ty Cobb's unique split-handed batting grip demonstrated here (**RIGHT**) was not only the key to his awesome batting prowess (giving him exceptional bat control, if reducing his overall bat speed and power), but it also is linked to one of the most famous of numerous apocryphal stories coloring the career of the legendary Detroit outfielder. Tired of journalists questioning him about Babe Ruth's newly unleashed home run power, which was setting new standards for the game by the mid-1920s, Cobb once reportedly downplayed the achievements of the boastful Babe by shooting back at reporters that hitting home runs was not in fact the mark of any special hitting talent. Cobb, it was obvious, had no love lost for either the boisterous Babe Ruth or the newfangled longball which had supplanted his preferred hit-and-run style of play. To cement his claim, Cobb reputedly slid his hands down the bat handle that day and immediately poked three roundtrippers himself in a game against the St. Louis Browns, launching two more the following afternoon to punctuate the issue. The most famous and least trustworthy Cobb anecdote, however, is one consistent with the boastful nature of the Georgia Peach, if not with the actual events. Supposedly asked by an interviewer in the late 1950s about how he would hit under modern-day conditions, Cobb is reputed to have said that he was confident he could check in with an average of .310 or perhaps even .315. "How is this possible," queried the amazed novice interviewer, "when you hit over .400 at least four different times?" "Well, you have to remember, I'm 72 years old now," Cobb supposedly replied.

The Magic of Baseball 33

ROGER THE ROCKET

Roger Clemens has maintained the title of baseball's foremost power pitcher since Nolan Ryan's retirement, and the recent achievements of an unprecedented fifth Cy Young Award and a fan-selected position on the roster of Major League Baseball's All-Century Team has seemingly assured a first-ballot Hall-of-Fame enshrinement in the first decade of the new millennium.

The Magic of Baseball 35

Roger Clemens is still most strongly identified with a Boston Red Sox uniform and perhaps always will be, especially among ballpark fanatics in the nation's northeastern corridor. It was in Boston, of course, that Clemens first burst upon the baseball scene and posted some of his most impressive strikeout performances. As a youngster in Texas the physically imposing and hard-throwing righty had idolized strikeout king Nolan Ryan. And in his own first half-dozen big-league Boston campaigns Clemens parlayed brazen confidence, unrivaled mechanics and control, and a 95-plus fastball into an achievement-laced career that quickly made him Ryan's clear successor as baseball most overpowering moundsman. The Boston ledger included back-to-back Cy Young trophies (the fourth pitcher ever to accomplish that feat), a major league record 20 strikeouts in a game (accomplished twice), and 18 shutouts in his first 139 starts. In recent years Rocket Roger has taken his lucrative free-agent act on the road, first to Toronto and later New York, and in the process has also revived a Cooperstown-bound career. While his fastball had waned somewhat by the mid-nineties, Clemens in Toronto successfully substituted craftiness for raw power and also successfully extended his dominance – to the stark surprise of many, especially disillusioned fans and club executives back in Boston. While he had won only 50 games for the Sox between 1993 and 1996, largely due to poor offensive support in hitter-friendly Fenway Park, with the Jays he tacked on two more Cy Youngs and in 1997 became the first American League pitcher in a half-century to pace the junior circuit in wins, ERA and strikeouts simultaneously. The following summer he won his final 15 without defeat, captured 20 victories for the fourth time, posted a fifth strikeout crown, and also "rocketed" past 3,000 on the career strikeout tally board. And finally, over in New York during the final year of the decade, there was a long-awaited opportunity to crown an already incomparable career with the greatest team triumph possible, a World Series championship ring. In the collage of photos on these pages baseball's ranking flamethrower is seen en route to a World Series win over the Braves in 1999 (**OPPOSITE**), earning one of his career-best 24 victories with Boston in 1986 (**TOP**), tossing the first pitch of the 1990 campaign (**MIDDLE**), and toiling for Toronto during his 1998 fifth Cy Young summer (**BOTTOM**).

YANKEE CLIPPER

DiMaggio was more than an exceptional athlete; he was the consummate professional ballplayer; his foremost badge was pride; his outfield grace was unsurpassed.

DiMag Streak Goes to 56!

Many revisionist baseball historians and sabermetricians today complain of DiMaggio's supposedly overblown stature and now-diminished career numbers: 40 players hold higher lifetime averages and 35 have now blasted more homers. Reputable baseball historian John Holway calls DiMaggio's 1941 streak "the biggest baseball myth of all" (observing that "two gifts from a friendly New York official scorer kept the streak going, as did a can-of-corn-flyball and topped 30-foot roller") and asks: "Take away the NY from Joe's cap and who do you have? Hank Greenberg?" One is, of course, hard pressed not to admit that DiMaggio's eternal rival Ted Williams was by far the greater hitter, although certainly never the complete ballplayer and silent team leader that could stand comparison with the incomparable Yankee Clipper. DiMaggio nonetheless is simply the most magnetic name among all baseball heroes of the past, even though Williams was the greater batting technician. DiMaggio was the kind of player you had to see to appreciate, one who roamed the outfield with matchless grace and style and who stroked a baseball with god like ease.

The images of the youthful Yankee Clipper are as vivid for the veteran New York baseball fan today as they were when the handsome youngster broke into the big leagues in 1936. Whether sliding into third in 1948 Opening Day action **(OPPOSITE TOP LEFT)**, posing with club owner Colonel Jake Ruppert before World Series action in 1937 **(OPPOSITE TOP RIGHT)**, signing autographs for his adoring fans in 1940 **(OPPOSITE BOTTOM)** or legging out another base hit during his miraculous 1941 hitting streak **(RIGHT)**, Joltin' Joe remained the very image of classical grace in action. The Yankee Clipper could do everything with unmatched talent, and for a large portion of baseball fandom he remains the greatest all-around player ever. For an even larger portion he stands forth today as baseball's most popular figure, and during the 1969 centennial celebration of the national pastime it was none other than DiMaggio who, by a landslide, was named the game's greatest living player.

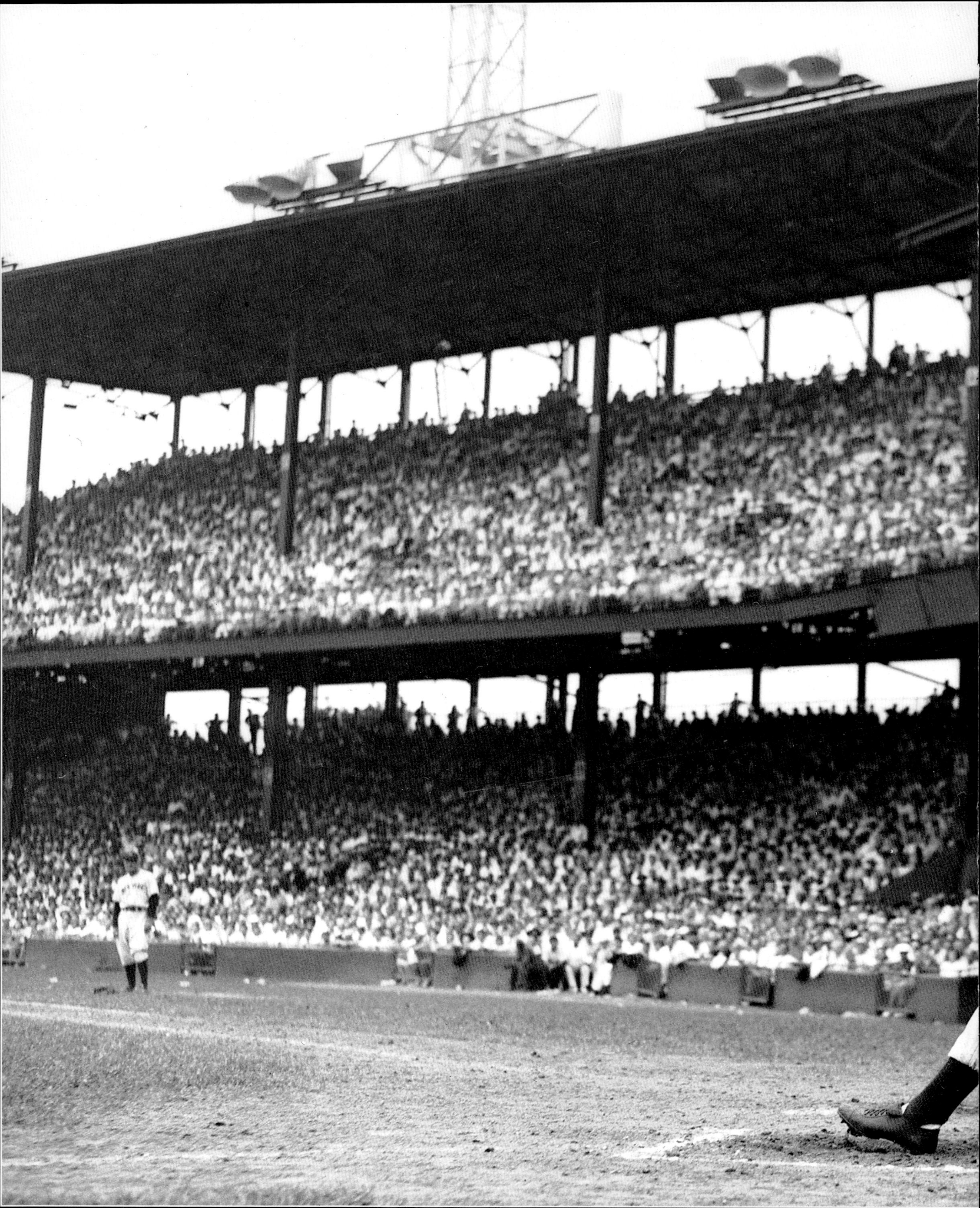

The Magic of Baseball 39

40 THE BASEBALL SCRAPBOOK

The Magic of Baseball

In his heyday in the 1940s Joe DiMaggio was a truly beautiful hitter, blessed with a classic swing **(PAGE 38-39)**. For decades after playing his final game, Joe D remained a top-drawing celebrity who packed fans into Old Timers Games **(OPPOSITE TOP)** and was a fixture at ceremonies like the one pictured here **(OPPOSITE BOTTOM)**, where he posed alongside Muhammad Ali as recipient of a prestigious Ellis Island Medal honoring the nation's most distinguished representatives of ethnic minorities. He became a living legend, a silent and proud demigod who towered above the adoring masses who worshiped from afar. Perhaps the beginning of the DiMaggio legend owes something to the silky voice and rapt portrait of Yankee Stadium action provided by the radio delivery of Mel Allen. The laconic, shy DiMaggio might not have fared so well amidst the frantic hype and relentless personal scrutiny of the later television age. Whereas radio always heightened the mystique of a great ballplayer, television inevitably works eventually to demythologize the famous and the legendary. It may be that one reason DiMaggio's fame is so lasting is because he was the final great hero of the radio age in American sport.

Nor does DiMaggio fare particularly well in a baseball age devoted to raw statistics. A new and arcane sabermetric yardstick devised by the popular baseball historians John Thorn and Pete Palmer, "Total Baseball Ranking," even suggests that Joe D was only the 37th best all-around performer ever to play the game (among major leaguers, that is), and in an equally nebulous category of "Production" these same pundits rank the Clipper's single 1939 campaign as 47th best. Ted Williams by contrast rates seven individual seasons among baseball's top fifty. But the game of baseball is composed of memory and myth, not just numbers. Its attraction is as much Edenic as statistical. Its appeal also lives in nostalgic memory, in which two eight-team leagues still play on real grass fields, not in a bloodless world where cold numbers silence passionate arguments over intangible skills. Most living fans who remember the mid-century epoch that marked the heyday of DiMaggio and Williams heard far more games over the airwaves than they ever saw from a grandstand seat. For them the graceful Yankee Clipper, seen at **RIGHT** with his son Joe Jr. in 1949, still looms as large as ever in the imagination.

RAPID ROBERT

The winningest pitcher in Cleveland history, he also owned the best fastball ever. Yet scout Cy Slapnicka signed him for a dollar and an autographed baseball.

Like a figure straight from some overly melodramatic baseball novel, young Iowa farmboy Bob Feller stepped out of a high school classroom at age 17, in the spring of 1936, and directly into the major leagues, immediately becoming the rare stuff of baseball legend. Striking out 15 Browns in his major league debut and 17 Athletics in his next outing, Rapid Robert Feller established a reputation that would live forever as the fastest pitcher of the inter-war period and one of the fastest of all-time. Yet Feller himself always insisted that the many strikeout records that were to follow over the course of his 18-year career were as much a product of his seductive curve and slider as they were of his blazing hard one. In addition to a then single-season strikeout record of 348 in 1946, Feller's career was highlighted by three no-hitters and a dozen one-hit efforts. One of the no-hitters came against the White Sox on Opening Day of the 1940 season (Feller's mother was in the grandstand and felled by a foul tip midway through the historic contest), and another was against the fearsome Yankees in New York on April 30, 1946. Yet perhaps his most truly satisfactory and memorable campaign was that of 1948, when despite persistent rumors of his declining talents, the flamethrower paced the American League in strikeouts for the seventh and final time, authored six straight victories down the season's stretch to lead the Clevelanders to their first flag in 28 summers and then pitched brilliantly in a losing effort in the opening game of the 1948 World Series with Boston. The collage of nostalgic photographs on these pages captures Feller striking out Joe DiMaggio during his memorable 1946 no-hit effort in New York's Yankee Stadium (**OPPOSITE BOTTOM**), pitching in Cleveland's Municipal Stadium during September 1946 (**TOP LEFT**) and posing with manager Lou Boudreau before the outset of March 1946 spring practice in the Indians' Clearwater, Florida, training camp (**BOTTOM LEFT**).

CHAIRMAN WHITEY

He was known as "The Chairman of the Board" for his business-like approach to the art of pitching, though the moniker was perhaps more fitting still because it attached to the star hurler on a team which was the very epitome of corporate efficiency.

The Magic of Baseball   45

Baseball history is crammed full of stories of young phenoms who burst upon the scene with spectacular rookie performances, only to fade into obscurity before they became household names. Super Joe Charboneau was such an instant legend, grabbing American League Rookie-of-the-Year honors in 1980, then tailspinning into the minors a half-season later and all the way out of baseball by 1983. So was Karl Spooner, who joined Brooklyn's Dodgers in late 1954 as an unheralded 22-year-old and soon set the baseball world on its ear with two consecutive shutouts and 27 strikeouts in his first two outings. But Spooner would win only eight more games before his big league career evaporated in 1956. And in the 1990 season there has been Dodgers rookie shortstop Jose Offerman, who homered on his first big league pitch, singled in his next two at bats, then played himself out of the lineup within a week. Yet when a young and previously unknown New York Yankee rookie named Edward Charles "Whitey" Ford celebrated similar debut success in the Yankee clubhouse with catcher Yogi Berra on September 25, 1950 (**OPPOSITE BOTTOM RIGHT**), few could imagine all that was yet to come. The 24-year-old lefty sensation had won nine straight games out of the gate and would lose only once by season's end. While that .900 winning percentage could not be expected to hold up, the .690 ratio (236-106, third best all-time and first among modern pitchers with over 200 wins) which Ford did post over the next fifteen summers could hardly have been expected either. And Whitey Ford's sensational rookie-season start was more than matched in World Series play of his freshman year as well, when he started and won the final fourth game (**OPPOSITE LEFT**), pitching 8 2/3 innings without allowing an earned run. It was, in fact, World Series play that was always Ford's forte, as he appeared in 11 Fall Classics, compiling all-time highs in wins (10), losses (8), games and games started (22), innings pitched (146), walks (34) and strikeouts (94), also breaking Babe Ruth's long-standing record for Series consecutive scoreless innings by reaching 33 in 1962. Whitey Ford's final two stellar World Series performances came in 1960 (**TOP LEFT**), when he shut out the Pirates twice, and 1961 (**BOTTOM LEFT**), when he hurled 14 more scoreless frames for two victories over the Cincinnati Reds.

ENTER THE RIGHT-HANDED BABE

He drank heavily, squandered his life savings, failed at numerous businesses and choked to death on a piece of meat. In the meantime, this fun-loving giant was also one of the game's most productive long-ball hitters.

The Magic of Baseball   47

There is something poignantly fitting about a wire service photograph (**BOTTOM LEFT**), widely circulated in 1954, which showed retired baseball immortal Jimmie Foxx conversing with a group of New York youngsters about his personally sponsored programs to battle juvenile delinquency in the nation's urban centers. Foxx, co-owner of the record for single-season homers by a right-hander, with 58 in 1932, had just teamed with Yankee outfielder Gene Woodling on a plan to have 20 big leaguers tour the country and provide "clinics" for disadvantaged urban youth. "If we can keep a kid here or there from going bad later in life," Foxx reported, "the whole project will be worthwhile." Foxx had every reason to be acutely sensitive to the need for a guiding light and a helping hand: a jovial and fun-loving man, he long balanced the oft-reported "highs" of a 20-year Hall-of-Fame big league career (9th on the all-time home run list with 534) with the less-publicized "lows" of personal dissipation (he drank heavily, lost most of his baseball earnings in failed business ventures and squandered the rest on fast living). Jimmie Foxx owed the launching of his own meteoric baseball career to the grandfatherly interest of that "grand old man" Connie Mack, who acquired the promising 17-year-old strong-armed youngster in 1925 and then kept him largely sequestered on the Athletics' bench for several seasons while painstakingly tutoring him in the fine points of the game. Fifteen summers later the grateful Foxx, his own career winding down in Boston, would repay the debt by taking a struggling young rookie named Ted Williams under his wing for much needed counsel on the "ins" and "outs" of big-league life.

His gigantic clouts were legendary in every American League city throughout the decade of the 1930s as Double XX starred with Mack's Athletics (**TOP LEFT** and **OPPOSITE TOP**) and later (1936-42) with Thomas Yawkey's Boston Red Sox (**OPPOSITE CENTER** and **OPPOSITE BOTTOM**), proving a fine all-around hitter who impressed with his RBI totals (driving in over 100 runs in 13 different seasons) and general stickwork (winning the Triple Crown in 1933) as much as with his mammoth circuit blasts. Yet Jimmie Foxx was doomed to play for two financially strapped owners and never earned the income his star status seemed to merit. In July 1967, at the age of 59, Jimmie Foxx choked to death while dining in a Miami restaurant with his brother.

IRON-HORSE LOU

He is baseball's lasting image of unbounded courage, a tower of strength who played every day for 14 years and then suffered the game's most publicized tragedy.

Ruth and Gehrig had the good fortune to play during baseball's two most flamboyant decades, the Roaring Twenties and the Explosive Thirties, decades which they themselves had a large hand in shaping. And the incomparable career of Lou Gehrig – as much as that of the Babe, in whose shadow he constantly lived – survives today not only in the numbers etched into *The Baseball Encyclopedia*, but as a collage of still-life images from a distant age of heroes before either radio or television gave lively voice or vision to the national game. There is the innocent gaze of the young Gehrig at Columbia University (**OPPOSITE TOP**), where he early became legend as both a hitter (compiling an unheard-of .937 slugging average his first season) and pitcher (once fanning 17 batters in a game he lost). There is the fearsome Yankee slugger seen here stroking a spring training base hit in 1929 (**OPPOSITE CENTER**) and crossing home plate with a ninth-inning homer in 1937 World Series Game Four (**RIGHT**). There are the poses with his teammate and rival Babe Ruth, this one taken before the 1933 inaugural All-Star Game in Comiskey Park (**OPPOSITE BOTTOM**). And there is the embarrassed demeanor of a proud Yankee star receiving a new auto as prize for his 1938 election as "Most Popular First Baseman" in a nationwide poll of baseball fandom (**BOTTOM**).

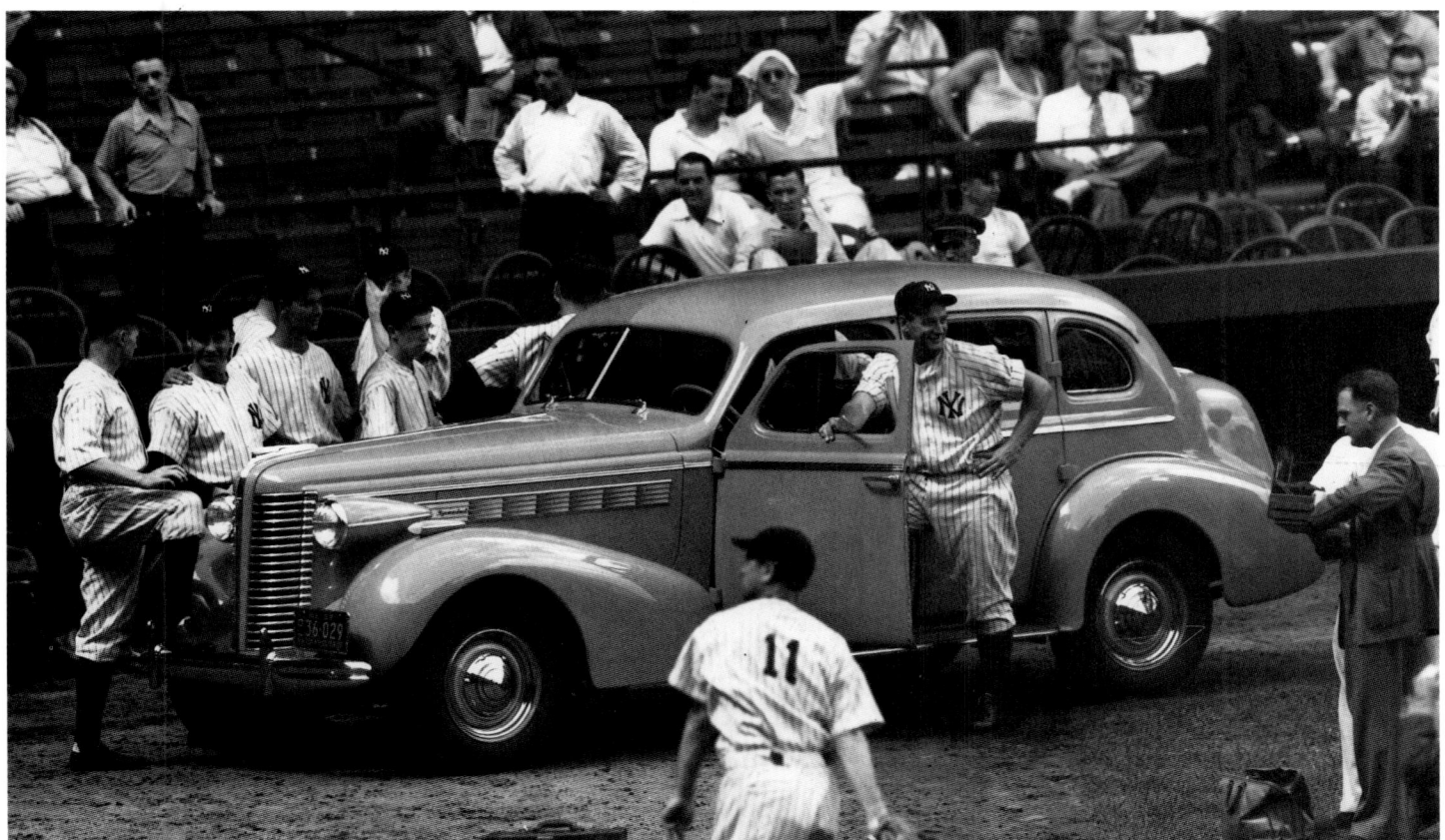

If ever a ballplayer was remembered and glorified for all the wrong reasons, it was the marvelous Lou Gehrig. Gehrig was doubly cursed in this respect. During his playing days he fell victim to the constant media barrage which surrounded the game's greatest all-time celebrity. Gehrig was an indisputably great player; he was a model of on-field and off-field consistency; he was the perfect baseball role model for the nation's fans and for its youth: but Babe Ruth was larger than life. Gehrig may have been the heart and soul of Murderer's Row and the glue that held together the Yankee clubhouse, but Ruth always made the great copy. And after his playing days and life were over, the unmatched ballplayer that was Lou Gehrig would fall victim to an even larger shadow – his own melodramatic legend. This is the legend of the strapping baseball hero struck down in the glow of youth by rare and incurable disease, by a tragic and inexplicable plague which robbed the star slugger of his life and the nation of its quiet baseball hero. It is a potent legend, fostered by wire-service, newsreel and Hollywood images of the dying slugger standing before microphones in Yankee Stadium on July 4, 1939, and pronouncing those unforgettable lines about being "the luckiest man on the face of the earth" **(RIGHT)**. Thus Lou Gehrig Day now stands as perhaps the most famous single ceremony in all baseball history. And if Gehrig's memory was robbed of its true richness by the presence of Babe Ruth and by his own legend as dying hero, it is also skewed by a single unforgettable number: 2130. Gehrig's record for consecutive game appearances – a mark that held up for almost six decades – casts an indelible shadow over his other career numbers which were just as impressive and which reveal far more accurately the true stature of Gehrig as one of the diamond's all-time greats. It is Lou Gehrig who owns the American League mark for single-season RBIs (184 in 1931), who stroked 23 major league grand slams, who hit for the cycle twice (while Ruth never did), who is the only American Leaguer other than Rocky Colavito to slam four homers in a nine-inning game, who led the circuit in RBIs five times and in runs scored four times, who topped 150 RBIs (a major-league record) seven times and who knocked in at least 100 runs and scored at least 100 more in each and every one of his thirteen big-league seasons.

The Magic of Baseball 51

THE THINKING MAN'S PITCHER

In an era when mound talent is measured seemingly only by scouts' readings on the radar gun, Atlanta's Greg Maddux has nonetheless built the most successful career of the 1990s more on "smoke and mirrors" than on his smoking fastball.

The Magic of Baseball 53

The often sad-sack Chicago Cubs franchise is known universally for short-sighted player transactions that have often short-circuited the ballclub's immediate future. There was the infamous Lou Brock trade to St. Louis for sore-armed moundsman Ernie Broglio, of course, and also there were deals that stripped the Northsiders of slugging Cy Williams (in the '10s), touted prospect Dolf Camilli (in the '30s), and substantial players like Andre Thornton, Joe Carter and Rafael Palmeiro in the modern era. But no bungled deal was more deadly for Chicago than the one that saw Cubs management decline handing over millions to free-agent Cy Young award winner Greg Maddux. Maddux had been spectacular enough in Chicago (where he is seen here, **BOTTOM**, facing the Mets at Shea Stadium in 1991). He reversed early-career shakiness in 1988 with an 18-8 ledger and then peaked at 20 wins four summers later. But when transplanted to Atlanta the scholarly looking Maddux overnight became the game's most unbeatable hurler – not for one or two seasons alone but for an entire Atlanta-dominated decade. He won 20 his first season with Ted Turner's fortunate club, and stretched out his Cy Young dominance three more seasons. Along with southpaw Tom Glavine and righty John Smoltz, he anchored the most effective rotation found anywhere in the game. (Here, **TOP LEFT**, Maddux pitches a complete game win over his former teammates in 1997.) A $28 million free-agent contract gave Maddux reason enough to smile during a 1993 spring training outing (**TOP RIGHT**), but it was Atlanta front office executives who were soon boasting the biggest smiles at the performances of their new prize catch. The key to the Maddux success story has been an unbending willingness – rare today but once the staple of all successful moundsmen – to learn the true art and craft of pitching. Rarely does a batter seem to see the same pitch in the same place from this hurling artist. His rather ordinary major league fastball is supplemented with unhittable curves, sliders and changeups delivered time and again with unfaltering pinpoint control. (**OPPOSITE**: Maddux displays his trademark style.) If there is a blemish on Maddux it is only his less-than-average successes in Atlanta's numerous post-season appearances. Baseball's all-time winningest lefty Warren Spahn (also a Braves' stalwart) once observed that hitting was timing and pitching was a matter of upsetting timing. Maddux is today's primary exemplar of Spahn's highly accurate theory. Today Maddux remains one of baseball grandest anachronisms, a strong-armed modern-era thrower who has more than mastered the art of pitching for a living.

REGGIE! REGGIE!

He could talk, he could hit, he was a sportswriter's dream. But in the end there wasn't enough mustard in the entire stadium to compete with one Reggie Jackson.

Reggie Jackson was the very definition of a baseball "Hot Dog." He was the flamboyant and outspoken self-promoter who arrived in New York City with a boast that he would be "the straw that stirred the drink" as long as he wore Yankee pinstripes. He had a huge, easily bruised ego and fought constantly with Yankee skipper Billy Martin and others who tried to dull his limelight. He was a grandstanding showman who announced his retirement a year in advance to benefit from a final grand tour around the league's ballparks. He was a media celebrity who had a candy bar named after him in New York and who collected outrageously expensive classic sports cars in California. He was the kind of colorful slugger missing from the game since the days of Babe Ruth, Jimmy Foxx and Babe Herman. And Reggie Jackson was also one of the truly great competitors and hitters of the past three decades. In a career stretching out over 21 summers and five different American League cities Jackson played on 11 divisional champion teams, six pennant-winning teams and five World Championship teams. Known as "Mr. October" for his World Series heroics, he amassed a lifetime .357 post-season average that stood nearly 100 points above his regular-season standard. He spent the final seasons of his career chasing down and surpassing Mickey Mantle for sixth place on the all-time career home run list (with 563), yet his lifetime mark of 2597 strikeouts has never been approached by any other free-swinging slugger. Whether a brash young rookie with Charlie Finley's Oakland A's at the end of the 1960s (**OPPOSITE TOP**), the proud and boisterous Mr. October with George Steinbrenner's Yankees in the late 1970s (**OPPOSITE BOTTOM**), the offensive and defensive hero of Oakland's World Championship teams in 1972 and 1973 (**BOTTOM RIGHT**) or a high-priced free-agent veteran with Gene Autry's Angels in the early 1980s (**TOP RIGHT**), Reggie Jackson was always in the camera's eye and in the nation's imagination as baseball's consummate celebrity hero.

THE SECOND WALTER JOHNSON

No other baseball superstar ever walked away from the game so dramatically at the very zenith of his career; for four glorious summers, no other hurler ever struck such pure terror into the hearts of opposing hitters.

The Magic of Baseball

Many players have tarnished Hall-of-Fame credentials by hanging on for several seasons after the timing has left and the reflexes have slowed; no player in baseball history has ever stepped away from the game at such a dizzying zenith of career achievement as did the incomparable Sandy Koufax. Koufax was another larger-than-life legend who might have achieved so much more had the fates been kinder. Just how great might he have truly been – what records might he have finally amassed – had not persistent arthritis in his pitching elbow sidelined this flame-throwing immortal at the tender age of 30? Perhaps only Dizzy Dean suffered as cruel a blow from baseball happenstance. Yet Koufax's numbers are all the more remarkable for the brevity of his dozen big league seasons: .655 winning percentage (165-87); a 2.76 lifetime ERA; seasons of 25-5 (1963), 26-8 (1965, **TOP LEFT**) and 27-9 (1966), the latter two in his final campaigns; 2396 career strikeouts, with individual season league-leading totals of 269 (1961), 306 (1963), 382 (the all-time major league standard for lefthanders and National League mark, set in 1965) and 317 (1966); and four no-hitters in four consecutive seasons. The numbers were complemented by off-field honors of almost unmatched luster: National League MVP in 1963, World Series MVP in 1963 and 1965, three Cy Young Awards (1963, 1965, 1966) and 1960s Major League Player of the Decade. Although the arthritic elbow that had plagued Koufax from 1964 on was common knowledge around the major league circuit and to the press, shock waves resounded throughout the baseball world when the Dodger's lefthander announced his premature retirement at the close of the 1966 campaign. No pitcher before or since had ever retired immediately on the heels of a Cy Young season; none had ever stepped down following a year of 27 victories (his career high), a 1.73 ERA (again a career best) and 300-plus strikeouts. Nor was another ever likely to do so. What was left was only the distant memory of pennant celebrations and World Series victory, like that which caused such spontaneous joy on October 6, 1963 (**OPPOSITE**), of the league strikeout records, like the one here being celebrated in 1961 with skipper Walt Alston (**BOTTOM LEFT**), and of the matchless southpaw delivery (**PAGES 58-59**) that befuddled hitters for a decade and more.

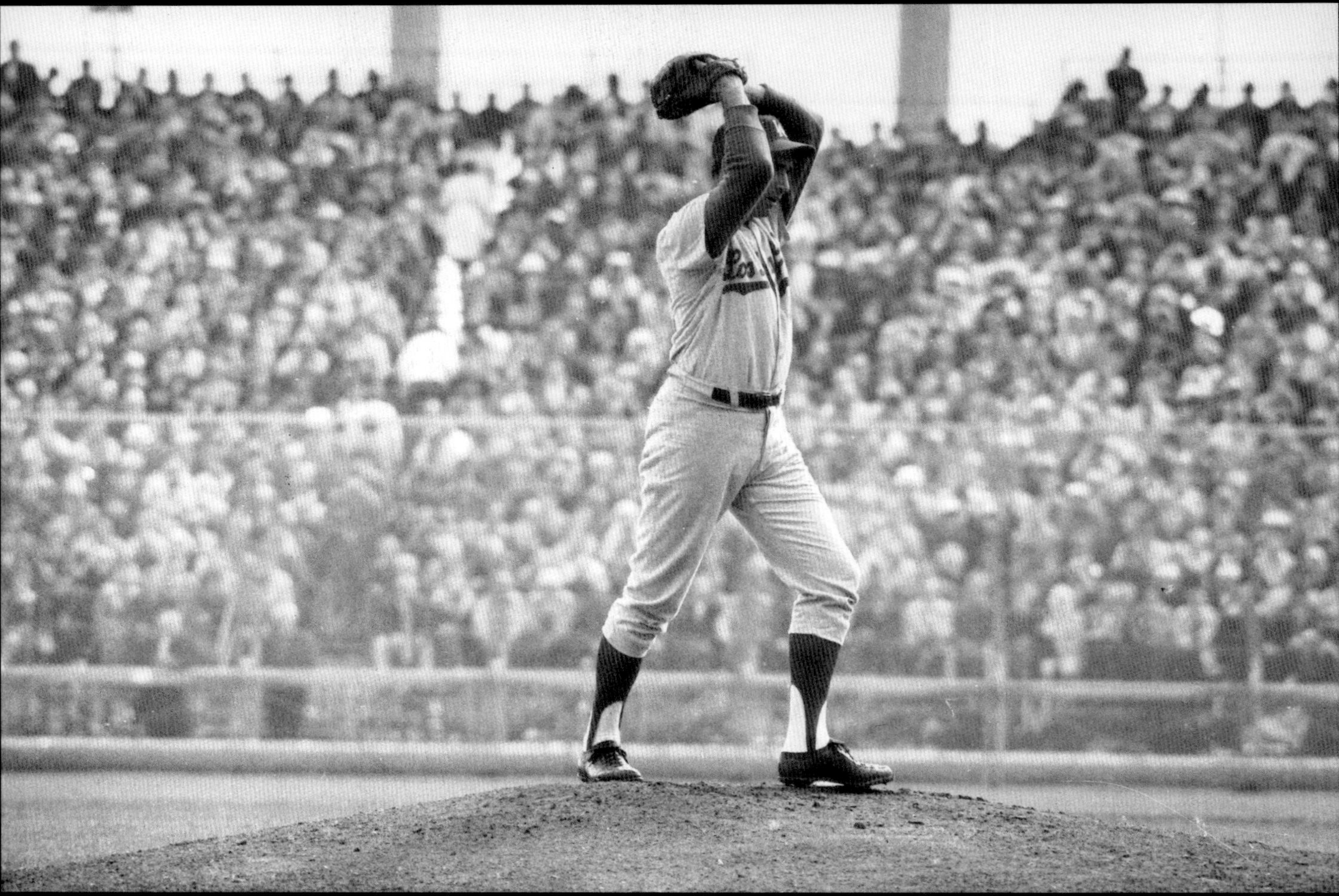

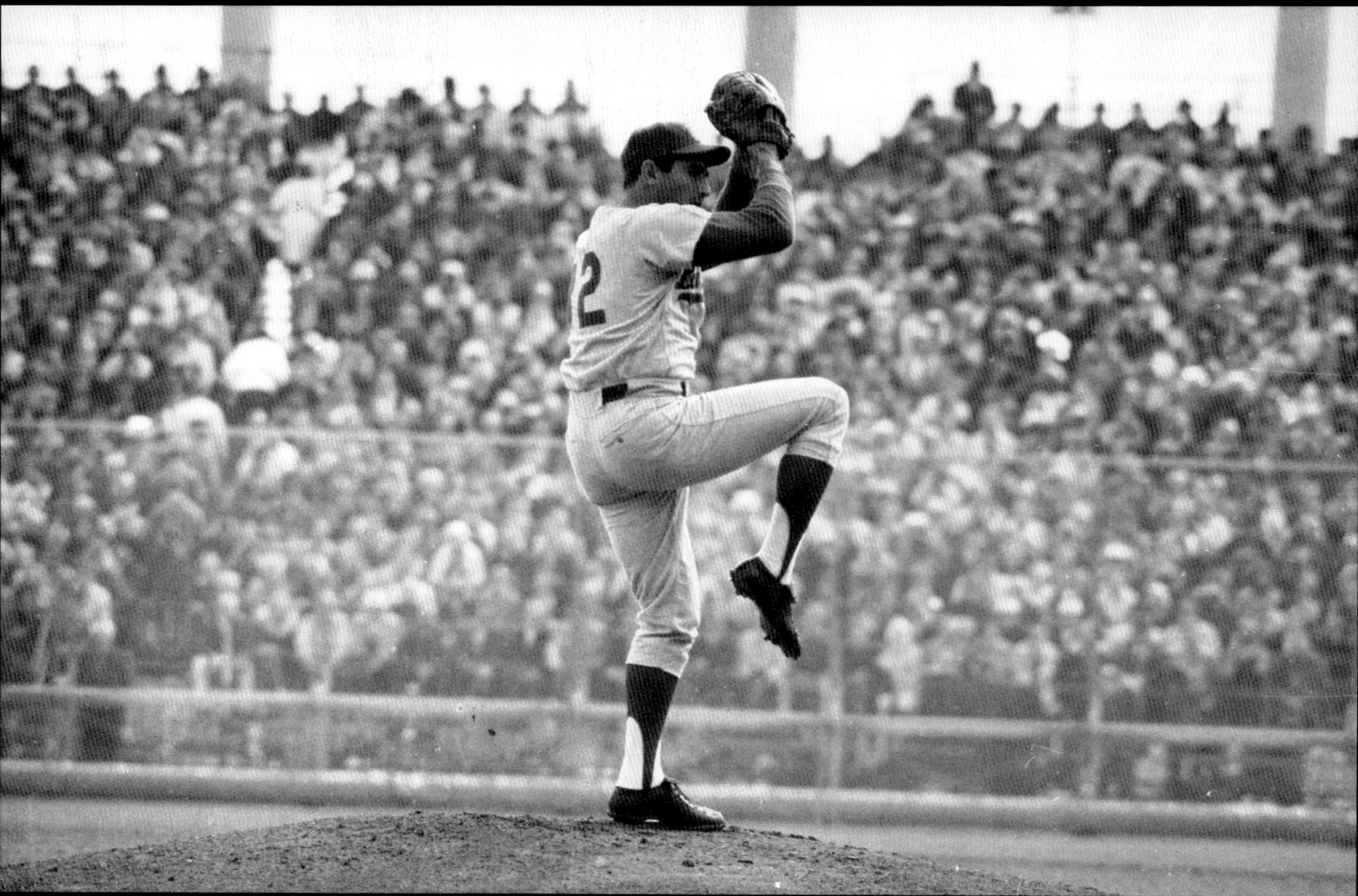

The Magic of Baseball

GRAND OLD MAN OF THE DIAMOND

For Cornelius McGillicuddy (a.k.a. Connie Mack) the game of baseball – a U.S. Supreme Court ruling of 1922 notwithstanding – was always foremost a business and only secondly a game; you had to show profits to keep going.

The life expectancy of a manager is today perhaps two or three seasons; with some franchises (Steinbrenner's Yankees and most expansion ballclubs come immediately to mind) it is perhaps more like six months. It is almost incomprehensible to the modern fan that a single manager (doubling as general manager and club owner at that) might sit on the same bench for a full half century! Yet Connie Mack did, taking the reigns of the Philadelphia A's ballclub in the inaugural season of the fledgling American League and finally stepping down from that post (at the age of 88) only two seasons before baseball's first western expansion during 1953. Needless to say, the records he would establish for games (7878), wins (3776) and losses (4025) will likely never be seriously challenged. And the genial Mr. Mack was also a personality unique in the game he so loved: a soft-spoken leader who would never raise his voice at a player, who rarely visited the clubhouse except for pre-game meetings, which he pioneered, and who remained unchallenged as the best-loved figure in the game for over six full decades. In two of his more classic images captured here, Connie Mack poses with his full American League All-Star team before the first midsummer classic held in Comiskey Park on July 6, 1933 (**TOP**), and with Yankee manager Miller Huggins against a backdrop Yankee Stadium crowd of 85,265 in attendance for a 1931 New York-Philadelphia twin bill (**RIGHT**).

The Magic of Baseball

While on the one hand, with his formal attire and dual post as manager and club owner, he seemed a kind of throwback to baseball's nineteenth-century past, Connie Mack was surprisingly modern in his views about the economic realities of America's pastime. For Mack the bottom line was not winning pennants but turning profits: "It is more profitable for me to have a team that is in contention for most of the season but finishes fourth," he once remarked, noting that "Teams like that will draw well enough during the first part of the season to show a profit for the year, and you don't have to give the players raises if they don't win." With the threat of financial failure looming over his Philadelphia franchise, Mack once sold off nearly his entire inventory of star players after winning four pennants in five years between 1910 and 1914. Having rebuilt his ballclub into a three-time champion (1929-1931), Mack found that declining attendance brought on by runaway pennant races forced yet another wholesale dismantling of what would ultimately prove to be his final great winning team. The last field manager to appear in suit and tie (symbolic of his conception of the game as a business venture), Mr. Mack is captured here in a classic bench pose during the 1930s (**TOP LEFT**) and mugging for the camera with skipper Joe McCarthy before the 1948 season opener in Boston (**TOP RIGHT**).

GREATEST SWITCH-HITTER EVER

First they hoped he would be the next DiMaggio, then that he would soon be the next Babe Ruth; there was no other player who so electrified a crowd, yet somehow he failed to match the greatness all expected of him.

The Magic of Baseball 63

Posing as a brash rookie in 1951 along with the two great hitters of the age, DiMaggio and Williams (**TOP LEFT**), Mickey Mantle was prepared to make his bid to join the ranks of such immortal sluggers. Only a few short seasons later – after his Triple Crown season of 1956, which saw him hit .353, smack 52 homers and drive home 130 runs – he was being hailed as already having surpassed the two unrivaled batsmen who had flanked him that rookie summer, as having surpassed Babe Ruth and everyone else in baseball history. But such premature fan enthusiasm tempted fate. Despite the glorious achievements of Mantle's subsequent years, none of the Babe's vaunted slugging records would ever be his own. Some would even contend by decade's end that his offensive and defensive play did not quite match his New York rivals at the centerfield position. Willie Mays of the Giants and the Dodgers' Duke Snider (with whom he poses here, **BOTTOM LEFT**, during the 1955 World Series). Yet after that explosive 1956 season Mantle would always be assured a place in baseball history as the game's greatest power-hitting switch hitter. He hit home runs of epic proportions from both sides of the plate, coming close on a half-dozen different occasions to hitting the first ball ever completely out of cavernous Yankee Stadium. He displayed a special talent for World Series stardom, playing in a dozen Fall Classics and establishing Series marks for home runs (18), RBIs (40), runs (42), walks (43), extra-base hits (26) and total bases (123). He also hit for average in a fashion rarely achieved by the game's great power hitters, enjoying ten seasons over the .300 mark and a career-best .365 season in 1957. A collage of Mantle memories captured here displays "the Mick" in 1961 World Series action against the Cincinnati Reds at Crosley Field (**OPPOSITE TOP**), in 1961 baserunning action against the Washington Senators (**OPPOSITE BOTTOM**), and posing with manager Casey Stengel and teammates (l to r) Bauer, Reynolds, Berra and Rizzuto (**CENTER LEFT**) during his sophomore 1952 season.

64 THE BASEBALL SCRAPBOOK

The Magic of Baseball 65

When he broke into the Yankee lineup as a rookie sensation in 1951, facing such talented American League hurlers as Bob Feller (**OPPOSITE**), his potential seemed unlimited. He seemed the heir apparent to DiMaggio in centerfield and the next in a long string of heroic Yankee sluggers reaching back to Gehrig and Ruth. But the fates were not kind to Mantle, for all his career milestones and Hall-of-Fame achievements. An injury in the 1951 World Series brought a disastrous end to his rookie season and resulted in leg damage which plagued the rest of his career. Mantle played with constant pain, and despite his prodigious home run totals throughout the 1950s, many in the press and grandstands thought his injuries overblown and criticized his apparent malingering. Finally it was one-year-wonder Roger Maris who achieved what all had long expected of Mantle, the breaking of Babe Ruth's home run standard. Yet the 1960s brought a new appreciation of the injury-riddled star as his career stretched out for 18 seasons. By the time of his retirement and the special Yankee Stadium day in his honor (**RIGHT** and **BOTTOM**), Mantle had emerged as one of the most popular Yankees in the long and rich tradition of New York baseball.

ROGER'S PUZZLE

For much of baseball's decade of the 1960s they were the famous "M & M Boys" – the most potent long-ball duo since Ruth and Gehrig; yet while Maris nabbed a cherished record it was Mick who drew the accolades.

Maris Beats The Babe's Record

The Magic of Baseball 67

Many of our baseball legends are shaped more by personality than performance, are more a matter of nuance than of pure numbers. Certainly there is no better test case for this maxim than Roger Maris, here about to rob a homer in Chicago in 1960 **(OPPOSITE LEFT)** and trying for one against Detroit that same summer **(TOP LEFT)**. For 34 seasons all manner of sluggers had pursued Babe Ruth's prized record of 60 homers in a single season, set during a 1927 summer when the Babe's total alone outpaced all other teams (let alone individuals) throughout the American League. Foxx, Greenberg and Hack Wilson had all come close, only to be turned back by injury and pressures of September play. And as each summer passed the Babe's feat grew in stature and the nation's sports pages were filled with early-season accounts of sluggers like Kluszewski, Kiner or Banks standing several games behind or ahead of the Babe's 1927 pace. Thus when Maris (who had never previously topped 39 in a single campaign) ran neck-and-neck with Mantle in hot pursuit of the Babe in 1961, the press and fans alike were first disbelieving, then somewhat uneasy, and finally seemingly annoyed that such unworthy challengers should threaten to dethrone the legendary Babe. When the "M & M Boys" posed for photographers **(OPPOSITE BOTTOM)** before a July 25th twin bill in which Maris socked four roundtrippers, bringing his total to 40 and his lead over Babe's pace to 24 games, the strain of the chase already seemed etched upon his drawn face. When he acknowledged the fans' cheers **(BOTTOM LEFT)** after lacing a Tracey Stallard delivery deep into the Yankee Stadium rightfield grandstand on October 1st, attaining the magic total of 61, the agonizing burden of the chase had been lifted from his shoulders, only to be replaced by the burden of owning the record itself. That record would stand only slightly longer than the Babe's mark before being shattered by Mark McGwire's big bat in 1998. Yet to many the Babe's 60 still seems the stuff of legend, and Roger's 61 a mere accident of history, a footnote to a compendium of baseball trivia. For some fans the record Maris set in 1961 didn't seem legitimate because the one-season Yankee standout would reach 30 homers only once more in his injury-riddled career; for others, because Maris had played a longer schedule than Ruth and had batted 50 more times; and for many simply because he didn't fit the mold of the true successor to the beloved Babe.

"BIG MAC" MARK McGWIRE
First it was Ruth and later Maris, but by century's end Big Mac was undisputed Kingpin of Swat.

The Magic of Baseball

With their record-smashing home run slugging in the summer of 1998 Mark McGwire of the St. Louis Cardinals and Sammy Sosa of the Chicago Cubs between them rekindled America's fanatical interest in our national pastime. It is perhaps not even an exaggeration to claim that McGwire and Sosa were almost singlehandedly reponsible for finally lifting baseball out of the sad doldrums that had plagued the sport ever since the disillusioning players' labor action and resulting management lockout that had cancelled a 1994 World Series and turned off an entire nation of frustrated ball fans. For future generations of fans the night of September 8, 1998, will always remain one of baseball's most special and cherished moments. Each of us will likely remember precisely where we were on that historic and unforgettable evening when the gigantic slugging redhead in the St. Louis uniform smashed yet another inside fastball into the leftfield grandstands and in that single instant broke a milepost single-season home run record that had stood unchallenged for nearly four decades. When Maris had wrested the cherished homer mark from baseball's first Sultan of Swat 37 seasons earlier there had been legions of naysayers and millions of doubters, and scepticism about Maris's achievement only increased when the Yankee slugger failed throughout the remainder of his career to ever again post Ruthian-type slugging records. But there was never any doubt throughout the decade of the nineties that McGwire, both in Oakland (**MIDDLE**) and St. Louis, was a true home run king with legitimate claim to the Babe's original title. Big Mac had belted more than 50 in each of two previous summers and had only missed the coveted Maris and Ruth records of 60 and 61 because injury had twice robbed him of full seasons. As a rookie back in 1987 (**BOTTOM LEFT**) he had obliterated the slugging standard for first-year phenoms, and with only a dozen seasons under his belt he was also already approaching the rare career benchmark of 500 roundtrippers. Mark McGwire would not only post Ruthian totals in 1998, of course, but he would stretch the longball standard to the almost unthinkable plateau of 70, and then reach the 60-plus milestone yet again during the century's final summer (**BOTTOM RIGHT**, Clouting homer 35 in 1999). Much of the joy surrounding the historic home run race of 1998 was found in the special relationship between Sosa and McGwire (**TOP**), who rooted each other on and shared their special achievements in heart-warming onfield camaraderie. But in the end it was Big Mac alone who wore the coveted home run crown, and his devastating single swing of September 8th (**OPPOSITE**) will likely remain the most memorable image of one of baseball's most glorious summers.

"BIG SIX" PITCHING IN A PINCH

He was the dominant pitcher of his age, one of five original immortals selected for Cooperstown enshrinement – a nation's first true baseball star, with the good looks and clean reputation of a classic American hero.

The Magic of Baseball 71

When the final ledger is read, baseball may prove to have been mostly a saga of instructive defeats and ennobling tragedies, its fictional archetype the boastful Casey of Mudville, who shatters the empty air with the force of his futile blow and strikes out for the once-more defeated hometown nine with the bases loaded in the bottom of the ninth. One of the true tragedies of baseball's "untold history" is the sad saga of those final years of the immortal Christy Mathewson (whose proud wife is seen here admiring his Cooperstown plaque in 1958, **BOTTOM RIGHT**). Matty was perhaps the greatest pitcher of an age replete with pitching greats. Featuring a "magic pitch" which was precursor to today's screwball, Matty today still ranks behind only Cy Young and Walter Johnson in total career victories. Yet more remarkably, perhaps, he breezed through most games throwing only 75 or 80 pitches and walking only 1.6 batters per nine innings throughout his 17-year career. As important to his legend were his boldly striking good looks (**TOP RIGHT**) and his college education, both of which, in an age of diamond ruffians, helped to make Matty the first genuine national baseball idol. Yet nearly all great baseball legends have their downsides, and all springtime heroes have their autumns. At the end of a sterling 16-year career, which saw him win 372 ballgames for McGraw's Giants, the immortal Matty was traded to the Reds of Cincinnati. Mathewson was never destined for success in the Queen City, however, and only a few short seasons after his arrival he was to depart in a cloud of intrigue and bitter personal disappointment. The true culprit here, seemingly, was a heavy-hitting yet highly unsavory character who held down the first baseman's post in Cincinnati for three seasons after 1916, one Hal Chase. Questions long surrounded the integrity of Chase's play, and rumors linked him to efforts by gamblers to fix games. So strong were these charges that Mathewson in his new capacity as manager suspended his first baseman for the balance of the season in August 1918. When Chase filed a civil suit against his manager, and subsequently was formally tried by the league itself, he was promptly found innocent of any charge or implication of impropriety. Matty, for his part, was disheartened enough by the affair to retire ten games from season's end and enlist promptly for military service. Tragically, that service would lead to a training accident involving poison gas, and that would lead to tuberculosis and Matty's premature death at age 47.

SAY HEY WILLIE!

Only Aaron and Ruth socked more homers, and had Willie played in a less cavernous ballpark he might have been the all-time home run king. Yet nothing could have made Willie Mays' legend any larger than it already is.

The Magic of Baseball 73

A generation remembers them now as simply "Willie, Mickey and the Duke" – the three greatest center fielders of all time playing in the same decade and in the same city. It was seemingly no accident that the title of Terry Cashman's famous song gave their names in that particular order. For the legions of New York Yankee supporters the Adonis-like switch-hitting Mickey Mantle was the favorite, the anointed heir to Babe Ruth's slugger's crown. For thousands of crazed Dodger faithful the graceful, if sometimes sullen, Duke Snider (**LEFT**) had his backers as the more talented defensive stalwart. But for the lesser numbers of Giants fans who populated the Polo Grounds there was never any contest, and the judgement of history now rests on the side of these Polo Ground denizens. Neither Mantle nor Snider, nor anyone else who ever came along, could match Willie Mays for all-around talent – for the unprecedented balance of offensive power, basepath daring and outfield acrobatics, or for the enthusiasm and verve with which he played the game. For many he was simply the greatest baseball player they ever saw, the perfect embodiment of that mythical ideal, the complete ballplayer.

THE BASEBALL SCRAPBOOK

Seen (**BELOW**) preparing to smash the 2000th base hit of his illustrious career in a 1963 game at Dodger Stadium, Mays stood alongside Hank Aaron as the leading slugger of the two decades that stretched between the beginning of the Korean Conflict and the end of the war in Vietnam. During his first eight seasons in San Francisco he produced in excess of 100 RBIs and 100 runs scored each summer. He stroked four homers in a single game on one notable occasion, and three in a game during two other outings. His 52 homers in 1965 left him in the rare company of Ruth, Foxx, Kiner and Mantle as the only longballers ever to amass 50 circuit clouts on more than one occasion. He hit 30 or more homers in each of 11 different seasons and surpassed Mel Ott as the National League's all-time home run king in May of 1966, eventually extending his lead over Ott to well over 100, with a life-time total of 660 roundtrippers. But for all his awesome power, Willie Mays will perhaps be best remembered for the enthusiasm of his earliest days in New York, when he played stickball with youngsters in the Harlem streets surrounding the Polo Grounds and addressed all his fellow players with the now-famous high-spirited "Say Hey" that became a trademark.

The Magic of Baseball

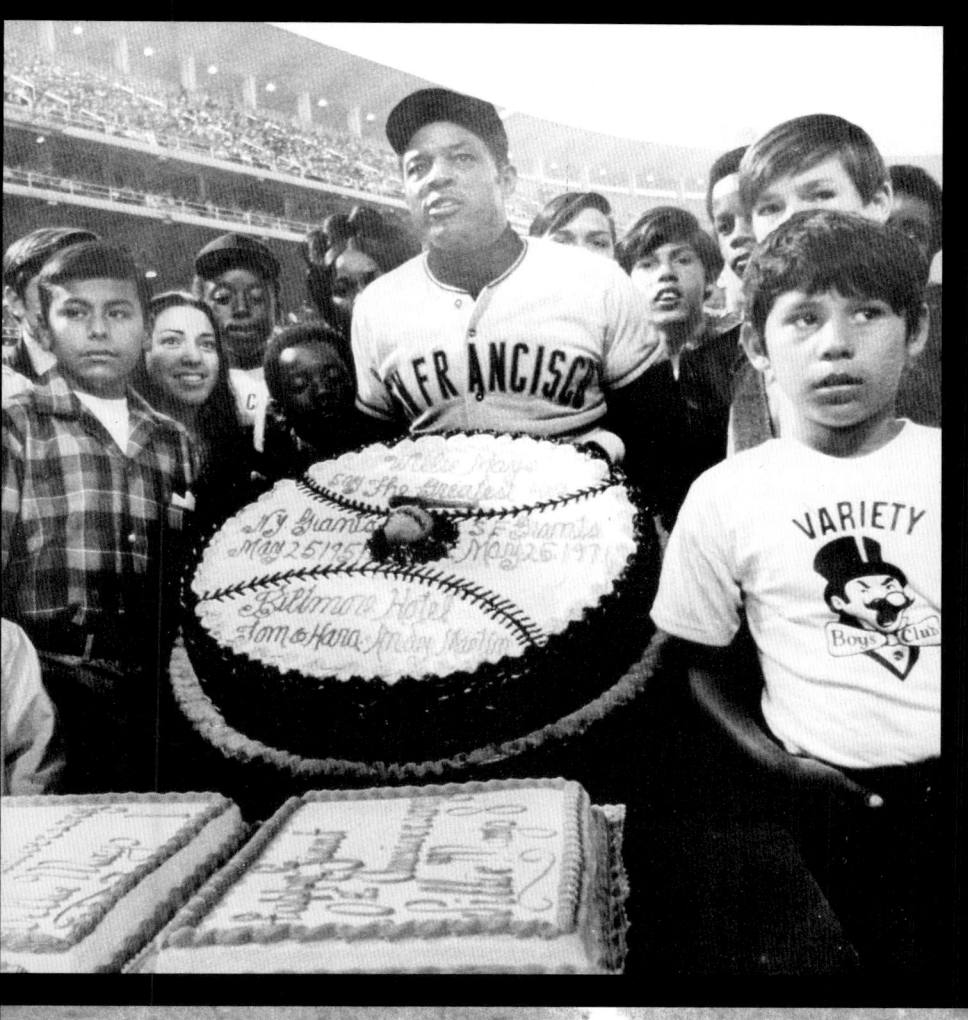

Willie Mays was a remarkably durable ballplayer, logging at least 150 games for 13 consecutive campaigns. And he was also the game's greatest gate attraction during a decade of the sixties, when baseball had seemed to lose something of its national appeal. For some, it was the fence-busting power that immortalized Willie Mays; for others it was the blazing speed and basepath daring that made him most memorable. Whether dashing to the plate for another Giants' run (**PAGE 72**), appealing a close play at the plate while wearing the uniform of the expansion Mets during the 1973 World Series (**PAGE 73, BOTTOM**) or bowling over the best of the league's catchers, like Reds Hall-of-Famer Johnny Bench in 1971 game action (**BELOW**), no player (even the ruthless Cobb or the daring Jackie Robinson) ever generated more pure baserunning excitement. For 20 full seasons Willie Mays plied his trade with unmatched grace and talent for the Giants, first in New York and later in San Francisco (**OPPOSITE TOP**). And fans around the league (such as the youngsters here celebrating his 20 seasons with the Giants in a special ceremony at Dodger Stadium, **LEFT**) always enjoyed the show, no matter what their hometown loyalties might be.

PEDRO MARTINEZ

If Marichal still rates a slight nod as top Latino moundsman of the ages, it is a slim fellow Dominican now toiling for the Boston Red Sox who is today's undisputed ace among Hispanic kings of the hill. Few would deny that Pedro Martínez has earned his niche as the most dominating hurler of the late 1990s and beyond.

The Magic of Baseball   77

A defining career moment for this nonpareil Dominican mound ace may well have been the 1999 major league All-Star Game staged on his home field in Boston **(TOP LEFT)**. If there was any lingering question that Pedro Martínez stood among baseball's finest hurlers of his era it was answered early on that night when the hometown hero mowed down the first four National League batters he faced, a feat that earned Martínez a cherished spot in the Midsummer Classic record books. Pedro faced only six enemy batters and struck out five, a performance earning MVP honors for the seven-year veteran. At the time of his debut back in 1992 with the Dodgers, the slender right-hander was recognized only as the younger brother of then LA ace Ramón Martínez, himself a quality NL starter. Debuting as a reliever because (despite his tantalizing fastball) he was deemed too slight of frame to log quality innings as a starter, Pedro's career blossomed only after being traded to Montreal straight up for journeyman infielder Delino DeShields. Martínez was quick to foreshadow his eventual dominance once he pulled on Expos togs **(BOTTOM)** — he lost a perfect game in the eighth at Cincinnati when he hit opposing batter Reggie Sanders (the no-hitter was also promptly lost); he pitched nine perfect innings in San Diego on June 3, 1995 but left the game after giving up a leadoff single in the tenth; and he struck out 200 batters for the first time in 1996. The big breakthrough would come a year later when Pedro earned his first Cy Young honors, logging 17 victories for the also-ran Expos but also fanning 305 enemy batsmen. Once established among the best in the senior circuit, Pedro Martínez suddenly became too costly a commodity for the cash-strapped Montreal franchise, which hastily peddled him off to Boston. Once in the American League Pedro Martínez only got better. He won 23 ball games in 1999 and mowed down 313 (logging 19 games with 10 or more Ks). Seemingly overnight the new Dominican Dandy **(TOP RIGHT)** was now the junior circuit equivalent of Randy Johnson. One stellar moment at the end of the fabulous 1999 season came in the Division Series with Cleveland. Pedro made a surprise relief appearance during the deciding contest, held the Indians hitless over the final six frames, and thus vaulted Boston into an LCS showdown with the hated New York Yankees (Martínez also posting the only Boston victory in the short-lived title series). At the year's end he had bagged a second Cy Young trophy, hoisting him into the company of Johnson and Gaylord Perry as the only trio to cop that honor in both major leagues.

THE RUGGED "LITTLE NAPOLEON"

Rarely has a ballplayer or sports star had any more fitting and descriptive nickname. This "Little Napoleon" was every bit the same arrogant, abusive, abrasive, combative, pugnacious mighty-mite as his famed namesake.

The Magic of Baseball

John McGraw was such a successful and renowned manager that it is easy to forget what a phenomenal player he once was during baseball's lost decades surrounding the turn of the century. He played 16 big-league seasons, compiled a lifetime .334 batting average (26th on the career list) and starred at third base for Ned Hanlon's fearsome Baltimore Orioles teams that won three consecutive National League titles (1894-1896). He was a skilled lefthanded batsman who perfected the hit-and-run play with teammate Wee Willie Keeler and batted over .320 for nine consecutive seasons. But above all, he was best known as a fiery competitor, maybe even a downright dirty player, an infielder whose continual blocking and tripping of baserunners is reputed to have led directly to the stationing of an additional umpire upon the modern field of play. As a manager, McGraw lost nothing of his "win-at-all-costs" approach to the game. The New York Giants teams that he managed between 1902 and 1932 won nine league pennants and three World Titles. These Polo Ground clubs featured the Hall-of-Fame hurling of Christy Mathewson and Joe McGinnity, but their games were most often won with the rough-and-tumble, hit-and-run style of offensive play at which McGraw was a master. At career's end he ranked behind only Connie Mack in total games managed and in career games won, and he stood second only to Stengel in World Series games managed. But these numbers do not really convey the larger truth about the man: that for the first three decades of the present century this "Little Napoleon" was arguably the most dominant figure in American baseball.

A year after his 1932 retirement a stately John McGraw would return one final time to the nation's baseball scene to manage the National League squad in the inaugural summer classic All-Star Game at Chicago's Comiskey Park. Later he would pose with his New York replacement, Bill Terry, as the victorious Giants celebrated the clinching of a National League title on the steps of New York's City Hall (**BOTTOM LEFT**). More casual portraits find the Giants skipper chatting with fellow immortal Honus Wagner of the Pirates (**TOP LEFT**) and striking a competitive stance in the Giants' gaudy 1917 checkered uniform (**OPPOSITE**).

A TRUE DOMINICAN DANDY

The greatest Latin pitcher of all time, Juan Marichal won more games (191) in the '60s than anyone, including Sandy Koufax and Bob Gibson.

Latin American ballplayers have long been victims of misunderstanding and underappreciation, if not downright discrimination. None suffered more blatant injustices during and after his career, however, than Juan Marichal (**OPPOSITE**) who shared the limelight during the '60s with Sandy Koufax, Bob Gibson and Don Drysdale. It today perhaps seems hard to believe that a moundsman who owned such a lengthy resume of milestones and records (including 243 career wins, 2,303 strikeouts, and a sterling .631 career winning percentage) would not have been automatically elected to Cooperstown in either his first or second year of eligibility. But the shadow of prejudice hung over Marichal's brilliant career, at least for a time. The underappreciated Latin athlete was the victim of the damaging public statements of his former manager Alvin Dark, who in one mood praised his ace as an athlete who "thrives on competition" and "always rises to the occasion," then in another mood blasted him as being "without guts" and careless with his talents. Equally damaging was a single unfortunate moment of indiscretion in which the star Giants pitcher bloodied Los Angeles catcher John Roseboro with a bat during an infamous bean-ball incident. But these shadows are obliterated by the brilliance of Marichal's career achievements. In 1963 Marichal defeated Warren Spahn 1-0 in a memorable 16-inning pitching duel. That season the Dominican Dandy threw the Giants' first no-hitter in more than three decades, and ended up with a 25-8 record and a 2.41 ERA. Not a flash in the pan, Marichal won more than 20 games six times during the '60s. In a happy scene the following decade, Marichal is mobbed by teammates (**TOP RIGHT**) in San Diego after his final pitch in the season's final game had clinched a 1971 division title and NLCS matchup with the Pittsburgh Pirates. Only four seasons later Los Angeles Dodgers manager Walt Alston extends a fond farewell to the Dominican Dandy (**BOTTOM RIGHT**) as he prepares to leave a big league clubhouse for the final time of his illustrious 16-year career. Marichal was about to retire after a brief season-opening stint with the 1975 Dodgers. In 1983 he was elected to the Hall of Fame.

THE HUMAN CORKSCREW

In the batter's box he looked like a contortionist peeking around the corner at a feared pursuer (the pitcher) he didn't want to face; in the record book he looks like the finest hitter ever to grace the National League.

The Magic of Baseball 83

As the last holdover from the great Cardinals teams of the wartime forties, Stan "The Man" Musial spanned two great eras of St. Louis baseball history during his remarkable 22-year career. As a sophomore member of the Cardinals' great World Champion team of 1942, the young Musial here slides home safely against the Boston Braves and famed catcher Ernie Lombardi (**OPPOSITE BOTTOM**). As a youthful slugging first sacker in 1946, he also poses here on the dugout steps with teammates (l to r) Joe Garagiola, Dick Sisler, Whitey Kurowski and Enos Slaughter (**OPPOSITE TOP**), on the eve of what would soon prove to be the final St. Louis World Series appearance for almost two full decades. And as a defensive standout on that same 1946 National League pennant-winning club, Musial stretches for an errant throw to first during pre-game practice in Brooklyn's Ebbets Field (**BOTTOM LEFT**). In the twilight of his career, two decades later, the ageless Stan Musial is also captured blasting a record-tying fourth consecutive home run in 1962 against Casey Stengel's young Mets, a mammoth blast launched in one of his favorite haunts, the venerable New York City Polo Grounds (**TOP LEFT**). Long home run balls were a signature of Musial's slugging career, and he belted out 475 in all, to stand alongside his 3630 career base hits (the senior circuit record before Pete Rose), 725 doubles (the third best all-time), 1949 runs scored and 1951 RBIs. But the true measure of Stan Musial's hitting prowess was his unparalleled consistency. Knocking out 1815 base hits at home, he recorded precisely the same number in road games. He batted over .310 for 16 straight seasons. And over 21 full seasons he averaged an incredible 172 hits, 92 runs scored, 92 RBIs and 23 roundtrippers per year. If this were not enough, the rugged Musial was also the first man ever to play more than 1000 games at each of two different defensive positions.

84 THE BASEBALL SCRAPBOOK

The Magic of Baseball 85

If Musial was the greatest player in St. Louis Cardinal history, he was also a runaway fan favorite. From his rookie season on, "The Man" wore an infectious and genuine smile that brought as much joy to the hearts of Cardinal faithful as it delivered terror to the hearts of opposing pitchers. Nowhere was that smile more in evidence than when Stan addressed an overflowing Dodger Stadium crowd in August 1963 after receiving two plaques from Southern California baseball writers honoring his last league appearance in the City of Angels (**TOP RIGHT**). And Musial's infectious warmth toward the adoring Cardinals fans is nowhere better captured than in a candid shot of the future Hall-of-Famer greeting his young fans on the roof of the Cardinals dugout at Sportsman's Park on Opening Day of his final season as an active player (**OPPOSITE**). Shortly after his retirement, the personable Stan Musial served a single season in the Cardinal front office as general manager, a most successful stint which saw the Redbirds under the field leadership of his closest friend and former roommate, Red Schoendienst, romp to a National League flag and World Series triumph over Boston's Red Sox. In his final official capacity with the ballclub he had served so long, Stan Musial here poses with friend Red Schoendienst behind the St. Louis Cardinals' World Series trophy on October 20, 1967 (**BOTTOM RIGHT**).

RANDY JOHNSON

Greg Maddux may be the most masterful hurler of the recent epoch, and Pedro Martínez may well have no peer when it comes to dominating rival batsmen. Yet no modern-era pitcher strikes more pure fear into the hearts of opposition hitters than beanpole southpaw Randy Johnson, owner of baseball's premier fastball.

Baseball has never witnessed a taller pitcher than Randy Johnson (6'10"), nor have there been many down through the ages quite as dominant as the fabled "Big Unit" who has toiled with even success for the Montreal Expos, Seattle Mariners, Houston Astros and Arizona Diamondbacks across his 15-year career. The resumé is easily as impressive as any hurler of the modern era—one no-hitter (versus Detroit in 1990), several seasons of 300-plus strikeouts (1993, 1999, 2000, 2001), a handful of Cy Young Awards (1995, 1999, 2000, 2001), and a pair of 19-strikeout games in the same season (1997). A fearsome fastball tinged with just enough cautionary wildness had made Johnson baseball's premier strikeout king by the century's end. He fanned 372 in 2001, missing Nolan Ryan's one-season mark by only 11, and two years earlier he matched Ryan with 23 games of 10 or more Ks. He is also one of but three pitchers (with Gaylord Perry and Pedro Martínez) to claim Cy Young honors in both leagues. When the D'Backs clinched the 2001 World Series victory over the Yankees it was Johnson who sealed the victory with a rare relief appearance (**OPPOSITE**). Gaining all four Arizona victories between them, Johnson and fellow D'Backs ace Curt Schilling shared post-season MVP honors (**TOP RIGHT**). But most impressive about Johnson is the awesome sight of his 6'10" frame staring down opposing batters (**BELOW**).

BASEBALL'S MOST NOBLE PIONEER

When it comes to great Dodger teams of the post-Depression era, there is only a single hands-down candidate for such accolades as "most exciting," "most daring," "most reckless" or "most inspired" – Jackie Robinson.

Jackie Robinson constructed a legendary Hall-of-Fame career that can neither be measured by the raw numbers catalogued in the *Baseball Encyclopedia* nor by any yardsticks so sedulously applied by baseball's ever-prevalent statisticians. Today Robinson does not even appear on most Dodger listings of career batting statistics, his highest post on any such list being seventh in all-time runs scored (947). Perhaps the most exciting basestealer of all time, Jackie played in an age when the steal was given a diminished role in the game – especially on a power-packed roster such as that of the 1950s Dodgers – and his career total of 197 stolen bases belies his true speed and daring on the basepaths. Yet Robinson did nevertheless achieve a remarkable list of distinctions and awards for so brief a career: the Major League's first Rookie-of-the-Year in 1947, National League MVP (**TOP RIGHT**) and batting champion (.342) in 1949, stolen base leader for the National League in 1947 (29) and 1949 (37) and a yearly All-Star selection between 1949 and 1954. A line-drive hitter with a .311 lifetime average and the speed and on-base percentage of a leadoff man, Robinson smashed 137 homers and often batted cleanup in his later years. Robinson's highest achievements had to do with his unparalleled abilities – not often recorded in box scores and thus not subject to quantification – to turn around ballgames in dramatic fashion and to beat his opponents by guile and intimidation. He repeatedly taunted and unnerved opposing pitchers from the basepaths. His daring baserunning feats produced numerous unearned runs by aggravating and frustrating opposing infielders into frequent costly mistakes. Those who actually saw it will steadfastly contend that a Jackie Robinson steal of home (he had 19 of them) was the most thrilling sight available in all of baseball. In this collection of memorable Robinson images we find Jackie signing autographs before his first big league game (**OPPOSITE TOP LEFT**), stealing third base in a 1947 pre-season game against the Yankees (**OPPOSITE TOP RIGHT**), chatting with Gil Hodges (l) and Branch Rickey before a 1949 World Series encounter (**OPPOSITE BOTTOM**) and pleasing autograph seekers at a final old-timers game appearance in 1969 (**BOTTOM RIGHT**).

CHARLIE HUSTLE

For three decades he was Cincinnati's showpiece of public pride as he chased down Cobb's seemingly unreachable hit record; then overnight he became its greatest source of public embarrassment.

The Magic of Baseball 91

Even the most casual ball fan knows that no player has banged out more base hits over the course of baseball's last century than Peter Edward Rose, the firebrand "Charlie Hustle" who is so intimately linked in baseball memory to the Cincinnati franchise, for which he played all but a fraction of his tempestuous career. It is equally obvious, if somewhat less quantifiable, that no player has earned more press coverage in the past decade than has this same Peter Edward Rose. The 1980s after all was the decade in which ballooning contracts and labor disputes had often driven base hits and pennant races from the front pages of even the daily sports sections, and if Rose was indisputably the silent heart of Cincinnati baseball in the 1970s, he was the acknowledged front-and-center media attraction upon his return engagement in the Queen City during the 1980s. At each turn the Cincinnati baseball story was seemingly another momentous Rose achievement or another cataclysmic Rose revelation. And while the news was always front-page stuff, it wasn't always good news, and it wasn't always strictly baseball achievements that were foremost in the public eye. Rose's failures as a field manager first disappointed the faithful throughout the decade's middle years. His revealed failures as a role model and baseball idol crushed the hometown Reds fans and the nation as a whole throughout 1989. What had begun with the glorious celebration of Rose chasing Cobb at the decade's dawning had dwindled to the sad image of Rose chasing his own lost stature as baseball hero by decade's dreary close.

Pete Rose is captured on these and the following pages in contrasting scenes which represent distinct stages of his rollercoaster career: legging out yet another base hit as a member of the 1981 Philadelphia Phillies (**TOP LEFT**), manning first base in 1985 game action for the Reds (**BOTTOM LEFT**), rounding first base after the 1985 single which at long last bested Cobb's seemingly unreachable record (**PAGES 92-93**) and pensively blowing a minor league bubble in the Reds' Spring Training dugout shortly after news broke concerning his ongoing investigation by the Baseball Commissioner's Office for his alleged gambling activities (**OPPOSITE**).

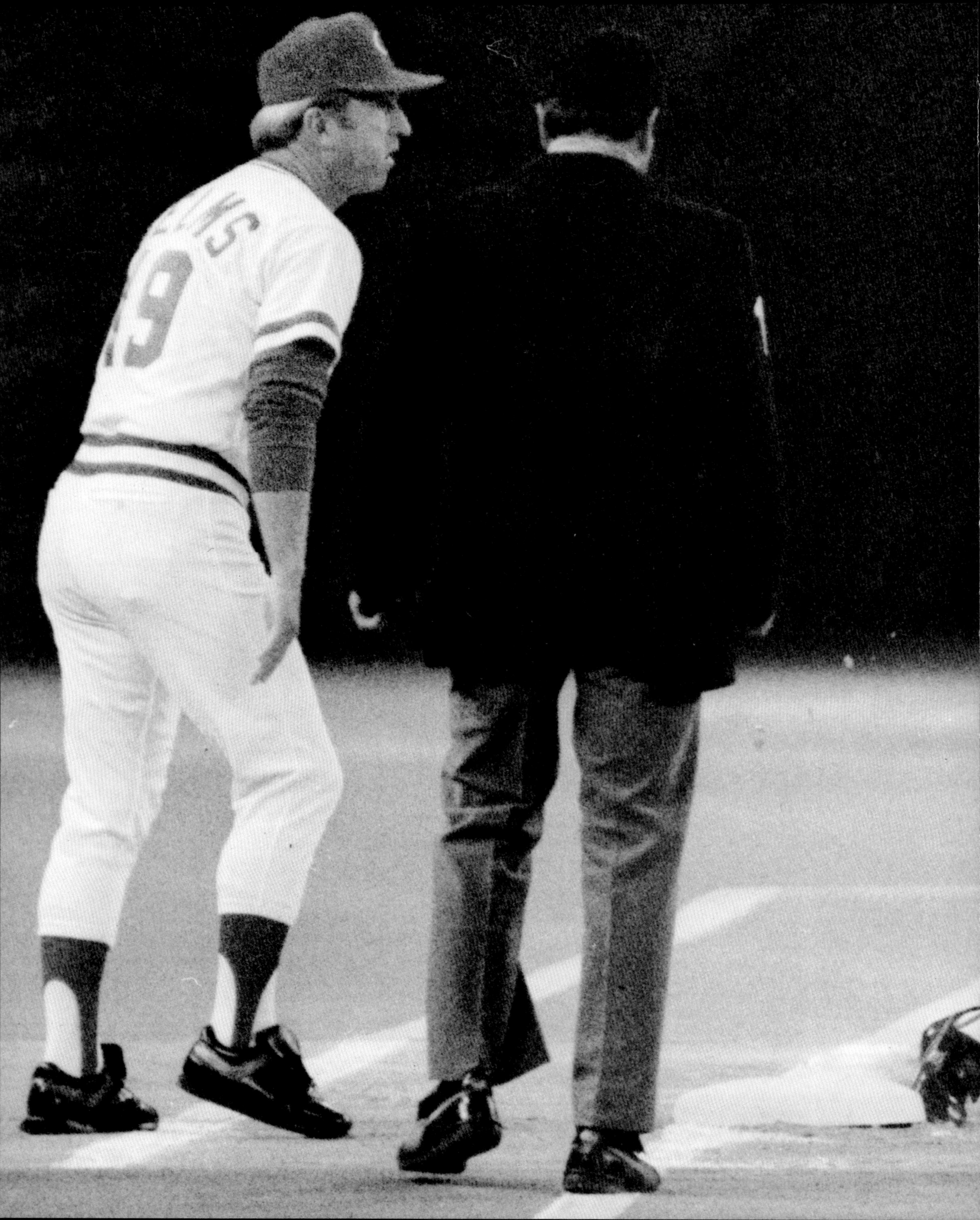

The Magic of Baseball 93

SULTAN OF SWAT

He holds the dubious distinction of being the only player ever caught stealing to end a World Series; but you can bet the farm that this isn't the reason most of a nation's sportsfans remember the man called Babe.

The Magic of Baseball 95

More than any player to swing a bat or hurl a fastball, Babe Ruth was the pure stuff of legend. With Ruth, in fact, the legend is often most difficult to separate from the facts. From his earliest days as a dominating Red Sox hurler (**OPPOSITE LEFT**), throughout the glory years as Yankee slugger (**OPPOSITE TOP RIGHT** and **OPPOSITE BOTTOM RIGHT**) and unparalleled fan favorite (**ABOVE**), and in the heart-tugging tragic moments of his final appearance in the "House that Ruth Built" (**PAGES 98-99**) – a frail figure wasted by cancer and making his last public appearance at age 53 – the Babe always seemed a figure almost too fantastic to be true. Did the Babe really, when informed that his salary had outstripped that of the President, shrug and say that he had simply had a better year than Hoover? Did he in fact "call his shot" when pointing to the center field bleachers before homering off Cubs hurler Charlie Root in the 1932 World Series? Did his final homer actually travel over 600 feet in Pittsburgh, as nowadays reported? And did he actually work a miracle for young Johnny Sylvester (**LEFT**), who lay gravely ill in a St. Louis hospital, by sending the sickly child a promise to "hit one for you tomorrow" on the eve of his three Series homers in St. Louis in 1926? The answer to all these questions, of course, is that we would rather not know. We baseball fans – especially when it comes to such legends as the Babe – prefer to take our strong shot of mythology straight, undiluted by any weak grains of truth.

96 THE BASEBALL SCRAPBOOK

The Magic of Baseball 97

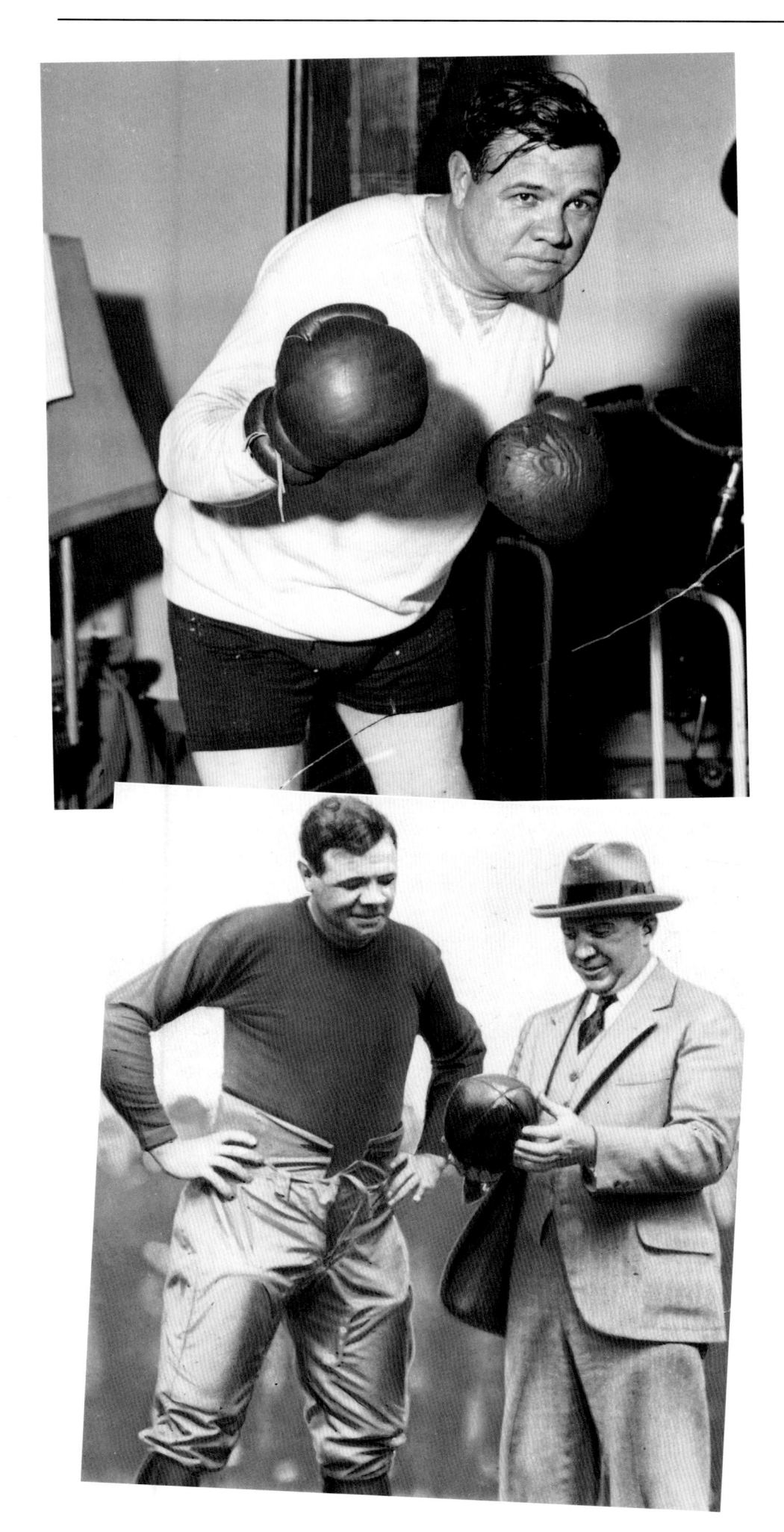

Unlike today's pampered and paraded multimillion dollar superstars, here was a sporting figure who really *was* larger than the game itself. While his "Sultan of Swat" glory years in Yankee pinstripes stretch for little more than a dozen summers, those legendary New York seasons were preceded by five Boston campaigns as the finest left-handed hurler in the American League. Before he was slugging the mammoth homers that revolutionized the game, the Babe was carving out legitimate Hall-of-Fame credentials as a moundsman – a ten-year career 2.28 ERA and lifetime .671 winning percentage (94-46); a record 29 consecutive scoreless innings in World Series play which stood unchallenged for 42 seasons; a league-leading 1.75 ERA and nine shutouts for the champion Red Sox in 1916. Sold to the Yankees in 1920 for a price ($100,000) twice that ever before paid for a single talent, Ruth soon rewrote the record books for long-ball heroics and revolutionized the game with his patented free-swinging batting style. In the half-dozen seasons of his heyday period (1926-1931) the Babe averaged better than 50 homers a year, eventually reigning as league home-run champion a record dozen times and posting a record career home-run ratio of one for every 11.76 plate appearances, easily outdistancing the nearest challenger in that department, Ralph Kiner (one for each 14.11 appearances). But it was not the ledger of the record book alone which made George Herman Ruth a living legend. Sportswriter Bob Broeg once said it best in suggesting that "to try to capture Babe Ruth with cold statistics would be like trying to keep up with him on a night out." It is as hopeless as trying to capture in limp prose the gargantuan appetites, limitless charisma and boundless ego which are as much a part of the indelible Ruth image as the unbalanced, barrel-chested, spindly legged figure circling the basepaths with his Santa-sized torso and delicate, choppy gate. The highest-paid athlete of his era, Babe Ruth was also a national celebrity of unprecedented proportions, as frequently seen before the newsreel camera as in the pages of baseball's record books. Here the Babe strikes a confident candid pose with manager Joe McCarthy and sidekick Lou Gehrig at the opening of pre-season practice in 1934 (**OPPOSITE TOP**), hauls logs on his own Sudbury, Massachusetts, farm (**OPPOSITE BOTTOM**), mugs in boxing gear for a 1933 publicity shot (**TOP LEFT**) and takes gridiron lessons from fellow legend Knute Rockne (**BOTTOM LEFT**).

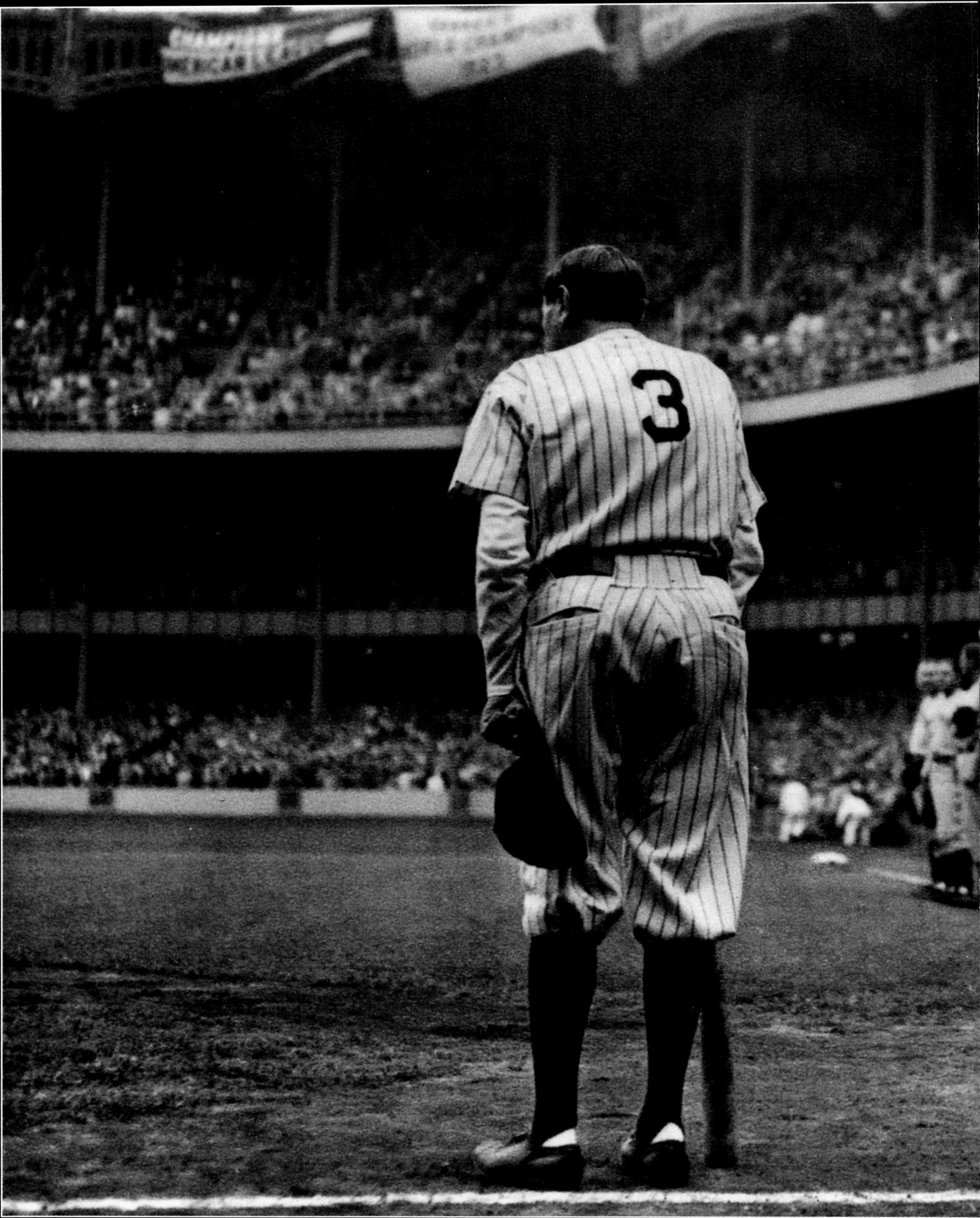

The Magic of Baseball 99

THE AYES OF TEXAS ARE UPON YOU

Perhaps baseball's most remarkable pitcher; assuredly its most incomparable physical wonder! Who else could overwhelm hitters with a 95-mph fastball and master an unthinkable 5000 strikeout barrier at the age of 42?

The Magic of Baseball 101

The unrivaled news story in the baseball-poor state of Texas during the summer of 1989 was one Lynn Nolan Ryan. Long labeled by skeptics as a ".500 pitcher" despite his awesome strikeout totals, Ryan led the circuit in walks more times (8) than in strikeouts (7) during two decades of flamethrowing for the Mets, Angels and Astros. But a much publicized free-agent signing with the Rangers provided showcase enough to demonstrate that there was still plenty of life in one of modern baseball's most enduring legends. The seemingly ageless Ryan (then 43) was, in fact, a clear choice as "Baseball Story of the Year" for 1989. In a season dominated by the relentlessly negative news of Pete Rose's betting scandal and controversial ban from baseball, the untimely death of Commissioner A. Bart Giamatti and the earthquake-plagued Giants-Athletics World Series, Ryan was perhaps the single inspirational diamond story of the summer. His unprecedented feat of 301 strikeouts at age 42, his relentless march past the unthinkable 5000 career strikeout barrier and his near misses during two occasions in which he flirted with an unparalleled sixth career no-hitter, all held the nation's baseball fans spellbound. And as if an encore were needed, Ryan's first marvelous season in Arlington was already proving no fluke when the certain future Hall-of-Famer opened the first month of the 1990 campaign with a sterling one-hit performance against the White Sox, tying Bob Feller's career mark for one-hitters at 12. Soon to follow were the long-awaited sixth career no-hit masterpiece and a final trophy with career-victory number 300. All agree today that the remarkable Ryan was an even better pitcher at age 43 than he was in his prime a decade earlier. The infectious Nolan Ryan is captured here at both the dawn and apex of his career. The brash youngster celebrates his league-leading strikeout total during a 1968 sophomore campaign with the New York Mets (**TOP RIGHT**). Twenty-five years later the veteran tips his cap after closing out his career in the final game played at Arlington Stadium (**BOTTOM RIGHT**). A wily veteran displays his unmatched fastball form at Seattle's Kingdome during his first start after a record career sixth no-hitter in the no-hit-crazy 1990 summer (**OPPOSITE LEFT** and **OPPOSITE RIGHT**). Amazingly, the following season Ryan threw his seventh no-hitter.

"NEW IRONMAN" CAL RIPKEN, JR.

If Babe Ruth rescued baseball from its Black Sox scandal, Ripken did much the same in the face of the sport's biggest public relations blunder, the 1994 strike-shortened season.

The Magic of Baseball

If Sosa and McGwire deserve credit for recapturing lost fans at century's end with their highlight-reel slugging feats, Cal Ripken, Jr., is perhaps more entitled still to the imaginary trophy for baseball savior of the greed-filled nineties. And Ripken worked his own brand of magic with fans not by prodigious momentary feats of long-ball slugging or dramatic game-winning contributions, but rather by the quite day-in and day-out workmanlike ethic of merely showing up for the job. While McGwire chased Ruth's and Maris's home run totals at decade's end, Ripken for a decade-long stretch had slowly but surely worn down another legendary baseball milestone – Lou Gehrig's mythic feat of playing in 2,130 uninterrupted games. It was thus Ripken's durability and not his performance numbers that authored an unmatched legend. Cal Junior finally outstripped Gehrig in mid-season of 1995 in a grandiose celebration at Baltimore's Camden Yards (**BOTTOM**) and then played on for three and a half more seasons before taking himself out of the lineup for the final home game of the 1998 season, the record terminating at 2,632. When it was all over Cal Ripken had gone an unthinkable stretch of not missing a single ballgame in more than 17 years. But one grand irony of Ripken's legacy for longevity was that it threatened to bury for most fans the true onfield greatness of his Cooperstown-bound career. Here was arguably the greatest all-around shortstop in the game's annals, surpassing even the legendary Honus Wagner for that accolade. His career began with a Rookie-of-the-Year 1982 campaign in which he slugged 28 homers and knocked home 93 runs, signs of a rare combination of middle-infield grace (**OPPOSITE TOP**) and slugging prowess (**TOP**) yet to come. As a sophomore (**MIDDLE**) Ripken earned himself an American League MVP honor and brought his team a World Championship, while in the process pacing the junior circuit in hits, doubles, and runs scored. While his batting marks did slide somewhat as his ironman stint continued throughout the decade of the '80s, Baltimore's standout was nonetheless an All-Star selection each and every season (**OPPOSITE BOTTOM**: Ripken autographs balls before the All-Star Game in 1997, his All-Star debut at third base.), and garnered another MVP for the 1991 campaign. And when fans selected an All-Century Team in 1999, Cal Ripken, Jr., was no surprise as the starting shortstop on baseball's greatest all-time mythical nine.

104　THE BASEBALL SCRAPBOOK

HOT-CORNER HERO

He was the best all-around third baseman of all time and baseball's premier power hitter for more than two decades. He was also a consummate ballplayer.

The Magic of Baseball 105

Mike Schmidt was at first strictly a blue-collar type of ballplayer, but the career which started out in the early 1970s as an economy-class Ford wound up at the end of the 1980s as a top-of-the-line Cadillac. Beginning as a strikeout-prone freeswinger nicknamed "A-choo!" by teammates for his prodigious whiffs, Schmidt ended up as one of the game's most potent offensive players and the ranking National League home run king of the past two decades, winning eight home run titles, hitting at least 30 roundtrippers in all but three seasons in his 16-year career and standing seventh on the all-time home run list, sandwiched between Mickey Mantle and Reggie Jackson. Such was Mike Schmidt's reputation and national popularity by the time he hung up the spikes in May 1989 that fans elected him as starting All-Star third baseman that season despite his retired status, a gesture that prompted the Phils slugger to make an emotional appearance in a nonplaying capacity at the 1989 Anaheim Classic (**OPPOSITE BOTTOM**). One of the most memorable features of Mike Schmidt's career was his marvelous regular season and post-season performances during the Phillies' single World Championship season of 1980. Powering the Phillies to their only World Title, Schmidt smashed a career-high 48 homers and amassed 121 RBIs for regular season MVP honors, then copped the Series MVP award as well. Here he is, celebrating his post-season heroics with teammates after the Series clincher against Kansas City (**OPPOSITE TOP**). Another milestone in the Mike Schmidt saga was his awesome hitting performances in Chicago's Wrigley Field (**BOTTOM LEFT**), including four homers in a single game there on July 17, 1976. Once he conquered the strikeout blues of his early years (he holds the fourth-highest career strikeout total in major league history), Schmidt seemed to feast on National League pitching. His slugging records are the proudest legacy in the history of Philadelphia Phillies baseball: five National League slugging titles and four RBI crowns; 11 Gold Gloves earned for his stellar defense at the third base position; team career offensive standards in 11 different categories (including base runs, hits, homers, RBIs and total bases); fourth all-time in career home run percentage; and three MVP awards (1980, 1981, 1983). As we see him round the bases once more (**TOP LEFT**), no other National League slugger has won as many home run titles as did the Phillies' heavy-hitting Mike Schmidt.

"SLUGGING SAMMY" SOSA

If Big Mac hadn't been around to hog the scene Sammy Sosa might well have been baseball's biggest story of the new millennium. This new Dominican Dandy ignited not only the city of Chicago but also Latino fans from New York to Santo Domingo.

The Magic of Baseball 107

Suddenly in homer-happy mid-summer 1998 America's pastime had a new and unexpected hero. For it was Chicago's Sammy Sosa and not the muscular Mark McGwire who seemed to capture the nation's innate love for an underdog and who charmed millions with his effusive personality and flamboyant playing style during the celebrated four-month home run chase. It was also Sosa who seemed to achieve the unthinkable by unseating basketball's Michael Jordan and baseball's Ernie Banks as Chicago biggest-ever sports hero and even as the city's biggest celebrity in any walk of life, first in the American League (with the White Sox in 1990, **TOP** and **BOTTOM**), then with the Cubs. And finally it was Sosa as well who suddenly emerged as the new hero for millions of baseball fans from countries like the Dominican Republic, Puerto Rico, Venezuela, Mexico and Cuba, where Spanish and not English is the native language, but where baseball is still the national passion. Overnight in 1998 Sammy Sosa had become America's most celebrated sports star since the legendary Roberto Clemente, whose uniform number he had always worn. The thrilling home run chase peaked in the month of September with some of the grandest excitement that baseball had known in decades. On August 30 and 31 Sammy had slugged his 54th and 55th (**OPPOSITE INSET**) to maintain his dead heat with McGwire. On September 2 Sosa slugged his 56th (**OPPOSITE**, and acknowledging the applause, **MIDDLE**). A climax came the following week when the two sluggers squared off head-to-head in a pair of Labor Day weekend games in St. Louis. It was then that McGwire reached and surpassed the record of Roger Maris that had stood unchallenged for 37 seasons. But while the nation erupted in celebration of the new record, the chase was far from over. Sammy soon blasted his own way into history with dingers number 61 and 62 in a single memorable game witnessed by a packed house of delirious Wrigley Field fans. And with his final homer of the season in Houston Sammy even finally overtook Big Mac and briefly held the coveted record, if only for the short span of less than an hour. When the season finally ended Mark McGwire was baseball's new slugging king with a remarkable total of 70 circuit blasts. But for Sammy Sosa there was little space for disappointment. He had carried his long-suffering Chicago Cubs into the playoffs for the first time in a decade. He shared several Sportsman-of-the-Year trophies with Big Mac and was the National League's Most Valuable Player by acclamation.

BEST CENTERFIELDER OF HIS DAY!

He played the shallowest center field in the history of the game, and many would argue he played the best center field anyone had ever seen as well. Add 3515 hits and a .344 career average and you have a legend.

For many who witnessed Willie Mays' amazing back-to-the-plate over-the-shoulder catch in deepest center field of the Polo Grounds during the 1954 World Series, that brilliant bit of fielding must have been a reminder of the kind of spectacular performance they had come to expect from another player of an earlier generation. For in the first three decades of the present century an equally flashy young outfielder, blessed with the same blinding speed and powerful batting stroke that would one day become Mays' trademark, had made a rare speciality of just such circus catches. The Grey Eagle, Tristram Speaker, roamed the center field pastures for the Boston Red Sox and Cleveland Indians (**RIGHT**) between 1907 and 1927 and was unanimously judged the "finest center fielder yet to play the game" by fans, sportscribes, teammates and opponents. And the similarity between Speaker's own dazzling style of center field play and that immortalized by the young Willie Mays during the 1954 Fall Series Classic was certainly not lost upon the press who had witnessed the memorable Mays catch. Two days after the event, on the eve of Series Game Three in Cleveland, Mays was posed before the cameras (**BOTTOM RIGHT**) with the still-revered Tris Speaker who had once so thrilled partisans of the hometown Indians. For the two decades of his own stardom Tris Speaker had played the shallowest center field in baseball history, and his daring method of playing in the long shadow of his infielders and then racing back for long pokes over his left shoulder had robbed many batting competitors of basehits. Not that the marvelous Tris Speaker had many more peers at the bat than he had in outfield play. A lifetime .344 hitter (7th all-time), the stellar fly-chaser copped only one league batting crown in a career that, unfortunately for Speaker, overlapped with that of the relentless Ty Cobb. Even so, he is the career major league leader in doubles, and his flashy baserunning (**OPPOSITE TOP**, where he avoids a tag at third from Heinie Groh) was second only to that of Cobb during the dead-ball era. But it was more as a spectacular defender that Speaker will best be remembered, and this all-time major league leader in outfield assists and double plays enjoyed his halcyon days as part of a legendary Boston outfield trio that included Duffy Lewis and Harry Hooper (seen posing together in a 1930 old-timers reunion, **OPPOSITE BOTTOM**).

"CAN'T ANYBODY PLAY THIS GAME"

The inimitable "Old Professor," Casey Stengel, best summed up his own career in a piece of classic "Stengelese" when he noted, "There comes a time in every man's life, and I've had plenty of them." He was a gritty player, a master of comedy, a true philosopher and maybe the most successful manager ever.

Few fans today remember Casey Stengel the ballplayer (seated third from right with the 1916 Brooklyn Dodgers, **ABOVE**); yet there isn't a fan alive worth his weight in Jose Canseco bubblegum cards who does not know and revere Charles Dillon Stengel the manager (captured in classic pose with the Mets in 1962, **LEFT**, and in Yankee Stadium on the eve of the 1949 season which launched his first Yankee dynasty, **OPPOSITE**). And no man or women in the nation whose blood pressure rises at World Series time and whose soul rejoices at the news of spring training can fail to admit a boundless fascination with Casey Stengel, the sage of baseball. If Casey may sometimes be given less than his due for his considerable ballplaying talent, or even for the success of his long managerial reign with the Mantle-Berra Yankees, he nonetheless has an undeniable claim on immortality for his invention of Stengelese, the convoluted prose in which the wry manager pontificated on the mysteries of life and baseball. "The secret of managing is to keep the five guys who hate you away from the five who are undecided," Casey intoned. Once asked about his own playing days by one who was too young to remember his 14 seasons with the Dodgers, Pirates, Phillies and Giants, Stengel encapsulated it all with the simplest possible Stengelese remark: "I chased all those balls that Babe Ruth hit."

The Magic of Baseball 111

112 THE BASEBALL SCRAPBOOK

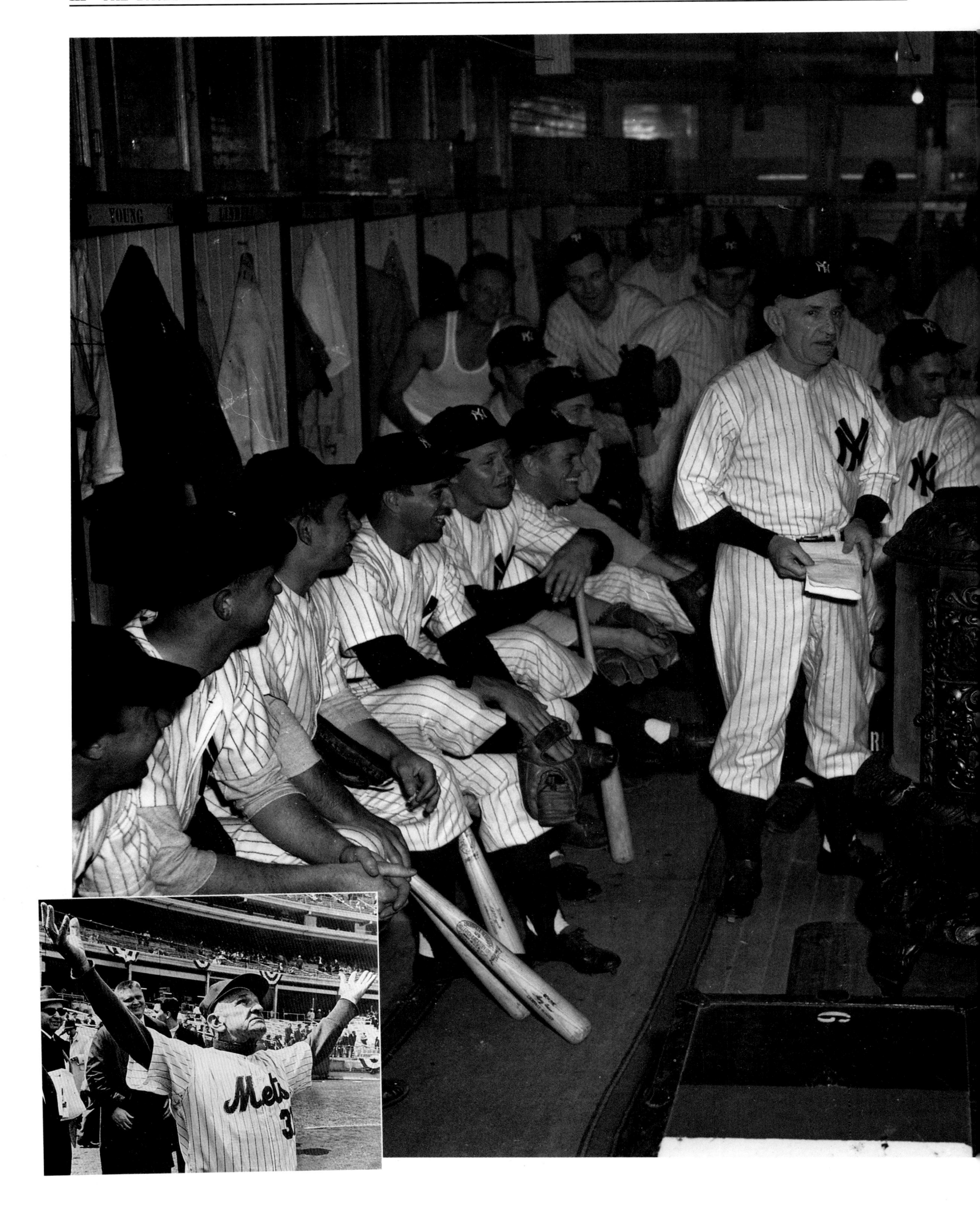

The Magic of Baseball 113

Until they got to know him, even Casey's admirers often took the elfish little man for being primarily a clown. It was an image that Stengel himself had done much to foster when he was a ballplayer. As mainstay of Brooklyn's outfield (1912-1917) he was more than merely adequate and enjoyed a remarkable, if checkered, career, soon becoming an unrivaled master of tricky caroms off the Ebbets Field right field fence. His playing days were from the first filled with big moments: a record 4-for-4 in his first big league game; a star's role in the first game ever held at Brooklyn's Ebbets Field; a .364 plate performance during the 1916 World Series; a first-ever Yankee Stadium Series homer (an inside-the-park job!). But his penchant for tomfoolery left the more memorable image, and the most truly unforgettable Stengel moment occurred when he set loose a live bird from his cap while standing in the batter's box for the Pirates in 1919 when they were playing his former Brooklyn mates. His early and middle years as a manager were not particularly successful (nine years at the helm for the Dodgers and Braves with no finish above 5th spot). It was therefore not surprising that when the same Casey Stengel was announced as a surprise choice for the Yankee post in 1949, the New York baseball world stood aghast. Stengel himself again did very little to calm alarm with his first statements to the New York press: "This is a big job, fellows, and I barely have had time to study it. In fact, I scarcely know where I am." Scribe Arthur Daley summed up local concern with the cogent observation that "I never saw such a bewildered guy in my life!" The usually businesslike Yankees had apparently turned over decades of proud tradition to a mere buffoon (here seen, **LEFT**, greeting his first pinstriped club at spring training). But if ever baseball pundits were wrong, it was in assessing the cagey "Old Professor" who assumed the reigns of the Bronx Bombers at the end of the DiMaggio years and the dawn of the Mantle years. What followed, of course, was the stuff of rare sporting legend – the greatest single reign in American sports history. Stengel was not treated kindly in New York for his bench miracles, however. By 1962 he was out as splendid guru of the Bronx and had taken up residence again across the Harlem River – in the Polo Grounds of his early playing days – once more the established Clown Prince (**FAR LEFT**) of the National League wars and manager of the most laughable baseball team ever.

BASEBALL'S MYTHICAL TRIO

"These are the saddest of possible words: 'Tinker to Evers to Chance'" – so wrote Franklin P. Adams, and so was born a baseball myth that soon grew far beyond the proportions of the diamond action that first gave it shape.

The Magic of Baseball

If one were to believe the popular doggerel that stands as baseball's second most famous poetic tribute (and often masquerades as baseball history), the Cubs' crack double play combination of shortstop Joe Tinker, second sacker Johnny Evers and first sacker Frank Chance, backbone of the Chicago 1906-1908 championship clubs, also served as one of the most tightly knit and invincible infields of the century's first decade. Certainly Frank Chance (**LEFT**) well earned his moniker as "Peerless Leader," a smart-sticking playing manager who never finished lower than third place in seven full seasons at the managerial helm for Chicago. Johnny Evers (**OPPOSITE**, seen at left with Joe Tinker) was the brainy center of the famed keystone combination, earning his lasting reputation for heads-up play in 1908 when he called for the ball and touched second to catch a napping Fred Merkle, triggering the diamond's most memorable "bonehead" play. The overly aggressive Joe Tinker himself sported a league-wide reputation for intelligent and deft fielding, yet never much cowed the league's pitchers with his mediocre bat. Several grand ironies, however, shadow this trio of solid Cub stalwarts, who were quickly turned from reputable ballplayers into undying legend by the catchy verse of New York *Globe* columnist Franklin P. Adams (**BELOW**). Adams had scrawled out his immortal lines on his way to a Giants-Cubs match after being informed that his day's column had run 8 lines short. While adept fielders, the trio turned few doubleplays by modern standards (16 in 1910). And for years while playing together the quick-tempered Evers and Tinker didn't even speak to each other, their open hostility resulting from an earlier clubhouse brawl. Finally, the very year (1910) of Adams' renowned verse was also the very last season the Cubs trio manned the infield together, the end of their eight-year stint on the infields of the National League.

TEDDY BALLGAME!

Ted Williams once wrote his own preferred epitaph: "I want people to say 'There goes Ted Williams, the greatest hitter who ever lived'."

The Magic of Baseball 117

Authors Brendan Boyd and Fred Harris were undeniably on the money when they reminded us that "in 1955 there were 77,273,127 male American human beings, and every one of them in his heart of hearts would have given two arms, a leg and his rare collection of Davy Crockett iron-ons just to be Teddy Ballgame!" Such was the status of one of the most revered sluggers ever to don the uniform of a big league ballclub. In addition to being called the greatest pure hitter ever, Ted Williams was also one of America's most familiar faces. Burned into collective memory are the cherubic features of the cocky young rookie taking pointers from manager Joe Cronin before seeing action in his first big league game (**OPPOSITE TOP LEFT**). And then there is the shy smile of the handsome curly haired batsman enjoying a relaxed moment with his rival, Joltin' Joe DiMaggio during the incredible summer of 1941 (**OPPOSITE TOP RIGHT**). Much copied but never mastered was the sweet swing (being demonstrated during 1949 spring training before Sox skipper Joe McCarthy, **OPPOSITE BOTTOM**) which would terrorize two decades of American League pitchers. Despite interruptions by two wars in which he patriotically served, plus numerous injuries which wreaked havoc with his career, "The Splendid Splinter" was nonetheless a permanent fixture in front of Fenway Park's infamous "Green Monster" left field wall for all but a fraction of the 1940s and 1950s. It was a demanding defensive post that rarely allowed the kind of relaxed respite he enjoyed (**TOP RIGHT**) on one extraordinary 1950 afternoon while leading his Bosox mates to a modern-day big-league-record 29-4 rout over the St. Louis Browns. Despite a reputation for open hostility toward the Boston press corps and an often uneasy relationship with his fans, Williams enjoyed the warmest friendship with teammates and competitors, as well as with past legends of the game such as Hall-of-Fame Boston pitching immortal Cy Young, seen here visiting the present-era Bosox star (**CENTER RIGHT**) upon occasion of the 50th Anniversary of the American League in 1951. And the aloofness with which Williams often treated the Boston fans during his heyday years in Fenway Park was belied by the warm response a mellowed Splinter (**BOTTOM RIGHT**) gave to young fans hovering above the dugout steps of Washington's DC Stadium in 1969 during Ted's final zenith year in baseball as American League Manager-of-the-Year with the upstart expansion Senators.

118   THE BASEBALL SCRAPBOOK

No one could have stats like those compiled by Williams without becoming a baseball legend, and the legend of Teddy Ballgame rests largely on four facets of his career. The first has to do with that incredible summer of 1941, a season still not dimmed by a half century's history but alive in memory as one of the most gripping and excitement-laced mano-a-mano batting races of any big league campaign before or since. In 1941 Ted Williams enjoyed one of the finest individual performances of any ballplayer in history. He hit .400 for the final time in the current century, claimed his first home run title while slugging at an awesome .735 percentage and single-handedly won the All-Star Game with the most dramatic hit of his glorious career, a ninth-inning two-out homer in Briggs Stadium. He missed the Triple Crown only by falling five RBIs short of DiMaggio, who himself burned up the league that summer with his own miraculous (and much more publicized) hitting streak. A second facet of the Williams legend is the "lost seasons," the seasons which prevented "The Kid" from amassing numbers almost unknown to any batsmen of the twentieth century: how many home runs might "The Thumper" have hit if four years had not been spent in Korea and the South Pacific? A third facet concerns Williams' reputation for cold-shouldered, even hostile treatment of both fans and press, an apparent abrasiveness that may have enhanced "the myth" yet probably harmed the career of this private and largely misunderstood man. And finally there was the Hollywood-like finale with which proud Teddy Ballgame would end his glorious Boston career. Batting .316 in his final season and pounding out 29 roundtrippers, Ted's final big-league at-bat (**RIGHT**) produced a dramatic home run into the Fenway right field bleachers. While hometown ceremonies like the one in which he received the league's MVP award at home plate from Commissioner Happy Chandler on Opening Day 1950 (**FAR RIGHT TOP**) were a matter of restrained public pride for an often reclusive star, none was more emotional than the farewell (**FAR RIGHT BOTTOM**) to the Boston faithful on the last day of his active playing career. It was then that Williams finally tipped his cap to the Boston fans, a practice he had vowed in 1940 never to follow during his playing career.

The Magic of Baseball 119

YAZ AND THE IMPOSSIBLE DREAM

As a brash rookie, Yaz replaced Williams in Fenway Park's left field in spring 1961; 3000 hits and 400 homers later, the slugger with the impossible name had nearly replaced Teddy Ballgame in the hearts of Boston fans.

For 44 long summer seasons the lush green pasture spreading before that famous "Green Monster" left field wall of ancient Fenway Park was patrolled with incomparable skill by two very special men. Williams had owned this territory, despite several temporary absences for military duty and to rest from injury, from the moment of his explosive debut in 1939 (as the first-ever rookie RBI king) until the hour of his dramatic farewell home run in 1960. The very next summer a new rookie was ensconced in left field, one who would own the space uninterrupted for 22 more years, establishing his own standards for playing caroms off the tricky Monster wall and eventually following Ted Williams as directly into Cooperstown as he had into Fenway Park. While it was but idle dreaming in 1960 to speculate that another Sox stalwart could ever even approach the living legend of Ted Williams, it came to pass less than a full generation later: Carl Yastrzemski (**OPPOSITE TOP**, second from left), known simply as "Yaz," not only filled Williams' shoes well but came within a hair's breadth of supplanting "The Splendid Splinter" altogether in the hearts of Boston's faithful. And it was not just that Boston fans had short memories, for Yaz would – incredibly – outstrip Ted Williams in almost all statistical categories, as well as in his overall outfield defensive skills, in his ability to bring championship play to victory-starved Fenway and even in his stature among adoring fans. Yaz did not possess Ted Williams' remarkable natural batting stroke – no one ever has. Yet he displayed a quiet charm that Williams lacked and an element of rugged durability that was tragically absent from Williams' career. When his own career was over, Yaz stood first in game appearances (3308) in the entire history of the national pastime. And there were other numbers to feed the argument that Yaz was, in fact, the greatest leftfielder Fenway Park had ever known. Here was the man who now ranked third in big league at-bats (11,988), third in walks (1845), sixth in total bases (5539), seventh in hits (3419), seventh in doubles (646) and ninth in RBIs (1844). Here was the only American Leaguer ever to have both 3000 hits and 400 homers in a career. Only in bases on balls, home runs and career average did The Splendid Splinter in the end outstrip the man they called Yaz.

There was plenty about Carl Yastrzemski to cause his legions of fans (**RIGHT**) to work up considerable fervor. Whether it was Sox Captain Yaz (**P.120, BOTTOM**) hustling upon the basepaths or the veteran flychaser (**P.121**) perfectly playing the Fenway left field wall, Yaz always generated enthusiasm throughout the league. Three times he reigned as league batting champion. One of these three times (1967) he owned a Triple Crown. Another batting title was distinguished on the surface by the oddity of its rank – the lowest average ever to cop a big league title. Yet Yaz's performance in the pitching-dominated year of 1968 was not to be measured by normal standards. Expert sabermetricians have assessed his true achievement as approximating a .400 season. Memorable as well were the high standards Yastrzemski set as the premier defensive leftfielder of his era. For 20 seasons he played the "Green Monster" better even than Williams. Yet despite these rare achievements, when fans begin rehashing the career of Boston's Yaz there is always one memory more vivid than all the others. This was the season of 1967, a summer enshrined in Boston baseball annals as the year of "The Impossible Dream." No franchise ever enjoyed a year quite like it, a year when decades of pennant frustration were washed away in a wholly unanticipated blaze of glory. And it was Yaz who single-handedly carried the Boston club down the stretch of its most joyous summer. He would win three batting titles, play in 18 All-Star Games and stand as the finest left field defender of his era, but all this pales next to his relentless performance in 1967. With four clubs virtually tied for the lead in final weeks, Yaz hit .523 and knocked five homers in the final 12 games. He went 7 for 8 in the last two desperate pennant-clinching games against Minnesota; he provided the defensive throwing gem that saved the season's closing game. He walked off with the Triple Crown that summer; topped the circuit as well in hits, runs, total bases and slugging average; and came within a solitary vote of unanimous MVP selection. For an encore the marvelous Yaz smacked three homers and hit at a .400 pace in the World Series as well. It was indeed the "Impossible Dream" for Boston and its pennant-starved Sox, and it was the greatest year for the great Yaz.

The Magic of Baseball 123

THE ART OF BASEBALL

Without doubt the hardest single thing to do in the realm of sports is hit a round baseball with a round stick. Even the diamond sport's greatest natural batsman, Ted Williams, was quick to admit that. And clearly no other athletic contest demands such a blend of physical skills, athletic artistry and balanced grace and strength from its participants. Nor does any other game make more demands upon its spectators – or reward them more deeply for their fidelity. The play on the field spreads before us in a fashion that seems deceptively lucid: you can always follow each flight and bounce of the ball, as well as the subtlest movements of the players. Try saying this about football or hockey. Yet such subtleties are endless, and they are always unfolding – the hit and run play or squeeze bunt; the strategic pinch hitters; the pitching changes and late-inning defensive maneuvers; the defensive alignment of outfielders; the intentional walk. The game can be watched and followed at so many levels that the dedicated fan must keep a score sheet and record each pitch and each moment of action for later reconstruction. Again, try this with football or hockey. Roger Angell had it right – baseball is the most intensely remembered game precisely because it is the most intensely watched.

No one can understand the true difficulty of hitting a major league fastball – the sheer terror of facing its plate-ward flight – who has not tried. Or the skill needed to turn a double play with split-second timing in the face of oncharging enemy spikes. Or the subtlety of a manager's juggling of the complex strategies of the game. Baseball, of all games, assuredly requires the greatest number of specialized skills. Players (even specialists like relief pitchers) must possess widely diverse talents: the outfielder must hit as well as shag flies; the slugger must field his position or be a liability; the pitcher (throughout most the game's history) has had to take his own turn in the batters' box, and despite legends to the contrary, many have done so with extraordinary batting talent. In all other sports players frequently come overnight to the big-time directly from the college campus – at times even from the high school gymnasium. In baseball, however, they still (with a few rare and highly touted exceptions) toil for years in the minor leagues to learn and perfect the kind of skills demanded at the highest levels of the game.

Much has been written suggesting that it is basketball players who are the most gifted pure athletes among our professional ballplayers. The raw physical demands of constant running, jumping and physical contact – without benefit of padding – are undeniably supreme in the hardwood sport of Dr. Naismith. Most football players, on the other hand, train more for brute power than finesse; baseball players are almost sissified by comparison.

Many of the diamond's legends – from Santa-shaped and profligate Babe Ruth to bent-shouldered and white-haired Phil Niekro – have reinforced this image. The paunchy Ruth looked more like a comic foil than a gladiator, and roly-poly Fernando Valenzuela was hewn from the same block. The cumbersome and bow-legged Honus Wagner was efficiency personified at the keystone position, but he was never grace and poetry. Little men like Ott, Rizzuto and Ozzie Smith have played baseball like giants, but equivalent feats are not even imaginable in the worlds of professional basketball or football. On the diamond, the poorly conditioned and barrel-bellied Hack Wilson, Bobo Newsom and Terry Forster – or the alcoholic Pete Alexander, Sam McDowell and Ryne Duren – have enjoyed far more than just fleeting moments in the summer sunshine. These cases of skilled performance by men who appear more like barroom spectators than trained athletes are, of course, the exception rather than the rule in baseball. Yet the status of such legendary diamond performance by bumpkins and weaklings has worked to reinforce the notion that baseball is truly a game for Everyman. And this conception is one of baseball's lasting charms, as well as its reigning illusion.

The essential difference between baseball and football players has been well captured by author Murray Ross with his contrast between Babe Ruth and pro football idol Jim Brown. The rotund Ruth provides the perfect embodiment for the diamond sport's essential "humanness." The Babe was a hero whose image was both comfortable and altogether mundane – round of shape, dressed in baggy uniform, with a schoolboy cap and bat which looked like a tiny wand upon his broad shoulders. He moved his Santa-sized torso on spindly legs and with quick, delicate steps and was thus the very model of comic disproportion, poignant and vulnerable. Brown, the Cleveland running back of the 1950s, was the perfect prototype of the "superhuman" football god – huge, distant, of perfect muscular physique, an expressionless mask under a depersonalizing helmet. There was absolutely nothing funny – or touching – about Jim Brown.

The contrast between Ruth and Brown underscores the fundamental differences among America's three national games. Football is stylized warfare, and this is only slightly less true of basketball, with its towering giants and flying gazelles. But baseball is a game meant to be played only by artists.

Recognizing the artistry of baseball opens the doors to the greatest pure joys of fandom. Arch-rooter Art Hill has stated this best. Each American male grows up wishing for no finer fate than to play on a major league diamond. When we fail and are resigned to mere fandom, the pill is sometimes so bitter that for a time we may even shun our spectator's role. Then comes the realization that on the big league diamond we can witness that greatest of rarities, a small field of human activity in which all the participants excel at the highest possible level. It is then that we echo Hill's wish about the next life: "If I do come back, I hope it's as someone who can go to his right on a hard ground ball with a little more haste – and, I hardly need add, hit a curveball. Failing that, I'd like to have season tickets."

The photos and text which follow in this chapter celebrate the artistic side of the game of baseball – its most recognized individual artists, some of its greatest artistic performances and its most sophisticated playing skills. First come a handful of celebrated players who conform to certain traditional measures of performance. These are the players acknowledged for superior skills by selection as the league's "Most Valuable" performers. Then there is a gallery of hitters and pitchers who have excelled by reaching baseball's rarest milestones, men who have pitched 300 victories, or have excelled in hitting skill as measured by 3000 base hits, or have reached the heights of power-hitting by banging 500 career homers.

And then there is baseball's purest artistic performance – the no-hit game. It is the no-hitter – that symbol of ultimate baseball perfection – that has captivated and thrilled countless fans like nothing else from the very earliest days of the past century. Every dedicated fan cherishes the day when he or she might be fortunate enough to witness personally just one such diamond spectacular. Thus no-hit wizardry paid special dividends for baseball boosters during the 1990 season – the greatest no-hit year in big league history. No-hitters have their allotted place in the pages that follow, along with a few exceptional hurlers who have somehow managed to spin this magic web upon the bats of opposing hitters on more than one occasion.

Found here, as well, are those who have mastered special tricks of pitching – knuckleball, curveball and the infamous illegal spitter. Also, we pay homage to the specialized skills of sliding, stealing, executing the squeeze play and other feats of baserunning artistry. Then we look at some breathtaking examples of defense play, some of the game's greatest catches. And to leave no single infield pebble unturned, we survey here as well those necessary peripherals, the equipment with which our favorite game is played, along with examples of the physical training which underlies all its skills.

So in this chapter we celebrate as best we can the subtle and many-faceted art of baseball. It is an art like no other, and it is an art that yields pride of place to no other.

MOST VALUABLE DIAMOND PLAYERS

With the cynical perspective of the hard-boiled sports scribe, the late Jimmy Cannon tabbed an MVP as "A guy on the club that wins the pennant." In fact, many (but hardly all) have led their ballclubs to pennant glories.

The Art of Baseball 127

They have always been the essential thread in the colorful fabric of big league baseball – the irreplaceable slugger or hurler or defensive wizard who can always be counted on to provide the key, rally-saving base knock or to squelch every opposition uprising. They seem single-handedly to carry their teams and no one questions that it is their contributions which, more than any others, glue a ballclub together. Since 1931 they have been honored by prestigious annual awards voted by the National Baseball Writers Association: league MVPs. And these awards have given rise in turn to other awards for heroes who have sparkled for lesser periods – World Series MVPs, All-Star Game MVPs, NLCS and ALCS MVPs. A handful of the most memorable, as well as some of the unfortunately forgotten, flash their hardware here: Chuck Klein and his Philadelphia Phillies teammates circling his 1932 National League award (**OPPOSITE**); catcher Elston Howard of the Yankees accepting presentation of his 1963 junior circuit trophy from league president Joe Cronin (**TOP LEFT**); Athletics slugger Jimmie Foxx grasping the hefty 1932 AL award which, along with Klein's, brought both honors that year to the City of Brotherly Love (**CENTER LEFT**); modern-day Boston Red Sox hurler Roger Clemens hoisting a silver trophy won for his stellar All-Star Game performance of 1986 in the Houston Astrodome (**BOTTOM LEFT**); and finally, the northside hero who was perhaps the very epitome of "Most Valuable" for the always cellar-dwelling Cubs: Ernie "Mr. Cub" Banks beams while accepting the 1959 plaque which made him the first National Leaguer ever pegged MVP in two successive years (**BOTTOM RIGHT**).

NO HITS! NO RUNS! NO ERRORS!

It is a dream of every living fan to see just one such game in person – the rare zenith of baseball perfection and athletic artistry in which a pitcher manages to weave a spell over all the opposition batsmen.

In the apocryphal wisdom of Casey Stengel, baseball is ninety percent pitching, "while the other half is hitting." It is certainly that way for all true connoisseurs of baseball artistry. If fair-weather and Johnny-come-lately fans grow ecstatic over a home-run-filled 12-11 slugfest, for the true-blue diehard a 1-0 pitchers' duel will do just fine anytime, thank you. There is nothing else that quite grips the imagination like that showcase of absolute diamond perfection, the "no-hit, no-run" game. So special is the status of the "no-hitter" in baseball lore that newspaper accounts of such games from the earliest decades of the century proclaimed of any no-hit pitcher that he had "entered the Hall of Fame," despite the fact that the archive in Cooperstown bearing that name was not officially established until 1936. And never has the no-hit game held a more binding grip on the nation's fans than when, in 1990, a record nine such masterpieces were pitched within the course of a single summer's play. Not only did this season witness more of these rare pitching moments than any previous single campaign, but there were oddities galore: Dave Stieb finally cracked the magic barrier for Toronto's Blue Jays, the only team never to have had a no-hitter; Andy Hawkins became the second hurler in a century to weave magic for a full nine-inning game and then lose the contest; and no-hit champion Nolan Ryan (**OPPOSITE**) capped a brilliant career with his own record sixth career pitching gem. Yet if 1990's outburst of no-hitters seemed unaccountable, one should recall that this rarest of all diamond performances (there have been barely 200 over big league baseball's first century, thus approximately two a season and one for each 1100 games) has often inexplicably come in handfuls. For two of our most memorable no-hit artists this was certainly the case. Virgil Trucks (**TOP RIGHT**) would cram both his career masterpieces into a single (1952) season, a campaign in which he would, ironically, win a grand total of only five ballgames. And as if Trucks' no-hit doings were not unprecedented enough, the Redlegs' Johnny Vander Meer (**BOTTOM RIGHT**) lived by no-hit fame alone, hurling back-to-back hitless games in 1938, the only time in baseball history.

THE EXCLUSIVE DIAMOND FRATERNITY

Only 20 durable men hold membership in that select circle of moundsmen who have been able to fight the ravages of time long enough to amass 300 career wins, and the man at the top holds baseball's most unreachable record.

It is clearly one of the game's most exclusive clubs, that group of immortal hurlers claiming 300 victories in their big league careers. A mere 20 pitchers own membership, and such Hall-of-Fame giants as Bob Feller, Jim Palmer, Robin Roberts and Whitey Ford never entered its charmed circle. For those who have made it, however, it is their singular lasting badge of fame. Take Nolan Ryan as prime example: despite an almost unimaginable standard of 5000-plus career strikeouts and an unmatched of six career no-hitters, Ryan was for many skeptical fans (and some voting sportswriters as well) never a legitimate Cooperstown candidate until the 300-win milestone was passed. Lately, however, the barriers to club membership seem to have been flung open with unsettling frequency. Steve Carlton (**OPPOSITE BOTTOM RIGHT**) was one of the first of the contemporary group to enter in 1984 (329-244), a four-time Cy Young selection and second winningest southpaw on the books. Don Sutton (**OPPOSITE BOTTOM LEFT**) was soon to follow (324-256) in 1986, now safely tucked in the twelfth spot on the all-time list. Most recent has been Ryan, on the heels of Gaylord Perry (314-265) and Phil Niekro (**LEFT**), the latter hanging around until age 48 to slip past Perry with a career total of 318. Topping off the list of those pitchers who played after World War II is the unchallenged greatest lefty ever, Warren Spahn (**OPPOSITE TOP CENTER**), with a lifetime ledger of 363-245, himself a 40-year-older when he climbed there in 1961. Only "Pete" Alexander (373-208) and baseball's earliest matinee idol, Christy Mathewson (**OPPOSITE TOP, UPPER RIGHT**), now join Cy Young (**OPPOSITE TOP, UPPER LEFT**) and Walter "Big Train" Johnson (**OPPOSITE TOP, LOWER RIGHT**) in perches above Spahn on the honor list. Johnson has long since been overhauled by Ryan as strikeout king, but his 416 victories will likely never be matched. Lefty Grove (**OPPOSITE TOP, LOWER LEFT**) holds the highest winning percentage (.680) of all who stand here. And Cy Young's incredible 511 victories over 22 summers remains today surely one of the most unchallengeable of all of baseball's sacred milestones.

The Art of Baseball 131

CY YOUNG'S UNIQUE LEGACY

His name evokes unparalleled achievements and traditions that uplift the game. Cy Young himself set standards that owners of the award that bears his proud name have only infrequently approached.

The Art of Baseball 133

Never has a prestigious baseball award been more appropriately named for a superhero of yesteryear. The namesake of the plaque presented to the year's outstanding pitcher in each league himself set standards for excellence which by today's measures can only be admired from afar. A career victory total of 511 is something almost certainly beyond the dreams of any modern pitcher. This grand total works out to 30 victories per year for almost 20 lengthy seasons! Impossible? Then think of it as nearly 30 20-victory campaigns. Any way you slice it, the result is staggering and could only be a relic from an age in which pitchers hurled 400 innings a summer and started 50 games a season as matters of course. And the placing of Cy Young's name upon the trophy which certifies unique pitching achievement is also fitting when one looks behind the mere statistics of Denton True Young's prodigious victory totals. There is no partiality as to league implied here, for Cy Young won nearly equal numbers of games in each circuit, having easily amassed Hall-of-Fame credentials as a National Leaguer in the last decade of the past century (285-167) before testing a new century and new league with the Red Sox after 1901, collecting 222 additional belt notches before a final brief swing through the senior circuit in 1911-12. Young was also the pitching hero of the very first World Series, with two wins for the Red Sox in the inaugural classic of 1903. And to clinch his unique position in baseball history, it should be recorded as well that Young began his pitching career at a time when the hurler stood in a "pitcher's box" that was but 50 feet from home plate and concluded it after the introduction of the present-day mound that is 60 feet, 6 inches from the batsman; that he pitched to the game's first great hitter of the past century, Cap Anson, and against the likes of Eddie Collins, who was still knocking down AL pitchers in 1930; that he was born in the shadow of a Civil War and was still fit well after the end of the Korean conflict. Baseball's all-time winner (and its all-time loser as well, with 313 career setbacks), the most durable pitcher in big league history, Cy Young is indeed the ideal symbol of the aspirations of every pitcher who ever has or ever will throw a ball.

134 THE BASEBALL SCRAPBOOK

Some pitchers proudly boast the coveted Cy Young Award as a final jewel in an otherwise already glorious pitching career. Catfish Hunter (**P. 133, BOTTOM**) won but one such award, yet flashed as dominant ace for two different teams at both ends of the decade now known as the "tumultuous seventies." Bob Gibson (**OPPOSITE TOP**) was a rare double winner, yet Gibson's glory was forever clinched during the 1968 "Year of the Pitcher" which found him posting an incredible modern-record 1.12 ERA. Dwight "Doc" Gooden (**OPPOSITE BOTTOM RIGHT**) launched himself on the way to greatness with one of the fastest starts ever, and the centerpiece of this rocket-launch to pitching fame was a marvelous "Triple Crown" pitching year in 1985, bringing NL bests for wins, strikeouts and ERA. Still others have collected the award in batches. Tom Seaver (**BOTTOM LEFT**) managed to garner three on his way to 311 career wins and five 20-win seasons. Roger Clemens (**P. 132 , LEFT**) was only the fourth man ever to take back-to-back awards, and had garnered five by 1998. For yet a final group of stellar moundsmen, however, the Cy Young Award has resulted from a single surprising summer in which past career mediocrity was set aside by a single glorious moment of super achievement. Vernon Law (**TOP LEFT**) was one such, for he flashed for a "career year" as he led the 1960 champion Pirates in his only 20-win season. Orel Hershiser (**CENTER LEFT**) is another single-time 20-game winner whose 18-year career wound up where it began, back in Los Angeles. Bret Saberhagen (**P. 132, RIGHT**) has mixed mastery with mediocrity, balancing 1985 and 1989 awards with a penchant for off-seasons in years ending in even numbers. Mike Cuellar (**P. 133, TOP**), despite a proficient career and rank as the fourth winningest pitcher of Latin American birthright, would hardly be remembered in baseball's archives were it not for a single marvelous Cy Young season in 1969, a year when he shared the lofty award with an equally brief supernova, Denny McLain. Frank Viola (**P. 133, CENTER**) was both unhittable over some stretches and inexplicable in others, yet lives in our memory for his sustained greatness in the Cy Young season of 1987. Mark Davis (**OPPOSITE BOTTOM LEFT**) remains freshest in mind as one who parlayed a single brilliant season and baseball's top pitching award into a huge personal contract, then apparently fell victim to his own surprising success.

The Art of Baseball 135

PROUD BATSMEN OF THE 3000 CLUB

To reach 200 hits in a single season is a mark of extraordinary batsmanship; to average that number for 15 or more summers is to earn admission into a select company of the national pastime's greatest paragons.

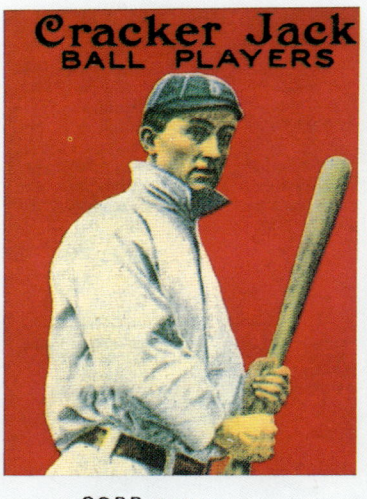

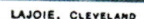

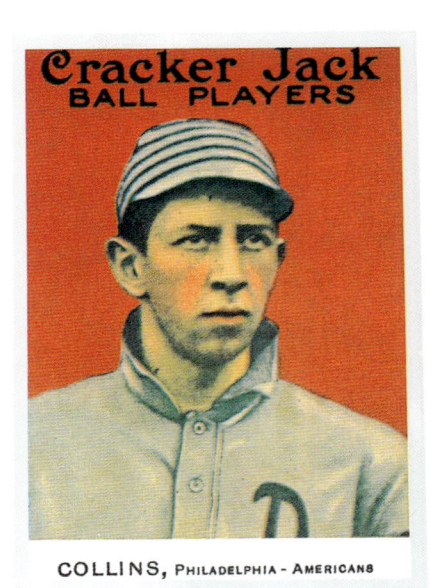

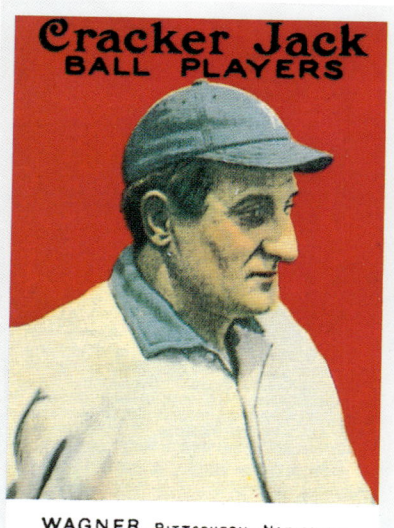

They stretch out before us on these pages like an honor roll of military heroes, resplendent in their colorful battle uniforms and framed on their pasteboard bubblegum card shrines (as with the seven cardboard collectibles displayed on the **LEFT**). They share the rare company of men who have stroked out 3000 base hits in a big league career, and to recite their names is to review the supreme achievement of baseball's most demanding skill. To hit a baseball thrown by a major league pitcher is a feat of speed, strength and coordination matched by few other athletic activities. And these men did it better and more often than any others. But like so much else in the national pastime, familiarity seems to breed contempt and the swelling numbers of one of the sport's most elite fraternities seems at one and the same time to diminish the achievements that earned initiation. For fans of the Golden Era fifties it seemed as though Ty Cobb's base-hitting exploits of an earlier generation would always remain untouchable. More than 4000 career safeties was seemingly a dream beyond realization for modern-era batsmen. Three thousand was the magic number that separated the super hitters from the rest of the talented magicians wielding Louisville ash wands. A handful of skilled swingers from the post-World War II era seemingly were on their way to posting numbers that would also likely remain unreachable for future generations. Incomparable Ted Williams was widely acknowledged as the greatest pure hitter ever, and yet he had lost far too much time in two separate wars to ever grace the magic circle. A kid named Aaron was clouting the long ball and stroking singles and doubles in Milwaukee, as was another named Mays out in San Francisco, but few yet suspected both would one day stand in the highest echelons among both baseball's greatest sluggers and its greatest swatters. It was perhaps Stan Musial of the Cardinals who seemed most likely to challenge Cobb, Tris Speaker, Honus Wagner, and the others who had once posted Olympus-like milestones. Musial would eventually surpass all previous National Leaguers and still stands in fourth place in the base hit hall of fame, trailing only Rose, Cobb, and Aaron. Yet by the 1960s and 1970s the fraternity began to grow rapidly meaning that one of baseball's most special laurels now somehow appeared not quite so special as it once had seemed.

The Art of Baseball 137

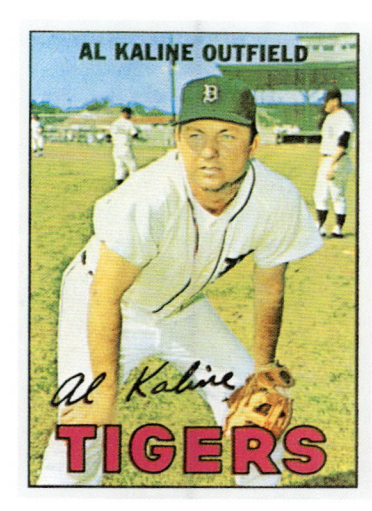

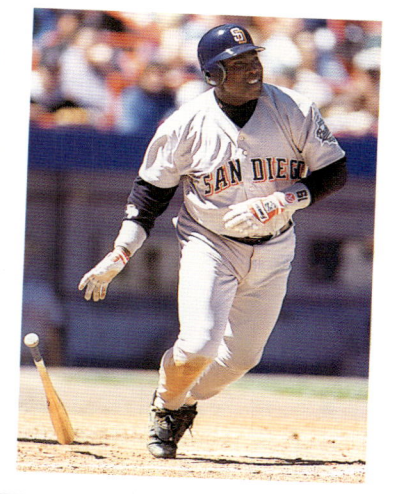

Pete Rose (**BELOW**) not only overhauled Ty Cobb's long-held slot as baseball's base-hit king, but also outstripped Hank Aaron (**TOP CENTER**) and Stan Musial (**THIRD ROW RIGHT OF CENTER**) as all-time National League pacesetters. Rose and Eddie Murray (**NOT SHOWN**) hold added distinction as the only switch-hitters in this highly select club.

Rickey Henderson (**IMMEDIATE RIGHT**), Tony Gwynn (**TOP RIGHT**) and Paul Molitor (**BOTTOM LEFT**) are among the most recent entrants in baseball's most charmed hitting fraternity. Members not shown on these pages are Eddie Murray (3255 hits), George Brett (3154), Robin Yount (3142), Dave Winfield (3110), and Cal Ripken, Jr. (3070).

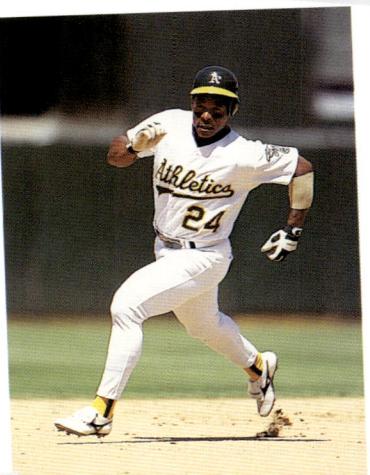

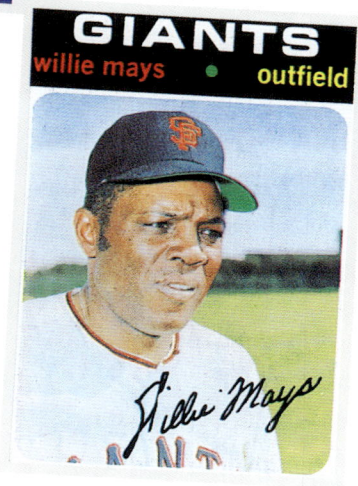

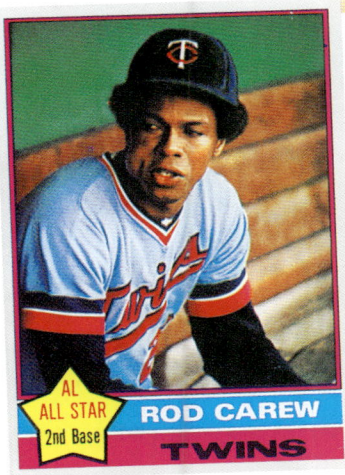

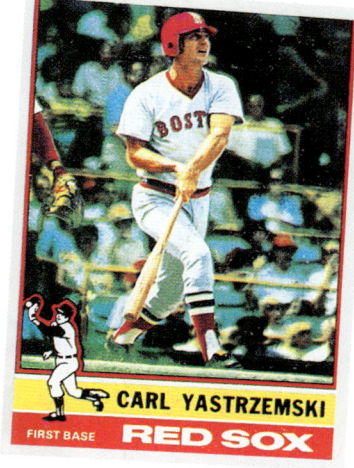

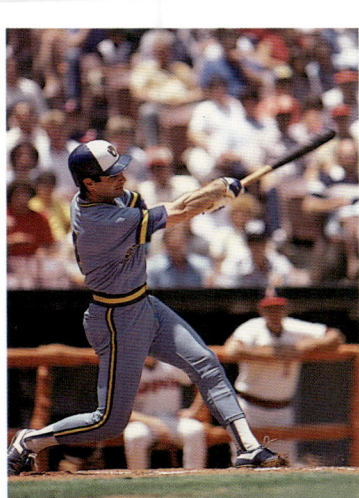

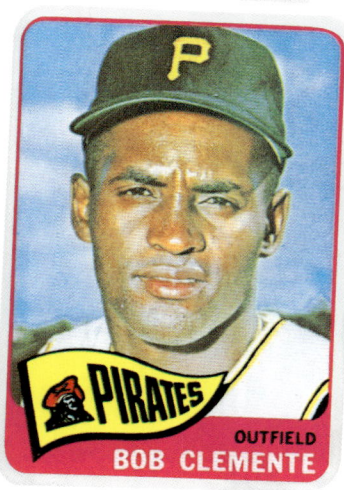

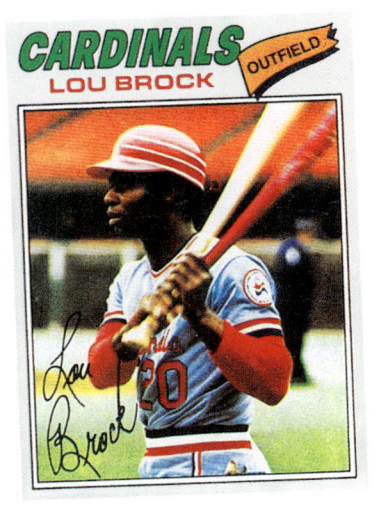

Roberto Clemente (**BOTTOM CENTER**) had his brilliant career and noble life cut ironically short only months after he stroked a final hit number 3,000. Among others barely reaching the elite circle of top hitters were Al Kaline (**TOP LEFT**) with 3,007 and Wade Boggs (**ABOVE FAR RIGHT**) who retired after climbing but ten safeties beyond the magic plateau.

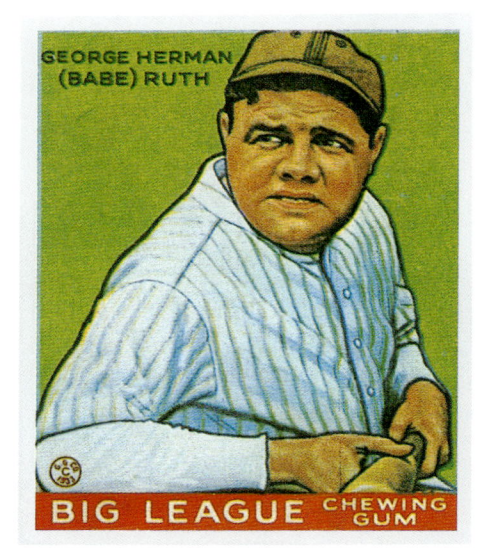

500 HOME RUNS!

Pete Rose once observed that singles hitters drive Chevys while home run hitters drive Cadillacs. If this is true, then each of the 17 awesome sluggers who have now climbed above the benchmark 500 homer plateau must have owned a full dealership!

For singles hitters who gain their standard of achievement merely by reaching base, the magical number is 3000; for pitchers, 300 wins signifies immortality; but for muscle-bound sluggers, the revered number remains 500. This is the touchstone of home run excellence, separating true slugging immortals from the near-greats. Babe Ruth (**OPPOSITE TOP LEFT**) remained for generations the measure of home run achievement until Henry Aaron caught and passed him. A next plateau is reserved for Willie Mays and Barry Bonds (**OPPOSITE BOTTOM**), the only pair lodged at the 600-homer level. Among those who challenged the lofty 600-plateau from the right side of the plate and fell ever so short were three he-men of legendary fame. Philadelphia's Jimmie Foxx (**TOP RIGHT**) challenged Ruth's single-year mark with 58 in 1932, then climbed into second spot on the career list, a perch he maintained until the sluggers of the 1950s and 1960s emerged to overhaul or outshine him in turn. In that latter crew were Harmon Killebrew (**BOTTOM LEFT**) and Mickey Mantle (**MIDDLE RIGHT**) of American League fame and Frank Robinson (**OPPOSITE TOP RIGHT**) who split time between both junior and senior circuits and ironically only once led the league in single-season circuit blasts, despite a fifth-place standing on the all-time list. Another right side swinger from the 1950s-1960s era who hit homers (512) with rare ease was the Cubs' personable Ernie Banks (**BOTTOM RIGHT**), a surprise entry, since his career began at the normally light-hitting shortstop post. From portside swingers there is the expected entry of American Leaguer Ted Williams (**MIDDLE LEFT**), whose perfect stroke provided 521 round trippers and whose several lost seasons likely kept him from joining Mays and Bonds in the exclusive 600-club. That Aaron's slugging Braves teammate, Eddie Mathews (**OPPOSITE MIDDLE LEFT**), finally made the cut was also little surprise. For years this duo pounded senior circuit fences, and together they rank as the greatest single-team home run pair ever to grace the field. A more remarkable entry is Mel Ott (**TOP LEFT**), hardly the mold for a slugging fence masher, despite his career 511 dingers. Ott socked more HRs in a single park (the odd-shaped Polo Grounds) than any man in history. Most recent additions to the club are Barry Bonds (**OPPOSITE TOP CENTER**), Reggie Jackson, Willie McCovey, Mike Schmidt, Rafael Palmeiro, and switch-hitting Eddie Murray (all not pictured), and finally modern-day bashers Mark McGwire and Sammy Sosa (**OPPOSITE BOTTOM**).

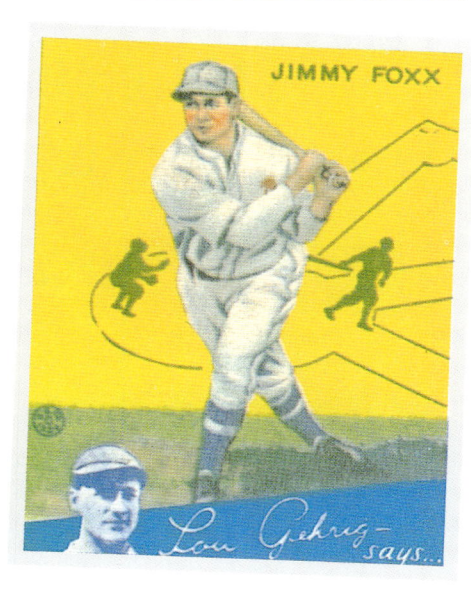

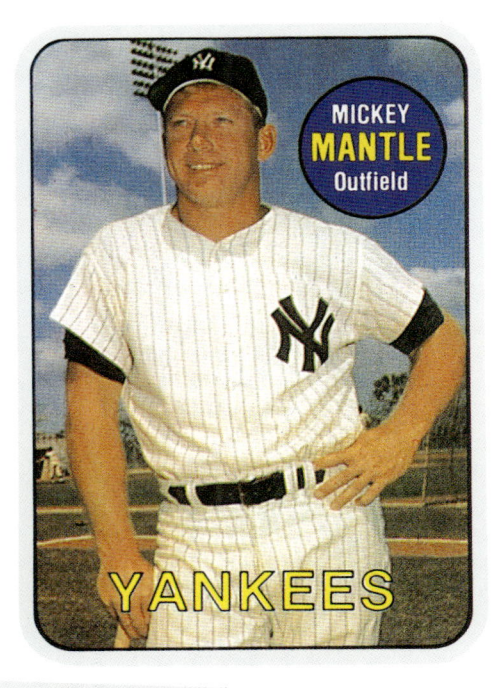

LEGENDARY DIAMOND LUMBER MEN

While pitching is baseball's subtlest art form, batting is its highly polished science; the former admittedly wins pennants, while the latter wins fans and spins turnstiles that are the sweetest music to any owner's ears.

The Art of Baseball 141

One of the secrets of baseball's lasting charm is the delicate balance maintained between offense and defense, between pitching mastery and batting prowess. If the most demanding of all athletic feats – one requiring immense concentration of reflex, coordination and concentration – is to hit a round baseball with a round stick when that baseball is coming at you at upwards of 90 miles per hour, then perhaps the second most difficult feat is to throw such a ball past a competent major league hitter. Many a journeyman or rookie hurler has lain awake nights in a cold sweat dreading the possibility of having to face such hitters as those pictured here. Tony Lazzeri (**OPPOSITE TOP LEFT**) was the lethal assassin of league pitchers who sandwiched behind Ruth and Gehrig in the most fearsome batting line-up ever assembled, the Murderers' Row Yankees of the late 1920s. For a brief time Hack Wilson (**OPPOSITE BOTTOM**) pounded National League hurlers as no power hitter had ever done before. While nearly the Babe's equal in bat power, Wilson was never a match for the Babe's lifestyle; while Ruth overcame his off-field escapades, Wilson was quickly done in by his. Blasters like Babe Ruth, Tony Lazzeri and Hack Wilson were showpieces of the lively ball era during the 1920s and 1930s, but hitting mastery was alive and well long before fence busting supplanted spray hitting. Even the pitching-rich dead-ball era had its wizards with the batting lumber. One of the first men who gave hitting respectability was a tiny artist who perfected place-hitting at the turn of the century and earned one of the sport's most famous epithets. "Wee Willie" Keeler (**OPPOSITE TOP RIGHT**) is immortalized in baseball lore for an ability to "hit em' where they ain't" and exploited his patented technique to compile some of the game's most impressive hitting statistics. No two hitters terrorized National and American League pitchers in the decades that stretched between Keeler and the sluggers of the Ruth era than did Honus "Hans" Wagner (**TOP LEFT**) in Pittsburgh and Sam Crawford (**BOTTOM LEFT**) in Cincinnati and Detroit. The former was one of baseball's first true all-around atheltes; the latter a rare power hitter of a dead-ball epoch more renowned for Willie Keeler's place hitting than for big-muscled latter-day fence busting.

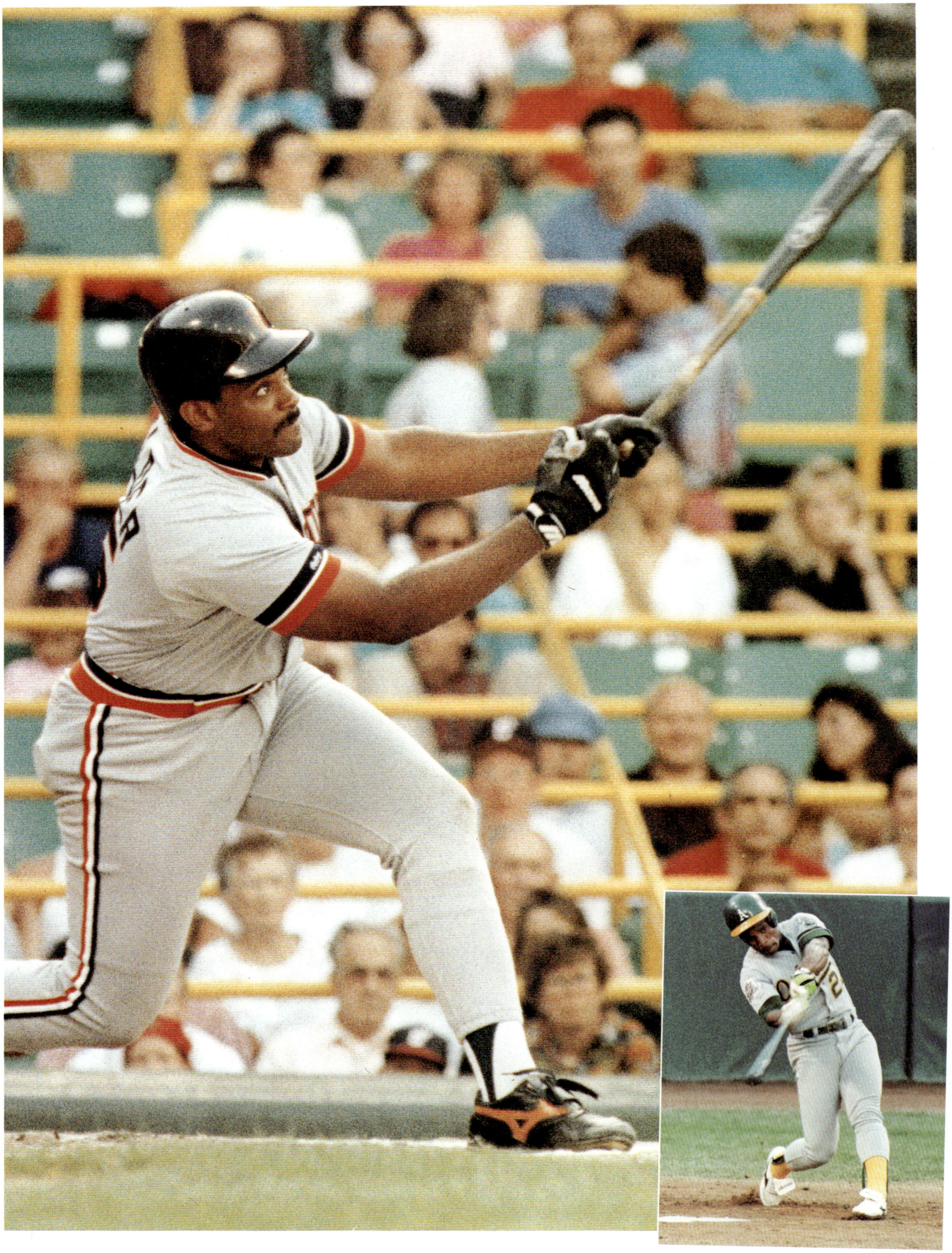

The Art of Baseball 145

The pundits who rule the American League decided that the slipping attendance and waning interest which accompanied the "football boom" of the late 1960s and early 1970s was attributable to baseball's lack of enough offense and scoring to meet the fancy of a generation of sports fans who were weaned on hard-hitting, fast-moving and wild-scoring gridiron action. The solution, as they assessed it, was to neutralize pitching, to liven up the plastic outfield "grass" if not the cork-centered ball, to provide temperature-controlled home run launching pads and to insert an extra slugger in the lineup in place of the pitcher. Neither the motives nor the solutions may have been well-reasoned, but their subtle impact upon the heretofore delicately balanced game of baseball has been far-reaching. The stolen base has again emerged as an offensive weapon. Free-swinging bashers have elevated both homer and strikeout totals over the past two decades. And a new brand of flashy slugger now fills our National and American League parks.

While 50-homer-a-year men are now nearly extinct, Detroit's muscleman Cecil Fielder (**OPPOSITE**) not only crushed a magic 51 dingers in 1990 but became the first American Leaguer to pace the circuit in RBI three consecutive years since Babe Ruth in the early '20s. Young Texas Rangers slugger Juan Gonzalez (**TOP RIGHT**) threatens to be the next 50-homer man, while Reds slugger Kevin Mitchell (**CENTER RIGHT**) has the swing and girth to break through for big numbers as well. In Oakland the power-bashing of Mark McGwire (**BOTTOM RIGHT**) was merged with the blazing speed of Rickey Henderson (**OPPOSITE INSET**), the diamond's new stolen base king, during the team's dynasty run. While the former slugger socked a record 49 roundtrippers his rookie season, the latter holds the major league record for lead-off homers. Cut in the mold of such power-and-speed boys as Henderson are other contemporary sluggers such as Bo Jackson (**BOTTOM LEFT**), who lost much of his speed to a pro football injury and hip-replacement surgery, yet still swings a potent long-ball bat. In vogue today also are trim bashers like Atlanta's Fred McGriff (**TOP LEFT**) with one of baseball's most picture-perfect swings. And the prototype of the modern slugger, of course, was one Reginald Martinez Jackson (**CENTER LEFT**), who emerged as one of the greatest home run hitters.

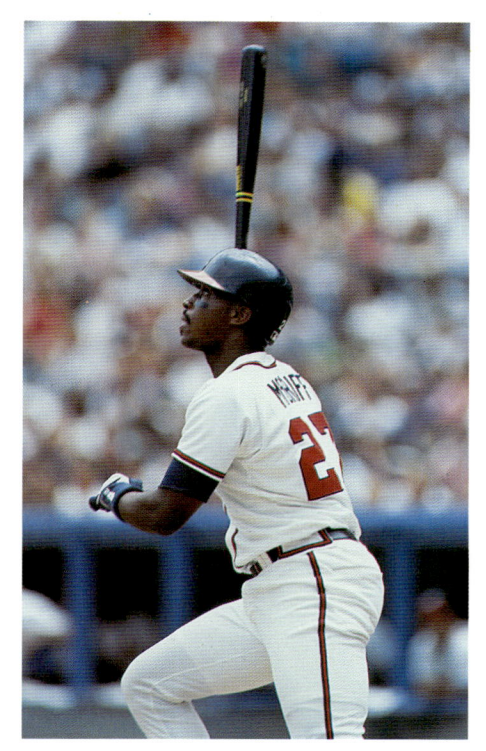

146 THE BASEBALL SCRAPBOOK

Nothing more readily evokes the awesome physical power that is one element of baseball's panoply of athletic skills than does the frozen photographic image of the slugger's roundhouse swing. Here hard-hitting catcher Tim McCarver (**OPPOSITE**) of the St. Louis Cardinals bears down on his tongue as well as the ball while he blasts a dramatic Series homer to defeat the Yankees in extra-inning play of 1964 Game Five at Yankee Stadium. One-time National League batting champ Dixie Walker (**OPPOSITE BOTTOM LEFT**) with Brooklyn provides a 1944 pose that was quite obviously one of those favorite action-packed yet totally unrealistic staged wire service shots (would any hitter ever pull his head out quite this much!). In more realistic game action "Big Cat" Johnny Mize (**TOP RIGHT**) displays during a 1945 spring training game the form that resulted in two league longball titles. Mize was batting grace personified, but the less graceful whacks made by the game's more hefty sluggers also provide potential moments of great drama. In one such case Yankees slugger Dave Winfield (**CENTER RIGHT**) lunges at a pitch in Toronto's Exhibition Stadium. In another, Boston's Don Baylor (**BOTTOM RIGHT**) breaks a bat cleanly in two yet still manages to drive a grounder through the infield at Fenway Park. Usually displaying somewhat better form, Winfield was later to become one of only 15 batsmen to register 1500 career RBIs. And frequently making better contact, Baylor would bang out 338 career roundtrippers before his 1989 retirement.

LAYING ONE DOWN FOR THE TEAM

The bunt was introduced by Dickey Pearce of the Brooklyn Atlantics in 1866; it was popularized by Tim Murnane of the Boston Nationals a decade later. Now bunting is baseball's lost art, as nearly extinct as real grass.

Old-time stars of the "Dead-Ball Era" (*e.g.* Edd Roush of Cincinnati, a .300 batter for eleven straight years, here demonstrating the science of "deadening the ball before the plate" in this pre-World-War-One game action, **OPPOSITE**) mastered the technique as their own not-so-secret weapon against league pitchers, who themselves stood armed with an array of spitballs, slimeballs, mudballs and every other deceit aimed to keep enemy hitters from making solid contact. For generations big-league ballplayers practiced the skill endlessly in spring training sessions, such as the one illustrated, in which former Dodgers backstop Roy Campanella (**CENTER RIGHT**) hones his craft with teammates Carl Erskine and Carl Furillo in the 1950s. While champion batsmen like Roush would bunt frequently to pad their average, maintaining the trick as an integral part of their full offensive arsenal, recent decades have seen this once-popular technique of reaching base relegated to the less-inventive tactic of sacrificing the batter in order to move along stranded baserunners. Pitchers, especially, were schooled in the art of "intentional" sacrifice, as practiced by Nolan Ryan (**TOP RIGHT**) of the Astros during spring training action in the early 1980s. The modern era of slugging has witnessed steady abandonment of bunting, especially among long ball hitters, and the consequent loss of the skill has often proven costly, as in this 1949 World Series action (**BOTTOM RIGHT**) in which Gil Hodges of Brooklyn fails to move two baserunners and thus kills an important Dodgers rally. Note Hodges' futile foul bunt glancing harmlessly off the mitt of Yankees receiver Yogi Berra.

DEADLY BALLS AND LIVELY ARMS

Cardinal catcher Tim McCarver once offered a classic Yogiism in testimony to the awesome talent of battery mate Bob Gibson: "He must be the luckiest pitcher ever, since whenever he pitches the other team doesn't score."

They seem to come in just about all known shapes, sizes, ages and possible temperaments. What they have in common is the rarest of abilities to throw a baseball in such a way that the game's greatest batsmen are stymied time and again by their mound mastery. Some are grizzled veterans, like contemporaries Nolan Ryan and Phil Niekro, or like that Ancient Mariner of an earlier age, Clarence "Dazzy" Vance (**CENTER RIGHT**). The very definition of a late bloomer, Vance didn't win his first big league game until age 31, yet he compiled 196 more in the 14-year career that followed. A minor league vagabond for ten seasons before landing his first major league assignment, Dazzy Vance was eventually a National League ERA champion on three different occasions, while reigning as unchallenged Senior Circuit strikeout king for a remarkable seven seasons (1922-28). While Vance saw 30 summers before winning a game in the Big Show, Waite Hoyt (**OPPOSITE**) of the same era enjoyed a tryout with the New York Giants at the raw age of 15. Hoyt did not officially appear in a league ballgame until the advanced age of 18, but he had already posted 176 victories (of his career 237 total) by the time he had reached the age of Vance's tardy debut. Yet while one was old in his heyday and the other still a strapping youngster, both Hoyt and Vance shared a trademark of their generation of moundsmen – they were durable all-purpose pitchers who amassed weighty totals of both complete games and innings pitched, even toiling in relief as well when occasion arose. Hoyt posted 23 wins for the Yankees in 1927. He also led the circuit in saves, with 8, and in seven National League seasons he also paced that circuit twice in relief wins. Both men were a breed apart from today's short-relief specialists, such as the Yankees' Goose Gossage (**BOTTOM RIGHT**) who pioneered the type in the late 1970s, flamethrowers who were called upon almost daily to overpower hitters, but for stretches of only three or four batters at a time. If pitching talent indeed comes in the widest possible assortment of packages, perhaps no man knew this better than catcher Wally Schang (**TOP RIGHT**). The only ballplayer ever to appear on three different World Championship clubs and for 18 years one of the best catchers of his day, Schang had the unique distinction of receiving most of the leading hurlers of the era – Herb Pennock, Eddie Plank, Chief Bender, Babe Ruth, Lefty Grove and even Waite Hoyt.

SOUTHPAW SCREWBALLS

Whether they are called southpaws or portsiders, they are usually known as flakes. Those who developed special pitches with funny names – the "fadeaway" or the "scroogie" – only enhanced their reputations for daffiness.

Lefthanded pitchers carry a reputation for wackiness: they are expected to be eccentrics by nature, flakes, oddballs, cut in the mold of "Spaceman" Bill Lee of Boston Red Sox fame or Phillies hurler Tug McGraw. This image holds fast despite the fact that some of the most workman-like craftsmen of the pitching persuasion have thrown from the port side. What moundsman, for instance, was better known for exemplary performance than Milwaukee's own Warren Spahn (**TOP RIGHT**), winningest lefty ever and fifth among all pitchers, who earned endless admiration for his year-in and year-out consistency as a 20-game winner well beyond age 40? Some lefties relish the screwball image, however, and labor to foster its continued application. The Santa-sized Fernando Valenzuela (**OPPOSITE**), with his Ruthian torso and spinning mound delivery, was something of a comic figure when he burst upon the National League scene in 1981. And one of the most formidable lefties ever, Carl Hubbell (**BELOW**), possessed a gaunt grinning face, huge floppy ears and an arm bent permanently by his "reverse curve" delivery, features more likely to inspire laughter than panic from the league's hitters. But there was more about both Valenzuela and Hubbell than their odd looks to inspire a lefty's reputation for flakiness. Each had mastered the game's strangest pitch – the "screwball," that murderous "fadeaway" breaking ball which made both men as unhittable as they were unorthodox.

The Art of Baseball 153

BREAKING CURVES

In a well-publicized 1959 experiment physicist Lyman J. Briggs provided the incontrovertible evidence that a thrown baseball can indeed be made to curve.

The Art of Baseball 155

The pitcher's ultimate artistic ploy, his special magic and sleight of hand, is to make the ball go where it does not appear to go. As the poet Robert Francis has perfectly expressed it, the pitcher's goal is "how not to hit the mark he seems to aim at, his passion how to avoid the obvious, his technique how to vary the avoidance." Pitching is in the end, after all, an act of deception, and no pitch is as deceptive as the curve. At the big league level it is the pitch that separates the over-touted minor league phenom batter from the true prospect. "I'll be home soon, Mom," writes the discouraged rookie from training camp, "they started throwing curves today!" Bob Feller often attributed the impact of his ballyhooed fastball to the equal effectiveness of his wicked curve. And other flamethrowers who have mastered this most basic of all trick pitches have lived handsomely off its magic. Pirates ace Bob Friend (**OPPOSITE**) will perhaps be remembered for achievements of somewhat dubious distinction. He is the only big league hurler to lose 200 or more games without also winning that many, a fact attributable mainly to his toiling for more than a full decade with punchless cellar-dwelling Pirate teams. He was the first league ERA leader from the roster of a last-place team. Though he twice led the circuit in losses and in hits allowed, hitters who faced Friend throughout the 1950s are far more likely to recall a curve ball that seemed to roll off a table top and which, at its best, was unrivaled across the league. One of the craftiest pitchers ever to wear New York pinstripes, Ed Lopat (**TOP LEFT**), earned credentials as the original junk man when he turned a lack of raw speed to his advantage, keeping hitters off stride for a dozen full American League seasons with dazzling mixtures of slowing-breaking pitches, all served up with unwavering accuracy. Juan Marichal (**BOTTOM LEFT**) employed the "bender" as centerpiece of his potent and varied arsenal, displaying pinpoint control of wicked sliders, screwballs and fastballs, as well as the ponderous curve, served up with a tantalizing variety of high-kicking motions. It was a confusing barrage, which the winningest of all Latin American pitchers parlayed into 243 career victories and a lasting plaque in the Halls of Cooperstown. Among contemporary hurlers, Burt Blyleven (**OPPOSITE TOP RIGHT**) exploited the premier curveball of his era to emerge by 1990 as active career leader in shutouts and active runnerup to only Nolan Ryan in strikeout totals.

FEARSOME FLAMETHROWERS

Babe Ruth once stood helpless as three of Walter Johnson's aspirin tablets sizzled over the center of the plate. "I didn't see any of them either," Babe muttered to the man in blue, "but the last one sounded kind of high."

For the seasoned connoisseur, pitching may be all deviousness and deception, a heightened art of trickery depending more on brain than brawn and designed more on mental strategy than physical prowess. Yet from the more distant perspective of the casual fan it is the raw speed of the overpowering fastball that is the stuff of big league legend. It is much the same with batting: we construct our legends around the prodigious longballs of Babe Ruth and not the adroit bat-handling of Wee Willie Keeler and Ty Cobb. With pitchers it is always the "heat" of Walter Johnson, Bob Feller or Nolan Ryan – not the equally unhittable "butterflies" of Hoyt Wilhelm and Phil Niekro – which we tend to extol. Feller, caught here delivering his famous "hard one" during a 1940 first-ever Opening Day no-hitter in Chicago (**OPPOSITE TOP**), was the modern-day type of the legendary fastball hurler. While he himself attributed his strikeout record to a prodigious curveball and slider, and while he became a dominant hurler only after his improved control reduced his lofty base-on-ball totals below those of his famed strikeouts, it was velocity alone that gained Feller his legendary status and famous nickname of "Rapid Robert." Other memorable power pitchers in the Feller mold were Robin Roberts (**OPPOSITE BOTTOM**), Jim Bunning (**TOP RIGHT**) and Robert "Lefty" Grove (**BOTTOM RIGHT**). His Hall-of-Fame career blocked from further luster by a dozen seasons with the dreadful National League Phillies, Roberts suffered another bane of the pure power-pitcher, the gopher ball, of which he yielded a then-record of 46 in 1956, while at the same time demonstrating unusual control for a flamethrower. Bunning employed his own lethal fastball with both the Tigers and Phillies, becoming the first man since Cy Young to win 100 games and to register 1000 strikeouts within both leagues. More impressively, he pitched a no-hitter in each circuit and closed his career in 1971 as second all-time strikeout leader behind Johnson, with the once-prodigious total of 2885. It was Lefty Grove, however, who possessed both the blazing fastball and a matching temper that were the genuine stuff of baseball legend. Rumor has it this hotheaded "bad boy" of the Connie Mack Athletics set several still-standing circuit mileposts with his shredded uniforms, cracked bats, trashed hotel rooms, smashed lockers, kicked buckets – and alienated teammates.

The Art of Baseball 157

SPITBALLERS – BASEBALL OUTLAWS

That fateful day when Carl Mays threw a twilight pitch that struck down Cleveland's Ray Chapman he fatally wounded more than a fellow ballplayer; he launched events destined to cause the demise of a whole era.

Today it looms large in baseball's prehistoric past – the nostalgia-laden Dead-Ball Era when banjo hitters like Ty Cobb, Honus Wagner and Nap Lajoie banged away at a deadened sphere that seemed to give all advantages to the iron-armed and iron-willed pitchers of the day. Batting averages were stratospheric, yet run production was scarce, and the weighty ball itself, as well as the pitchers' prowess, was more responsible for low scoring than were the defensive skills of the day. Folk history has it that bounceless balls were subsequently "livened up" after 1920 to provide Babe Ruth with a proper showcase for his popular home run slugging technique, thus deflecting attention from the shame of the 1919 Black Sox scandal. Yet both the "dead ball" and the reasons for its demise are probably more the stuff of hearsay than of history. What tipped the scales to the pitcher's clear advantage before 1920 was arguably more the color and condition of the game's single ball than anything about its internal construction. Clean new baseballs for each batter were unheard of, and pitchers were allowed (with the help of their tobacco-chewing infielders) to "doctor" the ball regularly, coating it with spit, mud, scratches, nicks and foreign substance of every imaginable variety. The hitter was often faced with a blackened and soggy sponge. One of the most lethal of these repellant weapons was the "brown spitter" laced with tobacco juice, the modern version of which contemporary spitballer Gaylord Perry (**TOP RIGHT**) righteously claimed never to have used. "I couldn't take the tobacco," Perry said innocently. It was, for the record, just such an invisible pitch that killed Ray Chapman and thus brought quick demise to the practice of "doctoring" the ball. But the art did not so much disappear as go underground. Spitballers on active club rosters (such as the Dodgers' Burleigh Grimes (**OPPOSITE**), here demonstrating his famous two-fingered application technique), were permitted to continue their favorite weapon until retirement. And the generations that followed them were filled with covert users. Most noteworthy among modern-day spitball outlaws was another Dodgers' Hall-of-Fame great, Don Drysdale (**BOTTOM RIGHT**). Drysdale (ironically named, for one whose career flourished with subversive "wet ones") was among the diamond's meanest pitchers. The brush-back was his flaunted trademark, yet the deadly spitter remained Don Drysdale's most effective secret weapon.

THE KNUCKLEBALLERS

Former major league catcher Bob Uecker reportedly took strong issue with the popular theory that, of all pitches, a knuckleball is the toughest to catch: "You just wait until it stops rolling and then you pick it up."

Famed batting coach Charlie Lau once told his charges that there were two theories about hitting the knuckler. The unfortunate thing, Lau continued, is that neither of them works. Manager Casey Stengel, on the other hand, once chided his catcher for signalling skilled knuckleballer Dutch Leonard (whose flutterball he seemed loath to catch) to throw a fastball which was then promptly knocked in the seats. "Don't you think," Casey demanded, "that if a knuckler's so hard to catch it might be a little hard to hit, too?" And Yankee Bobby Murcer once described facing Phil Niekro's elusive bouncing delivery like "trying to eat Jell-O with chopsticks." Such is the lore that surrounds baseball's most infamous pitch, and with good reason. Down through the years a few moundsmen so mastered this special brand of pitching wizardry that they became the bane both of rival batsmen and their own bedeviled receivers. Ed Cicotte (**OPPOSITE**) of Black Sox infamy is today credited in diamond lore as the first to exploit this brand of junkball trickery, perhaps as early as the 1908 season. With a wide repertoire of deceptive off-speed pitches, Cicotte, like all later masters of the exasperating flutterball, relied mainly on pinpoint control and a psychological edge to befuddle his lumber-wielding enemies. (It might be said of Cicotte that he was a pitcher who "never beat himself" – except, of course, in 1919, when he accepted a sum of $10,000 from gamblers and gangsters to do so.) Others have relied on this complete opposite of the "power pitch" to revive tired arms and keep major league pitching careers alive well past the geriatric stage: (**BOTTOM RIGHT**) Atlanta teammates Phil Niekro (left) and Hoyt Wilhelm (right) are the prime examples, the latter appearing in more games (1070) than any other pitcher in history, while the former – thanks in part to his devilish dancing delivery – was able to stretch his big league tenure to the ripe age of 48. In a rare moment of knuckleball history, Brooklyn Dodger Fat Freddie Fitzsimmons displays here (**TOP RIGHT**) the experimental canary-yellow baseball used in an Ebbets Field doubleheader on August 2, 1938. Fitzsimmons complained loudly that the dye-coated ball was altogether too slick to grip, and the side of his uniform was soon stained by his efforts to wipe off the offending substance. One can only speculate what hitters thought of a sphere the size and color of a grapefruit when delivered with Freddie's "flutterball grip."

GREAT CATCHES

They make the weekly television highlight films and are sources of delight on TV scoreboards in stadiums across the land. The circus catch is pure diamond poetry.

Perhaps no dramatic baseball moment more pleases the fan's eye than the leaping or diving circus catch which nips a rally, cuts down an enemy run or simply foils a hopeful batter. New York Yankees right fielder Lou Piniella (**OPPOSITE LEFT**) reaches unsuccessfully for a home run blast by Rusty Staub of the Tigers in the third inning of a July 2, 1977 game at Yankee Stadium. In this case fans had no more luck than the lunging outfielder, as the errant ball dropped in the gap between fences, to the considerable dismay of all the New York faithful.

While some outfielders leap high, others dive low to keep the ball from making its way disastrously into plush outfield pastures. Chicago Cubs left fielder Billy Williams (**BOTTOM RIGHT**) provides one of the more spectacular examples as he lands on his head after making a rolling grab of a blast from the bat of San Francisco batsman Tito Fuentes during a May 1971 contest in Wrigley Field. While the dramatic catch seemed to save the day at the time – cutting off a rally and preventing two Giants runs from crossing the plate – in this case the effort proved futile, as the Cubs went down to a 7-3 defeat.

With the taste of World Series victory on their lips, exuberant Pittsburgh fans look on as, behind third base, Pirate infielder Don Hoak (**OPPOSITE RIGHT**) makes a difficult "sun field" catch of a high pop by Gil McDougald during the opening game of the 1960 Fall Classic. Hoak's grab was only the earliest of many thrills to come the way of Pirates fans that week, as the local heroes battled their way to a first Series title in 35 long seasons.

Infielders are much more likely to thrill fans with lunging stops of hot ground balls than with leaping snags of airborne blasts, and one popular technique for gloving the wicked smash is deftly demonstrated here in spring training practice by stellar third sacker Eddie Yost (**TOP RIGHT**), who manned the hot corner for the Washington Senators throughout the decade of the 1950s. While best remembered for his ironman streak of 838 games during the first half of that decade, Yost retired with a then-record 2008 games at the third base position, as well as with league records for putouts, assists and chances at the position. And many of those chances were as adroitly handled as the one being demonstrated here.

164 THE BASEBALL SCRAPBOOK

Often, potential outfield defensive gems end suddenly in comic disaster for a pair of daring defenders. In one clear example here (**OPPOSITE TOP**), Los Angeles Dodger outfielders Duke Snider (right) and Wally Moon (left) collide as they pursue a fly ball off the bat of White Sox catcher Sherm Lollar in 1959 World Series action. Snider was not able to hold on to the drive and the resulting error allowed the Chisox hitter to reach second on a play that opened the floodgates to an 11-0 Chicago victory. Another such moment (**OPPOSITE BOTTOM**) finds Red Sox shortstop Luis Aparicio colliding on the outfield grass with hatless second sacker Doug Griffin, with neither able to hold the weak pop of Detroit slugger Norm Cash. While serious injury was avoided, a dent in the Boston defense was not.

More textbook cases of proper defense play are here displayed by Yankees stalwarts Graig Nettles (**TOP**), who makes a sensational diving stab at a vicious grounder by Steve Garvey of Los Angeles in 1978 World Series play, and late backstop Thurman Munson (**RIGHT**), who prepares to snag a rain-making pop fly behind home plate during regular 1973 season action against Cleveland at Yankee Stadium.

Often the most spectacular of fielding plays are those which are ultimately unsuccessful, yet which still provide ballet-like poses and colorful split-second dramatic action. In one illustrative case, Baltimore Orioles third sacker Craig Worthington (**TOP LEFT**) lunges after an infield pop from the bat of Cleveland's Joe Carter, after first badly misjudging the hit which nearly fell unattended at his side. Ozzie Smith (**BOTTOM LEFT**) of the Cardinals is similarly caught in a rare moment of imperfection, here bobbling a ball hit by Alan Trammell of Detroit in the 1987 All-Star Game in Oakland. Smith earned an error on the play, a rare enough occurrence because "The Wizard of Oz" is a phenomenal defensive shortstop whom many label the best ever at his position and whom St. Louis manager Whitey Herzog once credited with saving upwards of 75 runs per season with his unrivalled glovework. Smith is a winner of nine consecutive Gold Gloves for his flashy play over the past decade in the St. Louis infield. And as proof that glove men at long last draw their due acknowledgment in the game, he ranked for a while in 1987 as the highest-paid player in baseball, drawing a reported salary of about $2.3 million.

No gallery of defensive gems – most especially those involving daring and spectacular outfield play – would be complete without a picture of the remarkable play that but a few short seasons back was burned into the collective memory of a spellbound national television audience of millions. The setting was the ALCS playoff battle between the Angels of California and the Red Sox of Boston, two potentially snake-bite teams locked in dramatic struggle for a World Series berth. With California closing in on victory, Boston center fielder Dave Henderson (**OPPOSITE**) leaped against the centerfield fence in a vain effort to corral a towering fly ball by the Angels' Bobby Grich. The ball at first seemed to be clutched in Henderson's mitt for a game-saving grab; then, before the astonished eyes of the TV viewers and the photographers lining the outfield wall, the ball popped loose and over the fence for a four-bagger. Henderson's near "Hail Mary" catch was not the final chapter, however, for the disappointed Bosox flychaser battled back a half-inning later to sock a game-tying homer of his own, with the Angels ballclub one out away from victory and the Series. It was then, fittingly, Henderson again who clinched the game and the league title with a sacrifice fly for Boston in the 11th frame.

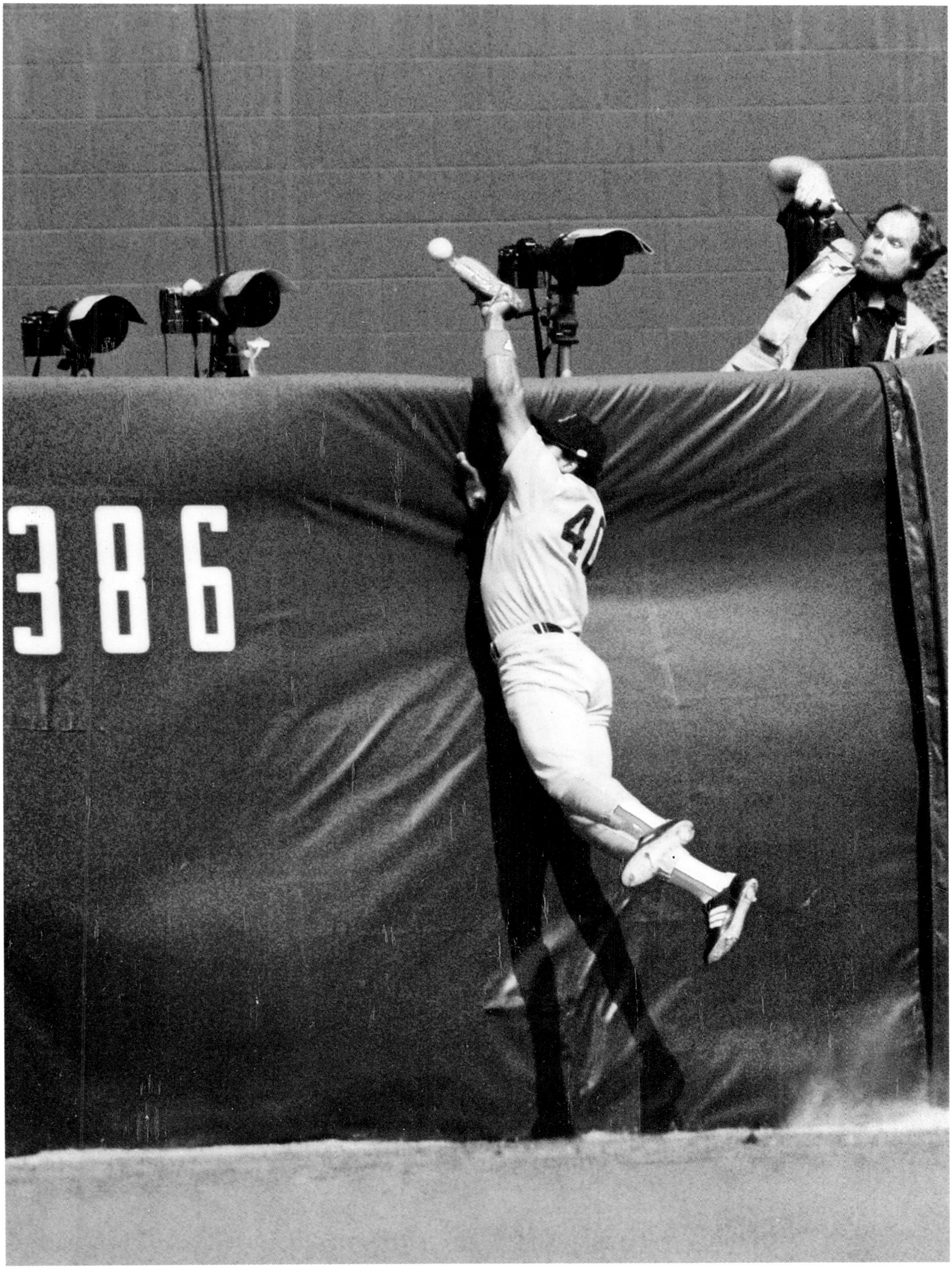
386

"SLIDE, KING KELLY, SLIDE!"

They dive feet-first or head-first, some with reckless abandon like Charlie Hustle Pete Rose, some with regal form like the princely Lou Brock, others with all the desperate gracelessness of stampeding buffalo.

The Art of Baseball 169

For hours on end the art is practiced during the heat of spring training workouts. It consists of throwing oneself on the ground toward a base in order to avoid the tag of a waiting infielder – or at times simply to keep from overrunning the safe haven of either second or third base. The slide can be performed either feet-first or in the more daring head-first manner; either way, the object is to make contact with the base by lunging with hand or foot, thus offering a much-reduced target for the swipe of the defender's tag. Two of the most famous practitioners of the more reckless headfirst style have been Yankees' diminutive shortstop Phil Rizzuto in the 1940s and 1950s and flamboyant Pete Rose of Cincinnati's Big Red Machine teams during the following two decades. In two classic samples, Phil Rizzuto (**OPPOSITE BOTTOM**) dives headlong at second during 1942 World Series action with St. Louis, and Pete Rose belly-flops into third (**RIGHT**) in a 1975 contest at Chicago's Wrigley Field, thus demonstrating the aggressive style underlying his "Charlie Hustle" reputation.

If any team was famed for wild basepath antics it was an untamed crew known as Gashouse Gang Cardinals. Throughout the mid-1930s this irrepressible collection of diamond clowns was led by the likes of Pepper Martin, Dizzy Dean ("gassy" enough all by himself!), Ducky Medwick, Leo "Lippy" Durocher (credited by at least some with coining the outfit's famous cognomen) and manager Frankie Frisch. Another version of the origin of this memorable epithet suggests that the ballclub once arrived in New York from Boston with uniforms so soiled (they were "a sliding team" and little attention was paid to laundering equipment in those days) that a local scribe reported "they looked like a team from the gas house" (referring to a rough-and-tumble district in Manhattan's lower East Side). If our lasting image of Gotham's Murderer's Row Yankees is that of roly-poly Ruth and statuesque Gehrig, posed with a fistful of lumber on their shoulders, that of the Dizzy Dean-era Cards will always be one of the roughneck Redbirds leaping headfirst into an anchored base on a sun-drenched infield. A cloud of dust, flashing spikes and a mouthful of loose dirt – this was the style that endeared Medwick, Martin, Frisch, Durocher, Ripper Collins and Chick Hafey to the nation's fans. The archetypal image is that of the crew's ringleader, Pepper Martin ("Wild Hoss of the Osage") diving hell-bent for third in typical game action at Sportsman's Park (**RIGHT**). Bellyflop slides were Martin's special trademark and helped him lead the senior circuit in stolen bases – as well as score more than 120 runs – over three successive seasons. Gashouse Gang manager Frankie Frisch (demonstrating the technique on **P.168, TOP**) had earlier pioneered the bellyflop style himself with the 1920s Giants, averaging 100 runs per season between 1921-1927 and stealing bases with reckless abandon. Frisch taught the devil-may-care basepath game to his Cardinals throughout the 1930s, as witnessed by a trio of his charges here (**P.169, TOP**) demonstrating their flashy style for the camera during a spring training sliding session. Captured in perfect illustration of hook, dive and fade-away versions are (l to r) Joe "Ducky" Medwick, Stanley "Frenchy" Bordagaray and Enos Slaughter.

The Art of Baseball 171

LEGAL LARCENY ON THE BASEPATHS

King Kelly, baseball's nineteenth-century idol, is credited with perfecting base stealing; Ty Cobb elevated it into a potent offensive weapon; and today's wing-footed thieves have made it pure poetry.

The Art of Baseball 173

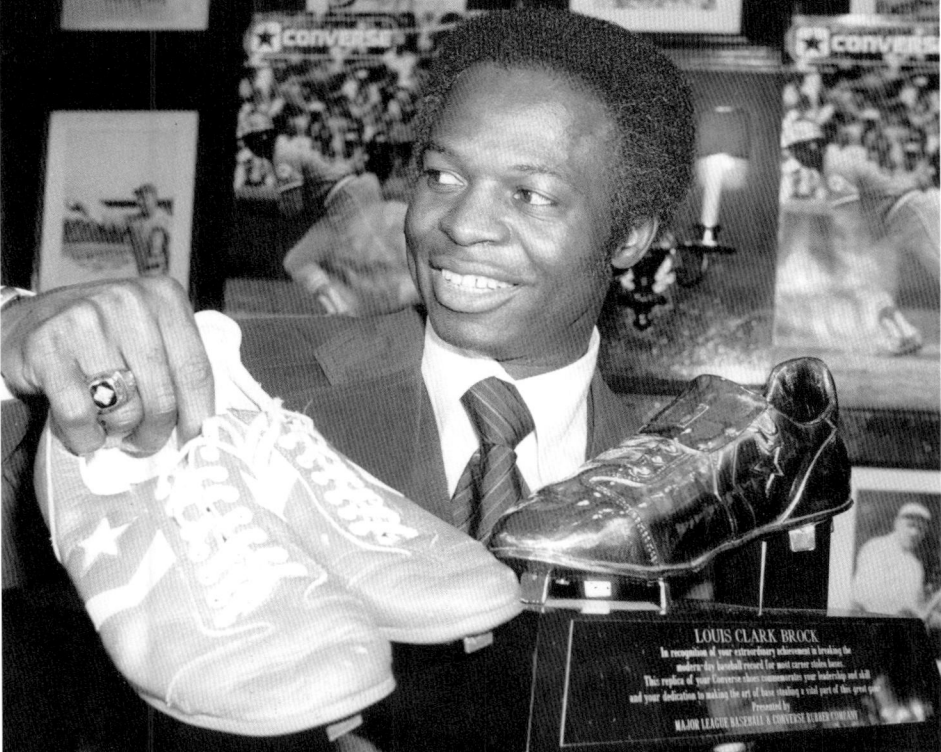

The ebb and flow of "stylish" ballpark play is nowhere better illustrated than in the history of the stolen base. The "scientific" style in vogue in the final decades of the nineteenth century featured diminutive spray hitters with almost unimaginable batting averages (Jesse Burkett hit .402 in 1899 and failed to lead the league!) and fleet-footed base thieves who pilfered at will (John McGraw stole 73 bases for the Orioles that same summer and also finished out of the running). Ty Cobb (**OPPOSITE TOP LEFT**) soon made his stolen bases as much an offensive weapon as his lofty batting average, and his dead-ball-era total of 892 thefts was seemingly an untouchable milestone. Cobb's rival, Honus Wagner (**OPPOSITE TOP RIGHT**), was a bowlegged, barrel-chested fireplug who resembled an octopus far more than a gazelle; yet the hustling Pirate shortstop displayed enough basepath daring in his day to amass 722 career steals, a total which still stands 8th on the all-time list. Cobb and Wagner were among the last of a breed, and with the onslaught of home run hitting ushering in the Roaring Twenties era the stolen base seemed to go the way of the dodo and the nickle cup of coffee. Stolen base champions often dipped to league-leading totals in the 20s and 30s during the decades bearing those same numerals, and two of the top basestealers of the World War II era, "Peewee" Reese and Jackie Robinson, paced the senior circuit with just 20 and 29 in 1942 and 1947 respectively. Then came a new stable of speed merchants, fueled by a change in baseball strategy, better nutrition and the miracle of synthetic fields, and once more records like Cobb's were an endangered species. First Maury Wills (**OPPOSITE BOTTOM**) burned the basepaths in 1962, reaching seemingly impossible levels as the first man since 1896 to commit basepath larceny more than 100 times in a single season, obliterating Cobb's modern mark of 96 (in 1915) in the process. Wills' new-found reign as stolen base king was short-lived, for he was followed in the second half of the decade by Cardinals speedster Lou Brock (**BOTTOM LEFT**, displaying shoes with which he passed Cobb's career record). Brock ruled as National League king for the next eight of nine years, streaking past Wills' single-season mark with 118 in 1974 and overhauling Cobb's career total by 1978 as well. Today baseball enjoys yet a new basepath king, as Rickey Henderson has overtaken both Brock's single-season record (**TOP LEFT**) and his all-time career mark.

LIVING OR DYING BY THE SQUEEZE

Never is timing as crucial, and no play in baseball's huge arsenal of offensive trickery puts more at risk, yet pays more dividends with games on the line. When it fails, it produces a desperate dash by a stranded baserunner.

It's the most daring play anywhere on the diamond. The runner on third breaks for the plate as his teammate with the stick attempts to bunt the ball just out of the catcher's and pitcher's reach. It is a matter of split-second timing, one that leaves the fielders helpless if the bunt is indeed properly executed. But a missed or unskillful bunt, one popped in the air or slapped back to the mound, will turn the committed runner into a sacrificial lamb. Such is the case in classic action captured here, as several victimized runners scamper for their very lives at the botched end of an unsuccessful "squeeze" play. Phil Rizzuto of the Yankees is trapped between third and home in 1949 World Series action in Brooklyn (**OPPOSITE**), unable to avoid the inevitable tag (**OPPOSITE BOTTOM**) of agile Dodgers' backstop Roy Campanella. Then it is the Yankees turning the tables on stranded Giant Tom Haller during the 1962 Fall Classic, as Haller scrambles hopelessly plateward with Clete Boyer in hot pursuit (**RIGHT**). Lance Johnson of Chicago (**BELOW**) looks over his shoulder as he also is about to be tagged by Tony Fernandez in a similar busted bunt attempt at the Toronto SkyDome in early 1990 action.

"BEATING THE BALL" BACK HOME

In other games the race is always against the clock or a fleet-footed human opponent. On the diamond it is the tiny ball which one races – across the diamond, around the bases and all the way back home.

The Art of Baseball

In infant days of a game first known as "town-ball" or "rounders" the play was much less civilized. A baserunner, for example, was put out by being struck down with a thrown missile, and play resembled a roughneck's version of schoolyard "dodge ball." Fortunately, the rules were soon altered, and the relieved runner was responsible only for avoiding a tag in his dashes from one post to the next. Now he only had to beat the ball to the safety of a base (thus avoiding being "tagged" out) if actually forced by a trailing runner onto the next station. And there began one of the most exciting contests of all sport – the action-packed footrace between human runner and thrown sphere. Baseball history is replete with such plays – runners stretching to beat the peg to first, sliding to avoid a baseman's tag at second or perhaps third, barreling down upon a waiting catcher positioned to block home plate. From earliest times such scenes have been the favorite of those who set out to record the game through the camera's lens. Three such images of this dramatic race to beat a tag at home plate here represent the sunrise years, high noon and glorious afternoon of our national pastime's century-long evolution. Fearless Fred Clarke (**OPPOSITE TOP**) of the National League's Louisville entry slides home in late nineteenth-century action, as the arriving ball eludes the catcher's waiting grasp in what appears to be a pre-season practice match. From the middle seasons of baseball's century, Detroit's Mickey Cochrane (**OPPOSITE BOTTOM**) demonstrates classic form as he lunges with ball in hand at an unknown opposition baserunner attempting to invade a backstop's precious homeplate territory. In a modern-day shot from the 1960s, Paul Blair (**BOTTOM RIGHT**) eludes a glove-hand tag from Boston Red Sox catcher Elston Howard in another dramatic homeplate tableau. The race to the first base sack is also captured here with runners seemingly suspended in mid-air flight: Gashouse Pepper Martin (**TOP RIGHT**) stretches for the bag in 1939 as Reds first sacker Frank McCormick turns to observe the call and umpire Reardon waves the runner safe. In similar tense action from a decade earlier (**CENTER RIGHT**), Boston Braves first baseman Dick Burrus stretches vainly for a toss that arrives moments too late to catch a successfully lunging Freddie Lindstrom of the Giants.

178 THE BASEBALL SCRAPBOOK

And the race goes on. "Too close to call" might seem to be the verdict on this homeplate collision between sliding Yankees outfielder Charley "King Kong" Keller and diving Indians veteran backstop Rollie Hemsley (**OPPOSITE TOP RIGHT**) at Yankee Stadium in May of 1939. But umpire Rue is Johnny-on-the-spot and signals "safe" as Keller completes his mad dash from first base to home (initiated when New York's Joe Gallagher singled into right, and Cleveland's Julius "Moose" Solters bobbled the troublesome base hit). Nowhere is the split-second arrival of ball and runner better illustrated than in the frozen action of Chicago's Shawon Dunston stretching to score in the 1989 NLCS while Giants pitcher Jeff Brantley waits helplessly for the seemingly suspended ball on its flight plateward (**P.180, BOTTOM**). A similar flight of the ball reveals a successful out made at second base (**RIGHT**), for Chicago's Nellie Fox has already unleashed his throw toward first, while sliding St. Louis Brown Ray Coleman has clearly yet to arrive at the second base goal. (This picture-perfect rally-killing double play occurred in 1951 Comiskey Park action.) It is the jubilant reaction of first sacker Will Clark of San Francisco (**P.181, BOTTOM**) that in another case signals that Cardinals baserunner Ozzie Smith has failed in his slide to first-base safety. Smith was doubled off first during a 1987 NLCS game when St. Louis batter Tom Herr lined a fly ball to Giants outfielder Candy Maldonado.

The Art of Baseball 179

THE RITES OF SPRING

For fans it's a joyous time of renewal; for rookie and veteran alike it's a time of sweat and strain.

Managers predict sure pennants, rookies are called "phenoms" and certain Hall-of-Famers, and even the umpires are lovable. What other time of year could it be but Spring Training? The practice – in a sport whose very lifeblood is tradition – outdates both the National and American leagues themselves. The semipro ballclub known as the Chicago White Stockings is reported to have made a spring training trip to New Orleans in 1870, a single year after Cincinnati's Red Stockings inaugurated professional play with their 1869 barnstorming junket across the nation. And the pre-season routine of mixing rigorous exercise with instructional training and relaxed exhibition play has lasted through all subsequent decades, though its venue has not always been the familiar Florida and Arizona locations of the modern era. Florida training camps have been a staple since the Washington ballclub experimented with the first Sunshine State encampment in 1888. A rare scene from the 1930s here captures Detroit manager Mickey Cochrane, himself a Hall-of-Fame receiver, giving tips on the noble art of backstopping to another future standout skipper, George "Birdie" Tebbetts, in the Tigers' 1938 Lakeland camp (**TOP RIGHT**). Another (**OPPOSITE TOP**) records early spring batting practice for the Brooklyn team under manager Wilbert "Uncle Robbie" Robinson (in topcoat, alongside the batting cage). A more typical staged promotional shot from a decade later (**BOTTOM RIGHT**) features four rookie prospects loading the first base sack at the Yankees' 1949 St. Petersburg camp. Pictured here (l to r) are Joe Collins, Dick Kryhoski, Babe Young (the leaper) and Jack Phillips, all locked in a struggle to wrest the position from incumbent Tommy Henrich. Yet such spring rituals have had more exotic settings as well. The lengthy 1930 pennant race trek begins for Chicago's Cubs (**OPPOSITE BOTTOM**) as they arrive at Catalina Island for the beginning of a California winter training session. Another "advance guard" of Brooklyn Dodgers reports (**CENTER RIGHT**) to the makeshift Durocher Field camp at Bear Mountain, New York, for a blustery wartime spring training session. This March 1945 scene captures the strange ambiance of spring baseball conditions prevailing when big league clubs moved their facilities northward as part of the economy-minded war effort. Baseball continued as usual on the home front, yet 1943-45 training camps were anything but the normal springtime fare.

Before the "snowbird" fans arrive in droves for the color and sunshine of pre-season exhibition play, it's a time devoted to fundamentals, repetitious drills and even a few minutes of rest and horseplay. Taking full advantage of a post-lunch rest period at Vero Beach in 1951 is Brooklyn Dodgers hurler Dan Bankhead (**BOTTOM LEFT**). Bankhead covers his eyes with his cap and starts his siesta in the "pepper pot" contraption used by pitchers during instructional drills. More standard spring training fare is the infield instruction being received by Baltimore Orioles veterans and hopefuls in Miami in 1987 (**ABOVE**) or the skull session (**OPPOSITE**) for a newly arrived Baltimore rookie crew checking into camp that same spring.

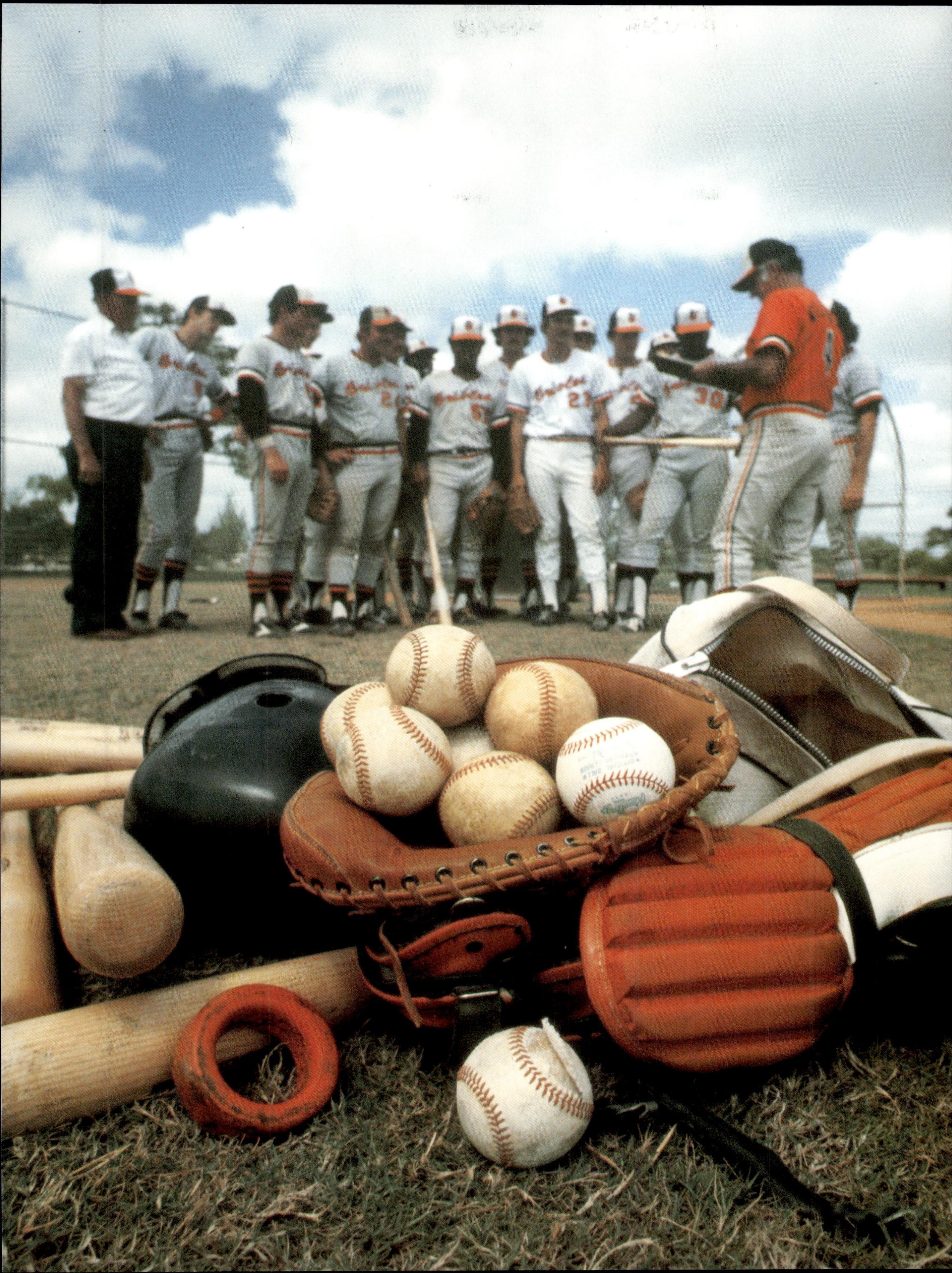

ONE, TWO, THREE AND STRETCH!

Baseball players have a bad name when it comes to physical conditioning. Diamond heroes from Babe Ruth to Greg Luzinski often look more like couch potatoes than athletes, and conditioning seems more a ritual than reality.

The Art of Baseball 187

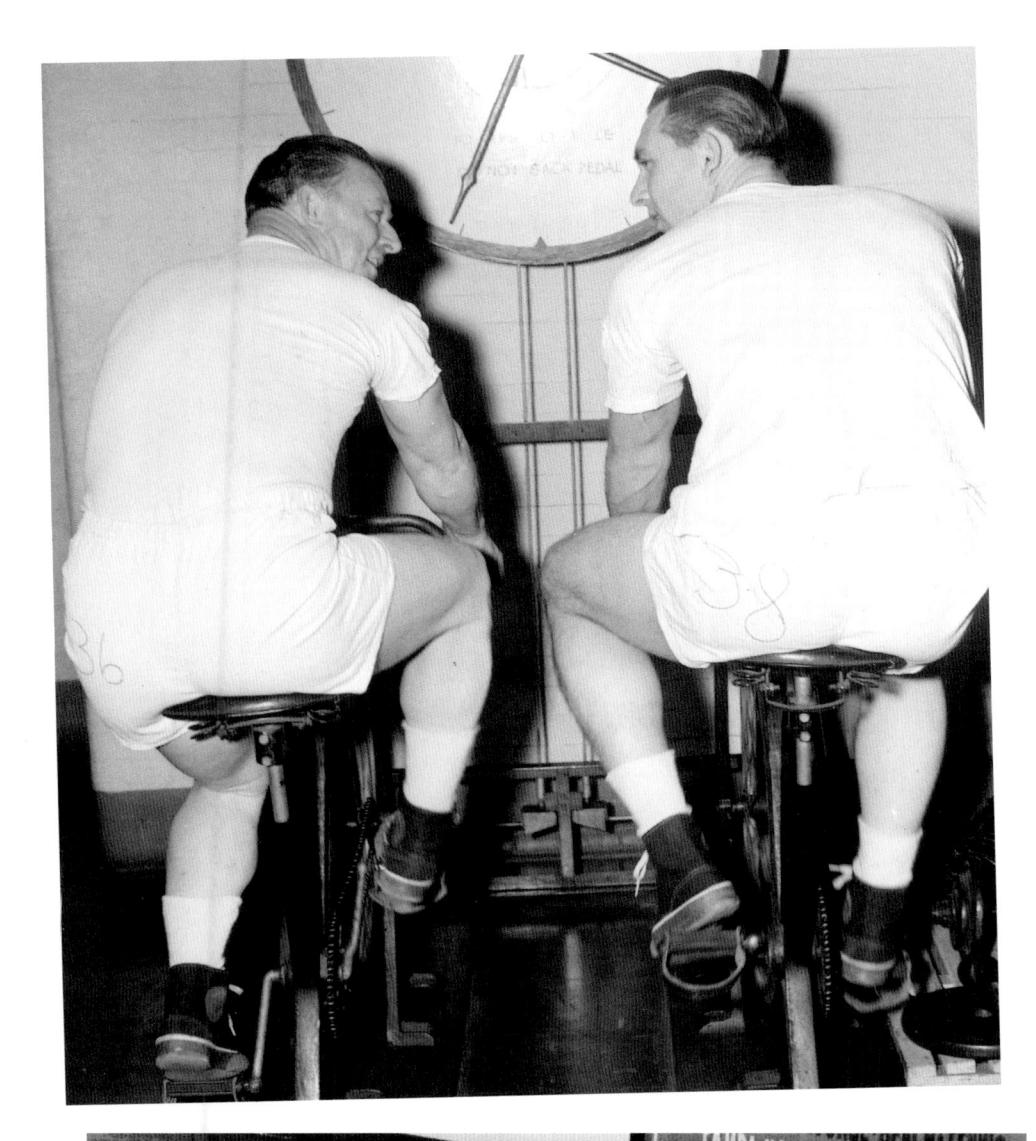

From the rigors of spring training to the long "dog days" of an August pennant race, physical conditioning remains a hidden element of the baseball culture, a daily reality in the lives of players struggling to fight their way back from mid-season injury or perhaps simply laboring to fortify against the aches and pains of the long season's play. At spring training sessions most veteran managers, like New York's Bob Lemon (**BOTTOM LEFT**), stand around like stern drill sergeants as their charges strain to reach playing shape. A few, however, like quixotic Yankee skipper Yogi Berra (**OPPOSITE TOP**), strike fashionable poses of their own during March pre-season calisthenics. "Boys of Summer" Dodgers boss Charlie Dressen was a field boss who was a practitioner as well as proponent of season-long conditioning. Dressen (**TOP LEFT**) seemingly enjoys a 1951 pre-spring training workout on the stationary bicycle with Dodgers star first baseman Gil Hodges (right) at the Brooklyn Crescent Health Club. No ballplayers have ever appeared more enthusiastic about a pre-game limbering up session, however, than the quartet of New York Mets who frolicked in a 1962 workout at the Polo Grounds hours before their first-ever season opener against the Cardinals (**OPPOSITE BOTTOM**). Displaying the unbridled enthusiasm of a typical expansion club roster, these light-hearted and light-stepping Mets are (l to r) Frank Thomas, Gil Hodges, Don Zimmer and Roger Craig. Three of the four would eventually enjoy their own turn as drill sergeants when they themselves became big league managers.

It's not always pure drudgery, this business of getting into proper shape for the rigors of seven months of day-in and day-out big league play. Sometimes the boredom of a pre-season conditioning session is broken up with a carefree game of "leap frog," like this one being practiced by a contingent of eager St. Louis Cardinals (**TOP RIGHT**) at the Redbirds' pre-season St. Petersburg training complex. The same contingent also tried substituting a friendly test of balance and strength for the usual stretching exercise (**CENTER RIGHT**). Sometimes there is time for a private moment of shared humor, such as that enjoyed in the midst of a stretching session by Los Angeles Dodgers mound ace Fernando Valenzuela (**BOTTOM RIGHT**). But in the end there is no escaping those seemingly endless sessions of leg lifts and wind sprints, demonstrated here by the Baltimore Orioles (**OPPOSITE TOP**) and Toronto Blue Jays (**OPPOSITE BOTTOM**). This is the price you have to pay during the first long sunshine weeks of February and March if your heart is set on being a big league pitcher.

The Art of Baseball   189

WHERE NONE BUT THE CHOSEN MAY ENTER

Other sports merely have benches – open and in full view of the spectator; baseball's dugout is the diamond sport's hidden inner sanctum, a place for strategy, horseplay, respite and inspired folklore.

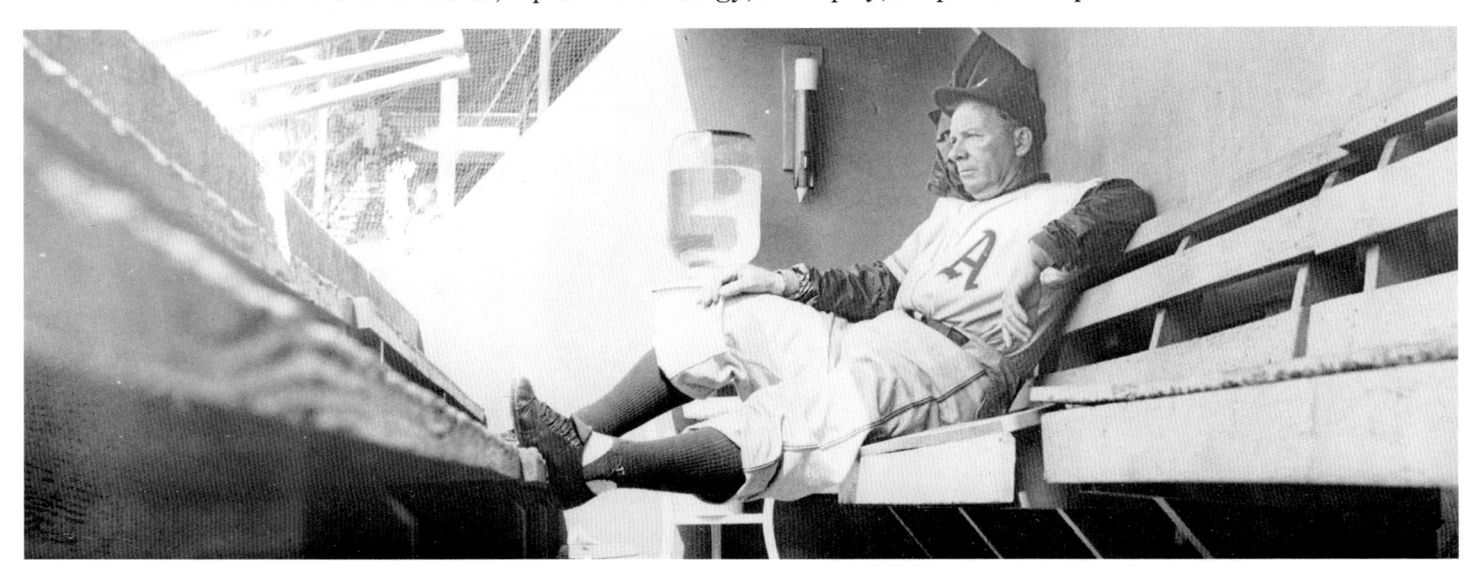

Every fan would love to spend a few hours here, to share in the look, feel and inner workings of a big league game from this forbidden inner sanctum of the ballpark world. It is from this private place that managers bark out instructions to their charges, that bench jockeys hurl their barbs at the opposition and that the players get their eye-level view of diamond action. Philadelphia A's manager Jimmy Dykes (**ABOVE**) wears a pensive look as he watches from the dugout's hidden recesses during spring training play in the early 1950s; Cardinals' skipper Whitey Herzog (**LEFT**) follows a tense moment of action from the same privileged perspective. But sometimes the view reserved for the "bench jockeys" is more distant, if equally as private - that from an outfield bullpen seat (**OPPOSITE TOP**). In this case the location is Yankee Stadium, and the observers are New York Yankees bullpenners Sparky Lyle and Lindy McDaniel. The dugout steps serve both as access to the sanctum sanctorum and as the launching pad for action on the field: here (**OPPOSITE BOTTOM**) the 1940 Philadelphia Athletics charge onto the field from their berth in old Shibe Park for season-opening action against the New York Yankees.

The Art of Baseball 191

TOOLS OF THE TRADE

You start with a bat, ball and leather mitt, plus a few sacks for the bases; soon you need a tight-fitting glove for hitting, an iron cage to shield a catcher's face, darkened glasses to block the sun, etc., etc.

The tools of baseball are often as much a part of the game's lore as the players and the action. Sometimes such tools are newfangled gimmicks quick to pass into oblivion. None was more bizarre an innovation than the light-fixture facemask rigged by White Sox players to protect the famous long nose of third base coach Joe Lonnett (**TOP LEFT**). From Lonnett's primitive protective gear it seems a space-age jump to the experimental glove being demonstrated by Senji Nobuta of the Mizuno Corporation (**ABOVE**), a mitt complete with an electronic gadget that allows beeps to replace the hand signals with which a catcher signals pitch selections to his pitcher. Lest one thinks such mechanical gizmos are entirely foreign to a sport so rooted in nineteenth-century traditions, consider the more familiar "Iron Mike" pitching machine. This Rube Goldberg contraption (**BOTTOM LEFT**) can pitch any style and, unlike its human counterparts, never tires during spring training workouts. But such innovations are the exception. The basic tools of our national pastime remain as simple as a ball, a wooden stick and a leather glove. Since the turn of the century Louisville Sluggers have been turned out in the millions by the Hillerich and Bradsby Company, always with the same painstaking process (**OPPOSITE TOP**) of calibration and lathe shaving. Roy Hobbs had his trusty Wonder Boy, and Shoeless Joe Jackson swung his sturdy Black Betsy, but future generations of sluggers may be marching up to the plate with "lumber" fashioned from aluminum tubes. Aluminum bats, now popular at all levels of amateur play, were developed by the Alcoa Company as early as 1930. Just like a big leaguer, an Alcoa technician (**OPPOSITE BOTTOM**) goes to the bat rack and selects a piece of tubing soon to be found smashing out doubles and triples somewhere in the schoolyards of America.

The Art of Baseball 193

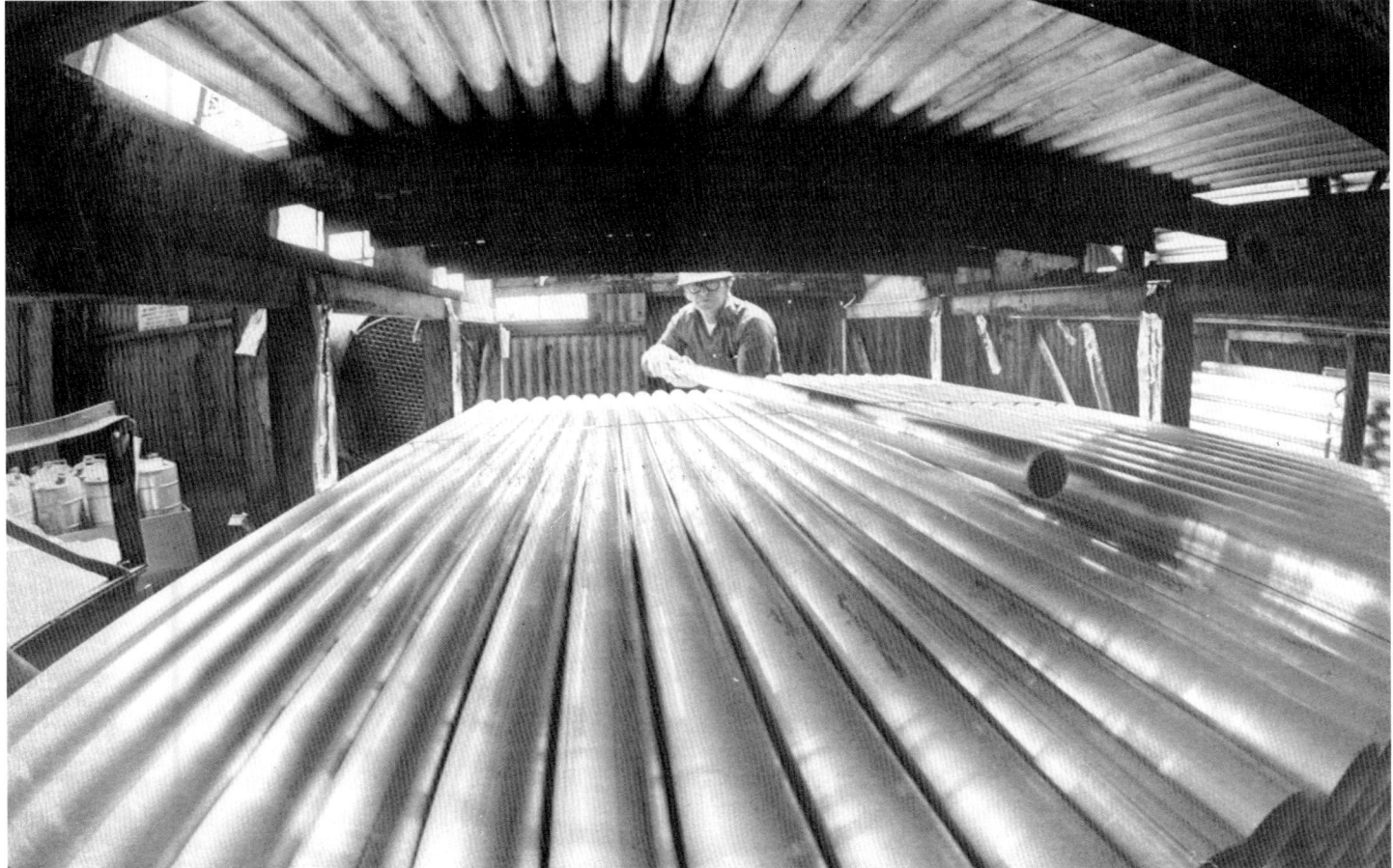

THE BASEBALL FAMILY

Poet Donald Hall sees baseball as a country unto itself, and certainly it is a country peopled by far more than skilled batting stars, celebrated magicians of glovework and strong-armed country boy pitchers. It also includes day laborers, umpires, managers, club owners and, most necessary of all, fans. Baseball's family includes the writers who record diamond events in polished prose and the announcers who bring the game to life over the airways. Alongside the ballpark superstars stand those legions of the game's colorful role-playing characters – the flakes, the flamboyant overachievers, the one-season and one-game wonders, the quickly forgotten "bonus babies" and the never-to-be-forgotten goats. Alongside the imposing legends of Babe Ruth and Ty Cobb there remains a piece of baseball immortality for Fred "Bonehead" Merkle, one-armed Pete Gray, reckless wall-crasher Peter Reiser, incorrigible Casey Stengel, "Lippy" Leo Durocher and the ultimate flakes, "Spaceman" Bill Lee, Jim Piersall and Pepper Martin. All have equal and well-earned claim to full membership in the warmly human and expansive baseball family.

Poet Hall has described the country of baseball thus: "The citizens wear baggy pinstripes, knickers and caps …seasons and teams shift, blur into each other, change radically or appear to change, and restore themselves to old ways again….Football is not a country…it's a psychodrama, brothers beating up on brothers….In the country of baseball the days are always the same." And it was Joseph Sobran who eloquently observed: "We are players or spectators of other sports, but citizens of baseball."

Ballplayers themselves represent a diverse and complex family, one drawn from the four corners of the globe. One true measure, in fact, of the sociological significance of baseball history is to note the successive waves of European and Caribbean immigrants who have entered the game during its past eight decades. For each of these new groups baseball was a broad avenue into the promised land of the American dream. First there were the Central and West European immigrants who filled the new American nation at the end of the nineteenth century – Irish, German and Slavic strains from the farmlands and industrial belts of middle America. Names like McGraw, Keeler, Kelley, Ewing, Schaefer and Donovan fill the entries in the *Baseball Encyclopedia*. Next came Jews from northeastern urban ghettos. Men like Hank Greenberg. Then came Italians – DiMaggio, Lazzeri, Crosetti, Rizzuto, Cavarretta, Lombardi, Cuccinello, Lavagetto, Garagiola.

Then came blacks after the second World War, speeding the process of integrating American society. And most recently there has been the Latin American invasion of the national pastime – Cubans, Puerto Ricans, Venezuelans, Mexicans, and especially Dominicans; nearly 50 percent of the 700-plus Caribbean and Hispanic ballplayers who have reached the majors donned big league colors for the first time after 1975.

The family connection in baseball has also been evident in the linking of one era to the next. Generations of older ex-players and coaches painstakingly teach the finer points of the game (usually at the minor league level) to their successors, for unlike basketball or football, baseball is an art which must be ever so patiently learned, often through years of arduous toil in bush league towns.

Among ballplayers at the big league level there is also the more outwardly visible link of fathers passing the mantle of big league fame to their sons, as well as brother playing alongside brother. Big league father and son combinations have been noteworthy. There is Hall-of-Famer George Sisler and his sons, Dick of the Phillies and Dave of the Red Sox. There is infielder Ray Boone and his more memorable catcher-son Bob Boone and grandsons Brett and Aaron; infielder Dale Berra and his more memorable catcher-father Yogi Berra. Sons of famous Latin players Roberto Clemente, Felipe Alou, Julian Javier and Sandy Alomar have been either noteworthy prospects or next-generation stars. And there are others: two Joe Colemans and two Dick Schofields, Bobby and Barry Bonds, Cesar and Andujar Cedeno, Gary and Buddy Bell, Mel Stottlemyre and sons Todd and Mel Jr., and finally two Ken Griffeys performing simultaneously in the same outfield. And there are many others.

Brother tandems and trios have been an even larger part of baseball history and lore. All of the following brother teams have impacted significantly upon the game: Delahanty (Ed, Joe, Frank, Jim and Tom), DiMaggio (Joe, Dom and Vince), Boyer (Ken and Clete), Waner (Paul and Lloyd), Perry (Gaylord and Jim), Niekro (Phil and Joe), Alou (Felipe, Matty and Jesus), Perez (Pascual and Melido), Ripken (Cal and Billy), May (Lee and Carlos), Torre (Joe and Frank), Cooper (Mort and Walker), Dean (Dizzy and Paul), Reuschel (Rick and Paul), Walker (Harry and Dixie). The Deans and Waners are perhaps most memorable for old-time fans, while the Perrys and Niekros have made greatest impact on contemporary rooters, but the Walkers still remain the only brothers both to win batting titles, and the Alous comprised the first all-sibling outfield. The Niekros and Perrys, on the other hand, both totalled 500 wins and 5000 strikeouts as tandems. All have established a sibling lore which is a fixture in baseball mythology.

These family connections between father and son – one generation and the next – are at least as strong for the baseball fan himself. As countless commentators have noted, baseball represents a common language in the American culture, one which cuts not only across racial, ethnic and economic barriers, but generational barriers as well. The daily scores and the season's action is something that can be discussed daily on street corners or at the breakfast table by men, women and children of all ages. The grade school kid knows the same stats and trivia as the businessman, the doctor and the ranch hand. Mothers and fathers share the lore of the game with their sons and daughters. Playing catch or going to the ballpark is a native American rite; some of the sweetest memories of childhood are those first baseball lessons lovingly administered by Dad at the local park. Perhaps only in his late twenties, Dad nonetheless becomes a grizzled bard of the game, passing on the great legends of his own childhood era. Thus do we inherit lifelong loyalties and attachments to favored teams: Dad's favorite often becomes the lifelong passion of son or daughter.

Such linking of generations is sustained by the game's unchanging rituals: spring training, Opening Day, the ceremonial tossing out of the first ball. Perhaps the "first ball" tradition is an especially meaningful rite, with its associations of seasonal renewal, rebirth, and the coming of spring. When President Harry Truman performed this function on the opening day of a pennant race at the end of World War II, all was right again in America. When politicians and media celebrities today perform the function, they sustain an old and venerable American tradition.

Finally, like any country, baseball has its special places – its shrines – as well as its people. There is only one Cooperstown, but there are dozens of storied ballparks, both old and new. Some are creaky steel and concrete monoliths of an earlier urban era; others are domed and carpeted all-purpose arenas of a modern suburban age. But all are the beloved homes in which the sprawling baseball family dwells.

HAIL THE GLORIOUS WARRIORS!

This game, like any other, has its trophies, honors and assorted promotional events – Cap Day, Poster Day, Fan Appreciation Day. But none evokes more nostalgia or sentiment than a special Player's Day honoring a local hero.

One of baseball's most popular promotional events is the practice of luring paying spectators to the park with the promise of a gala ceremony honoring one of the local favorites. The designation of a special day or night named in recognition of some hometown star – player, manager or even coach – usually involves a ceremony during which the honoree is showered with gifts, tributes and even large sums of cash. The practice is known to stretch back into the early days of the present century, Cy Young being the recorded recipient of one such "day" in Boston on August 13, 1908. Ty Cobb was given such a Player's Day on May 11, 1924, and on that occasion (**OPPOSITE**) a game in the nation's capital between the local Senators and visiting Tigers was preceded by ceremonies in which the great Detroit batting star was presented with a set of books representing his lengthy service in the national game. Here Senator Harris of Georgia and Representative McLeod of Michigan present the "Georgia Peach" (center) with his special parcels, while Senator Walsh of Michigan and other congressmen look on. Gifts to favored players on these ceremonial occasions take all forms, from cash to automobiles to artwork. Milwaukee Braves' hurler Warren Spahn (**OPPOSITE BOTTOM LEFT**) was so honored on September 17, 1963, when 34,000 fans turned out in County Stadium to present the lefthander with a painting of the hometown ballpark and the honor of a $30,000 scholarship fund established in his name. One of the more emotional of such tributes took place in late season in 1940 when a packed Yankee Stadium throng listened to a moist-eyed Joe DiMaggio present a speech of thanks to the thousands of admirers who saluted him during "DiMaggio Day" ceremonies. A wall of gifts surrounds the Yankee Clipper and popular New York Yankee broadcaster Mel Allen as Joltin' Joe (**TOP LEFT**), still shaky from a bout with near-pneumonia, returned to the lineup for the first time in more than a week for a vital game with the rival Boston Red Sox. Three decades later DiMaggio's heir, Mickey Mantle (**BOTTOM LEFT**), surveys banners paraded on-field during "Mickey Mantle Banner Day" in the venerable and tradition-rich Bronx ballpark.

ALL IN THE FAMILY

They come in pairs, and sometimes even in threes, sometimes making their opponents think they suffer from double vision. These double-trouble packages are rare, but some of baseball's brother combos have been legendary.

Major league history of the most arcane sort was made in New York's famed Polo Grounds on September 10, 1963. On that date, San Francisco's Giants became the first ballclub ever to employ three brothers in its line-up within the same ballgame. The Dominican Alou brothers all batted in the eighth inning that day, yet failed to provide a Frank Merriwell script as all three made quick outs. Jesus (l), Matty (c), and Felipe (r), here posing before that historic game (**BOTTOM RIGHT**), remained teammates throughout the 1963 season, thus becoming the first and only all-brother outfield in big-league history. While they remained together in San Francisco through only the opening months of 1964, the three Alou brothers were, individually, scourges in the National League ballparks of the 1960s: Felipe starred with the Braves and cracked 206 career homers; Matty won a 1966 league batting title with the Pirates; Jesus lacked Felipe's power and Matty's speed, yet performed admirably with the Giants and Astros and provided valuable pinch-hitting service with Oakland's 1973-74 World Championship club. While the Alous were the first single-team brother trio, they were by no means the only or even the most potent of brother acts in diamond history. Each decade seemed to feature a sterling sibling combination of its own. In the 1940s it was the DiMaggios – the Yankee Clipper in the Bronx; Dom matching Joe's superb centerfield play in Boston; and Vince, the oldest, who served five National League clubs and stroked a homer, triple and single while representing the Pirates in the 1943 All-Star game. Not often seen together in uniform, the three famed DiMaggios here pose (**CENTER RIGHT**) in the flannels of San Francisco Seals before appearing in a 1956 Pacific Coast League Old-Timers game. If the DiMaggio's were the most memorable brother act of the 1940s, the 1930s could boast famous Gashouse siblings in the persons of Dizzy and Paul Dean (**TOP RIGHT**), as well as a pair of Hall of Famers, Lloyd and Paul Waner, who simultaneously patrolled the outfield in Pittsburgh for 14 long seasons. Posing with brother Travis (**OPPOSITE BOTTOM**) – a young prospect who failed to make the big time – Lloyd (l) and Paul (r) were the most prolific fraternal batting combination in history, compiling 5611 safeties between them. Anticipating the Waners were the Sewells of Cleveland (**OPPOSITE TOP**), Joe (l), a Hall-of-Fame shortstop with a career .312 BA, and Luke (r), a dependable catcher whose career stretched for 20 full seasons.

200   THE BASEBALL SCRAPBOOK

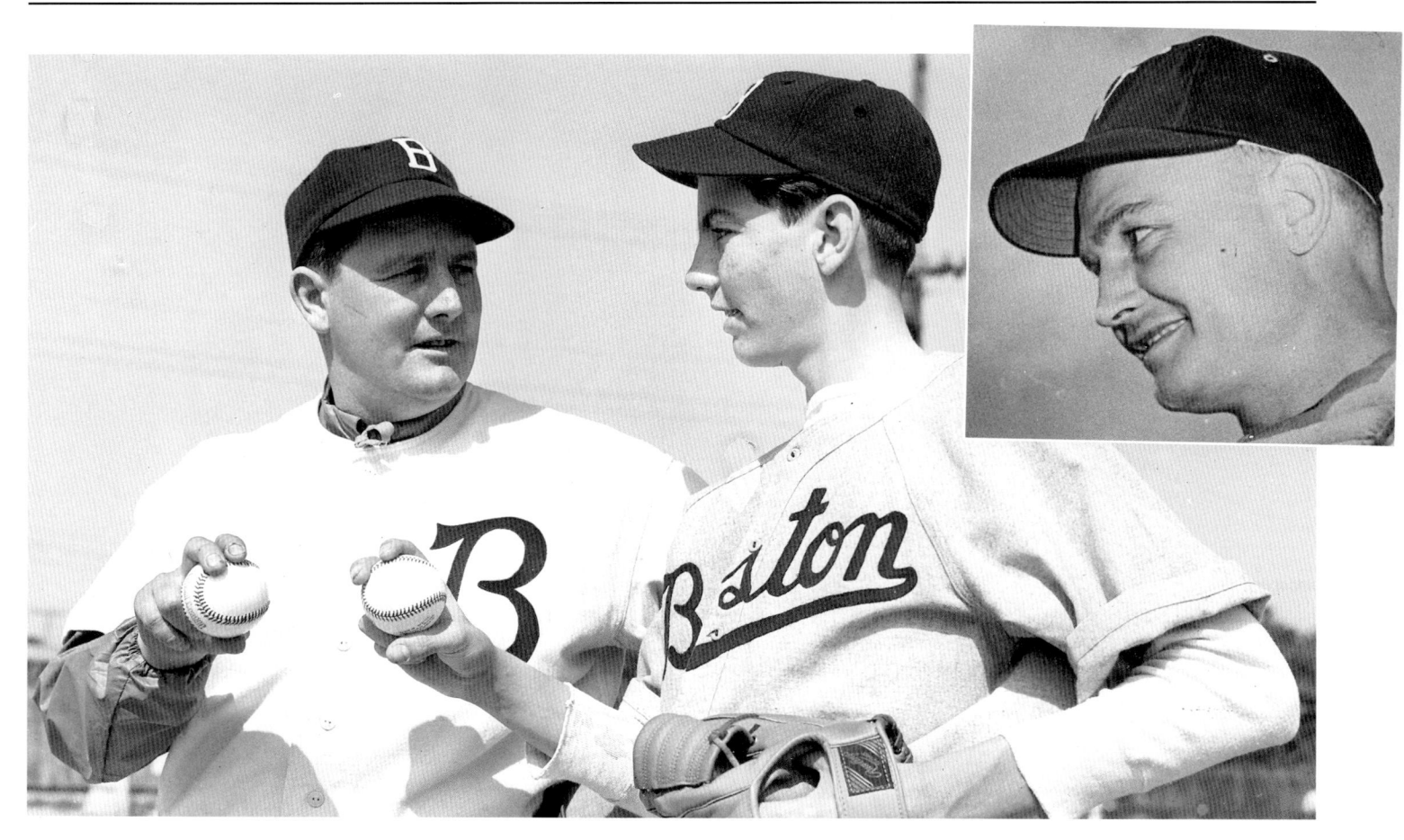

The Baseball Family

Baseball has had its share of tragedy. Sometimes it is the tale of a promising youngster cut off in his prime by some crippling injury; sometimes it concerns an old veteran turning goat in the heat of a pennant race or staring bleakly at the end of his fading career. Occasionally it is the painful discovery by a hopeful prospect that he simply lacks the talent possessed by some other member of the family who has already made his mark in the big leagues. Baltimore second sacker Billy Ripken (posing with father Cal Sr. and brother Cal Jr., **OPPOSITE BOTTOM**) now struggles for recognition in the long shadow of his iron-man all-star older sibling, with whom he forms a talented keystone combination. Paul Dean was lost in the glare of brother Dizzy's showmanship, and Vince DiMaggio could never measure up to either Joe or Dom. Yet at least all have fulfilled the dream of a productive big league career. Such was not to be the lot of Travis Waner, Sam Cooper or Ben Banks. Infield prospect Ben Banks (**BOTTOM RIGHT**) poses with his Hall-of-Fame old brother Ernie (r) at the Cubs' 1956 training camp, where Ben received a brief trial before seeing his own diamond dreams go up in smoke. Sam Cooper was a starry-eyed youngster when he took pitching instruction from his older brother and ace Boston Braves moundsman Mort Cooper (**OPPOSITE TOP LEFT**). Sam, however, soon had to face the painful reality that his dreams would never include big league stardom like those of three-time 20-game winner Mort or brother Walker (**OPPOSITE TOP RIGHT**), an 18-year big league catcher. Yet when it comes to tales of sibling tragedy, probably none approaches the joint fate of Boston's talented Conigliaro brothers (**TOP RIGHT**). Top draft choice of the Red Sox in 1967, Billy Conigliaro (l) broke in with 18 homers in 1970, then feuded with Boston teammates and management and faded rapidly from the major league scene. Multi-talented older brother Tony (r) was the youngest home run leader in American League history when he blasted 32 in 1965. Felled by a fastball which broke his cheekbone in 1967, Tony struggled bravely to regain his great potential, yet was soon kayoed again by failing eyesight. But tragedy was far from over for the luckless Conigliaro brothers. Tony suffered a paralyzing heart attack at age 37 (while riding in a car with his brother), which left him severely incapacitated for more than a decade until his eventual untimely death.

202 THE BASEBALL SCRAPBOOK

The Baseball Family

Baseball binds generations of fathers with their sons and daughters. Among the most cherished shared memories of both generations are those hours spent on the playground tossing a hardball and knocking out endless flies. It is a treasured rite of childhood, a ritual of springtime to be handed from one generation to the next. And professional ballplayers relish this ritual at least as much as any other parents. Big leaguers, however, enjoy the added privilege of sharing the game with their offspring within the grounds of the big league park itself. Padres coach Sandy Alomar (**OPPOSITE TOP**) poses with sons Roberto (Padres) and Sandy Jr. (Indians) during 1990 All-Star Game warmups, while Ken Griffey Jr. (**OPPOSITE BOTTOM**) and Sr. shared roster spots in Seattle. And Pete Rose (**BOTTOM LEFT**) limbers up in the 1979 Phillies spring training camp, with attentive son Pete Jr. imitating every move of his famous father. In recent seasons such on-field moments between major leaguers and their knee-high youngster have been formalized into Father-Son-Daughter Games held annually in big league ballparks throughout the land. On one such occasion, Minnesota Twins batting star Rod Carew (**ABOVE**) instructs his one-year-old daughter, Charryse, in the fine art of proper batsmanship during a 1975 Fathers-Sons game; in another, catcher Carlton Fisk (**TOP LEFT**) surveys the action before him while holding the large plastic bat soon to be employed by two-year-old Casey Fisk during a 1974 Red Sox Father-Son-Daughter pre-game contest.

EXPANSION FRANCHISES

Long gone is the world featuring but eight teams in each major league. Equally moribund is a big league universe in which expansion clubs are relegated to years of hopeless residence in the league's basement.

The Baseball Family 205

In days of yore—when sunshine, edible grass and Sunday doubleheaders were still baseball staples—eight teams in each league battled all summer in a marathon winner-take-all race, which was often all-but-over long before the dog days of August had settled in. The goal was to select a single league champion to do battle with the other league's kingpin in a true "fall classic" of meaningful proportions. Today's major league fare relies on a month-long post-season marathon tournament of divisional champions, plus the best among the runners-up, designed to crown an eventual title-holder. And it seems that each new decade has added to the roster of major league cities—with new teams in Minneapolis, Houston, Atlanta, Anaheim, Oakland, San Diego, Seattle, and Montreal (Canada) during the sixties; Arlington and Toronto (Canada) in the seventies; and Denver, Miami, Phoenix, and Tampa/St. Petersburg in the nineties. The new clubs were usually laughing-stock affairs for years after they debuted: witness the 120 losses of the woeful New York Mets in 1962; the parallel 100 losses by the Los Angeles Angels and new Washington Senators of a season earlier; San Diego's long run in the NL West basement at the outset of the 1970s; and the woeful Milwaukee Brewers and relocated Texas Rangers (nee original Senators) of the same decade. But such is no longer the case for the recent vintage of Johnny-Come-Lately ball clubs joining the big league fray. Free agency and an overall thinning of talent has seen to that. Colorado's Rockies (a 95-game loser out of the gate in 1993) took but two years to climb into post-season wars as a wild card contender; Colorado's 1993 expansion partner, the Florida Marlins, housed in the converted football home of the NFL Dolphins (**OPPOSITE BOTTOM**), walked off with World Series bragging rights in only their fifth campaign. The stunning victory was achieved on the strength of an instant free-agent makeover and such surprising overachievers as celebrated Cuban defector Liván Hernández (**LEFT**). Miami washed away the existing record for rags-to-riches miracles once owned by the storied 1969 Miracle Mets. The overnight success of the novice Miami franchise would be quickly outpaced by another instant winner plunked down in Phoenix only a year after the Marlins' own postseason triumph. Playing in their space-aged palace, The BOB (Bank One Ballpark), the newborn Arizona Diamondbacks chalked up 97 losses but raked in valuable dollars to stoke free-agent building plans. With Randy Johnson aboard for season number two the club leaped from last to first with a 35 game upswing in the win-loss column. Grabbing a second free-agent mound ace, Curt Schilling (**OPPOSITE TOP**), the Diamondbacks were also surprising World Champs by 2001.

SEEING RED WITH A MAN IN BLUE

It is the most heated rivalry on the diamond, and neither combatant ever wears a glove or swings a Louisville Slugger; one of the game's great mysteries is that manager or umpire never see close plays quite the same way.

It's as thoroughly American as mom's apple pie, dad's old '49 Chevy and Teddy Ballgame – to give the umpire a piece of your mind on any controversial play which doesn't favor the home side. Some truly classic moments of heated diamond confrontation display the trials and tribulations of a big league umpire's daily existence, for hardly a game passes without one such scene. Veteran Dodgers skipper Tommy Lasorda (**OPPOSITE TOP**) appears to be telling home plate umpire Fred Brocklander which direction to go, and just how far, as the arbiter patiently explains that Los Angeles batter Bill Madlock was hit by a foul tip rather than the pitch from Phillies hurler Tom Hume. Brocklander himself is considerably more animated in his response (**OPPOSITE BOTTOM RIGHT**) to Houston coach Matt Galante and Astros runner Craig Reynolds, both of whom angrily dispute a close inning-ending double play during 1986 National League playoff action. Sometimes an umpire listens patiently, as is the case with plate judge Bill McGowan when accosted by veteran umpire baiter Leo "The Lip" Durocher (**OPPOSITE BOTTOM LEFT**) during 1941 World Series play; or with veteran Bill McKinley (**BOTTOM LEFT**), who tolerates an ear-full from Cardinals catcher Tim McCarver and his manager Johnny Keane during 1964 World Series Game Two. Yet occasionally the arbiter can dish out a little outrage of his own, as does Ron Luciano (**TOP LEFT**) at the expense of Twins' field boss Bill Rigney during a 1971 Minnesota-Baltimore contest.

The Homer in The Gloamin'!

PUT ME IN, COACH

Playing managers now seem a relic of baseball's past; often they were senior players who concentrated on bench duties. But a few were their own brightest stars.

The Baseball Family

Pete Rose was seemingly the last of a nearly extinct species when he wore two caps as Cincinnati player and manager during the 1985 and 1986 seasons, in order to chase down Cobb's all-time hit record. But in an earlier day – when managers were tyrants and cheerleaders rather than club psychologists – it was not at all rare for a single man to fill out the daily line-up card and then take a regular spot in the batting order for himself. Hall-of-Fame catcher Gabby Hartnett did it his last three summers with the Cubs. And never has a playing manager figured more dramatically in a team's moment of triumph than when Hartnett circled the bases with his legendary ninth-inning "Homer in the Gloamin" that aided a Chicago pennant drive in September 1938. Here (**OPPOSITE TOP**) he is seen being escorted from the field in Chicago after the game. Nor has a manager ever been more of a team's on-field mainstay than was seven-time National League batting champ Rogers Hornsby (**OPPOSITE BOTTOM LEFT**) during his bench stints with the Cardinals, Braves, Cubs and Browns. The Rajah's final two hitting titles (including a .403 year in 1925) were garnered while wearing the skipper's cap as well. Over an incredible 29-year career Stanley "Bucky" Harris (**OPPOSITE BOTTOM RIGHT**) would eventually become baseball's third-ranking bench boss in games managed and games won, standing second all-time in career losses to boot. Yet the Senators' "Boy Wonder" manager would also enjoy his finest seasons during his first two years at the helm, leading Washington to back-to-back pennants in 1924-1925 with his able bench strategy, as well as his inspired second-base play. And switch-hitting Frankie Frisch (**BOTTOM LEFT**) enjoyed a similar fate as crack second sacker and manager for the Gashouse Gang Cardinals between 1933 and 1938, batting as well as coaxing the St. Louis club to a 1935 title with a reputable .305 season's average. One of baseball's all-time great home run sluggers, Frank Robinson (**TOP LEFT**), made diamond history as the game's first black skipper when Cleveland named him playing manager in 1975; Frank promptly responded with a game-winning Opening Day pinch homer in his first day on the job. Another playing skipper who enjoyed storybook success was Boston Red Sox catcher Bill Carrigan (**P.210-211**). A dependable but unspectacular platoon catcher, "Rough" Carrigan took over a dissension-ridden club in 1913 and piloted the Sox to world titles in 1915-1916.

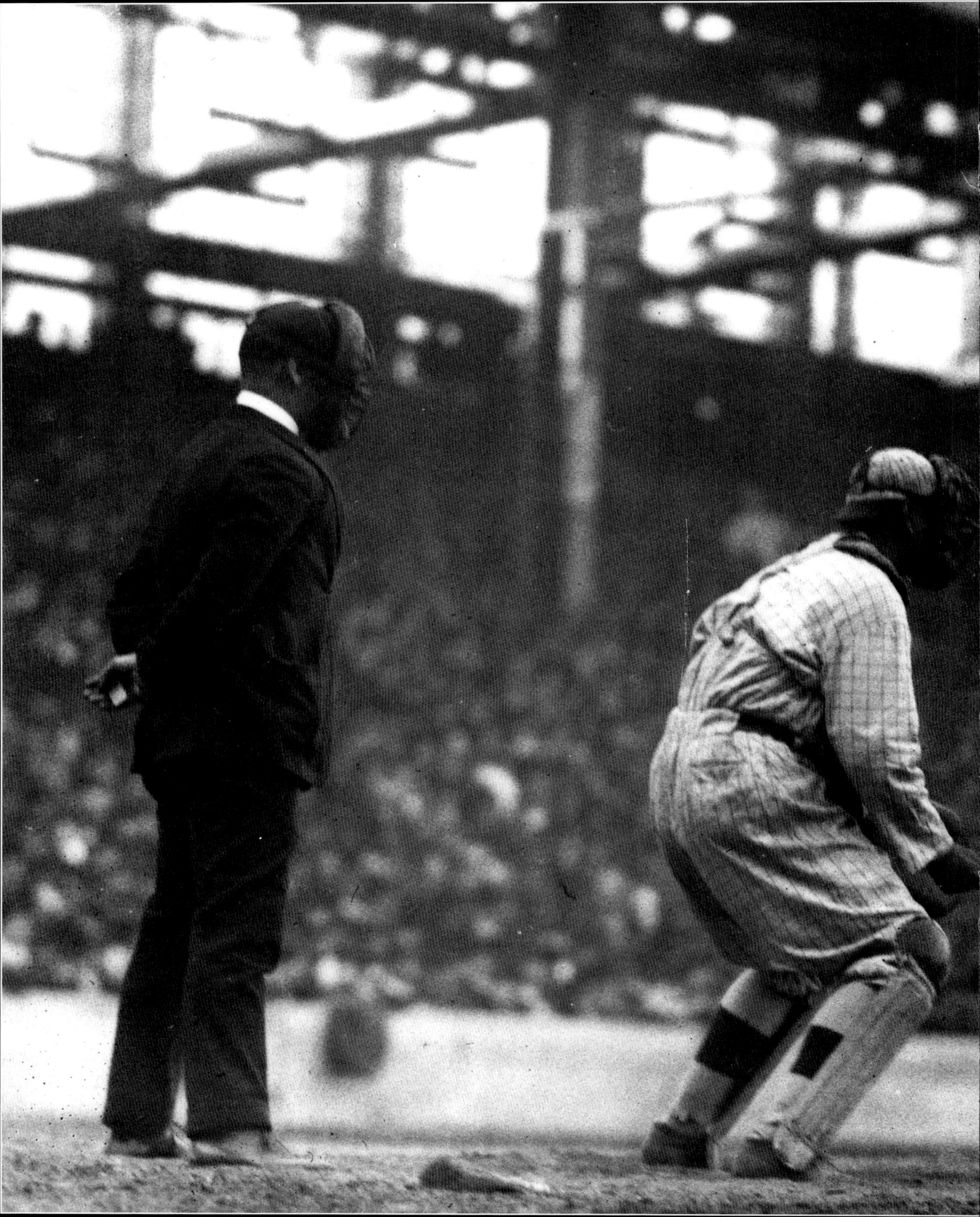

The Baseball Family 211

WHEN IN DOUBT FIRE THE MANAGER

Few would deny that when a ballclub loses, the manager receives far too much of the blame for inept performance; few would contest, on the other hand, that winning managers can sometimes receive more than their due praise.

Jennings, Grimm and Huggins. Nowhere in the pantheon of great managers is there a more colorful and combative trio than this triumvirate of long-lived bench bosses. Hughie Jennings (**OPPOSITE**) was the Horatio Alger of the trio. As one of the true "characters" and best loved sports figures of this century's first two decades, Jennings rose dramatically from bleak prospects as a breaker boy in the anthracite fields of Pennsylvania to a hallowed place in baseball's Hall of Fame. A redheaded firebrand of a ballplayer with the rough-and-ready Baltimore Orioles of John McGraw and Willie Keeler, Hugh Jennings was able to hang on for three decades in a major league uniform – as player, coach and manager – despite an incredible string of mishaps and injuries. During five full seasons in Baltimore before the turn of the century he never batted below .328 and once registered a .398 season that still stands as best-ever for a shortstop. His superior skills as a strategist and field leader kept "Ee-Yah" Jennings regularly employed on the diamond long after his playing skills waned. His 14-year managerial career was highlighted by its three initial seasons, which brought three consecutive pennants (though no World Series title) to the Motor City of Detroit. "Jolly Cholly" Charlie Grimm (**TOP LEFT**) stood without peer as Baseball Clown Prince. As a fun-loving fellow with glue-coated fingers, Grimm frolicked through 20 big league seasons as the most skillful first baseman of his era. When it came to managing with the Cubs (where he won pennants in 1935 and 1945) and Braves, gentle Charlie was a laid-back and tolerant skipper who always seemed to find a way to coax career-best seasons from his mediocre players, while giving free reign to the most talented among his stars. Miller Huggins (**BOTTOM LEFT**) reigned, by contrast, as the game's supreme strategist. The scrawny "Mighty Mite" was a hard-nosed leader who turned a bunch of carousers and bad actors, whom he inherited in Gotham in 1918, into the invincible Murderer's Row Bronx Bombers of the late 1920s. It was Huggins' Yankee teams which put an end to the dead-ball era forever; and it was Huggins, as much as Ruth himself, who established the long tradition of Yankee pride which would reign for so many decades to come.

214 THE BASEBALL SCRAPBOOK

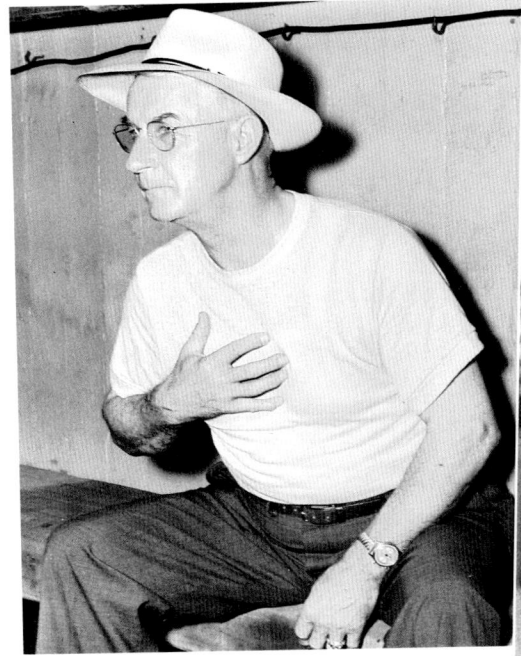

The Baseball Family

When it comes to colorful characters as managers, some teams seem to have an inexplicable and unfair monopoly. Take, for example, the Dodgers, Cardinals and Orioles. In Brooklyn, it is perhaps Leo Durocher (**OPPOSITE TOP**, chatting with fellow skippers, l to r, Mel Ott, Bill McKechnie and Frankie Frisch) who stands out above all others as being cut from a unique managerial mold. Over the course of his 24-year bench career (nine full seasons with Brooklyn), Durocher won three pennants, feuded with his equally bull-headed GM Branch Rickey, cavorted at the gaming table and racetrack and kept company with criminal types and known gamblers. He also inspired an endless string of epithets – like brash, bold, abrasive, umpire-baiting, bench-jockeying and the now infamous "lippy," which became his best-known moniker. Durocher's replacement, Burt Shotton (**OPPOSITE CENTER LEFT**) was cut from a distinct yet equally memorable mold. He was the last to manage from the bench in street clothes (after the fashion of Connie Mack), and while not the tactical genius that Durocher was, Shotton was a steadying influence ideal for a Brooklyn team breaking in Jackie Robinson as baseball's pioneer black big leaguer. Yet for all the Dodger tradition, no Brooklyn or Los Angeles field boss can ever be adequately compared with one Walter Emmons Alston (**OPPOSITE BOTTOM LEFT**). Alston was the quiet, inspirational leader behind a generation of Dodger teams that brought Walter O'Malley world titles and numerous pennants on both coasts. The numbers themselves are truly impressive: 23 seasons at the helm, 2042 victories against 1615 losses, for a career .558 winning percentage; 10 different seasons with 90 victories or more; seven pennants, along with four world championships; 17 of 23 seasons in third place or higher. And all this accomplished without benefit of today's managerial standby, the long-term contract. Baltimore, in the meantime, experienced managerial superiority with one exceptional man, Earl Weaver (**BOTTOM LEFT**). The irascible Weaver here demonstrates one of the ploys on which his reputation as the game's most original umpire baiter is based: covering home plate after being ejected for arguing with umpire Rocky Roe. What Weaver was to Baltimore during the 1970s, Whitey Herzog was to St. Louis in the 1980s. Herzog (seen with Angel Jim Fregosi, while himself manager of Kansas City, **TOP LEFT**) reigns as most successful bench boss of the past decade.

216 THE BASEBALL SCRAPBOOK

While Brooklyn, St. Louis or Baltimore seem to spawn true bench legends, a few unfortunate towns stick out as wastelands of managerial talent. Occasionally these cities will have a successful field general or two who weaves his magic for a few brief campaigns, but this only serves to heighten the contrast with so many bleak years of uninspired dugout leadership. Boston is a case in point, a baseball town of endless disappointment, where Hall-of-Famer Joe Cronin (**P.214, BOTTOM RIGHT**, in action from the third base coach's box during the 1946 pennant season) resided for a dozen seasons in the years between the mid-1930s and the close of World War II. It was Cronin who brought Beantown its last 100-victory season almost 45 summers ago. Montreal is yet another such managerial graveyard, where a promising expansion franchise has long languished with the memory of inaugural skipper Gene Mauch (**TOP LEFT**). The stately Mauch retired in 1988 after having managed more games for more seasons than anyone outside of Connie Mack, John McGraw and Bucky Harris. He patiently presided over Montreal's slowly improving expansion seasons and copped a league Manager-of-the-Year citation for his sound 1973 performance. Nowhere, however, has the dearth of managerial talent been as apparent as in Atlanta over the past 20 seasons. Here it is perhaps Joe Torre (**OPPOSITE**) who alone stands above the others as memorable. It was Torre, during his first Atlanta campaign in 1982, who guided the Braves to only their second divisional title in 17 seasons south of the Mason-Dixon line. It was Torre, again, who then brought home two second-place finishers the subsequent two summers, before management saw fit to let him go. Torre's dismissal was predictably a move followed by an evitable slide to six consecutive second-division finishes for the hapless Braves. Yet while colorful and productive managers remain as rare as honest politicians in cities like Atlanta, Montreal and Boston, the beat goes on to the ever-renewed tune of pennant fever in the baseball capital of Los Angeles, where Walter Alston's 23-year reign has been succeeded by the 14-year joy ride of Tom Lasorda (**BOTTOM LEFT**). Lasorda almost topped Alston overnight, as the first National League field boss ever to win back-to-back flags his first two seasons on the job.

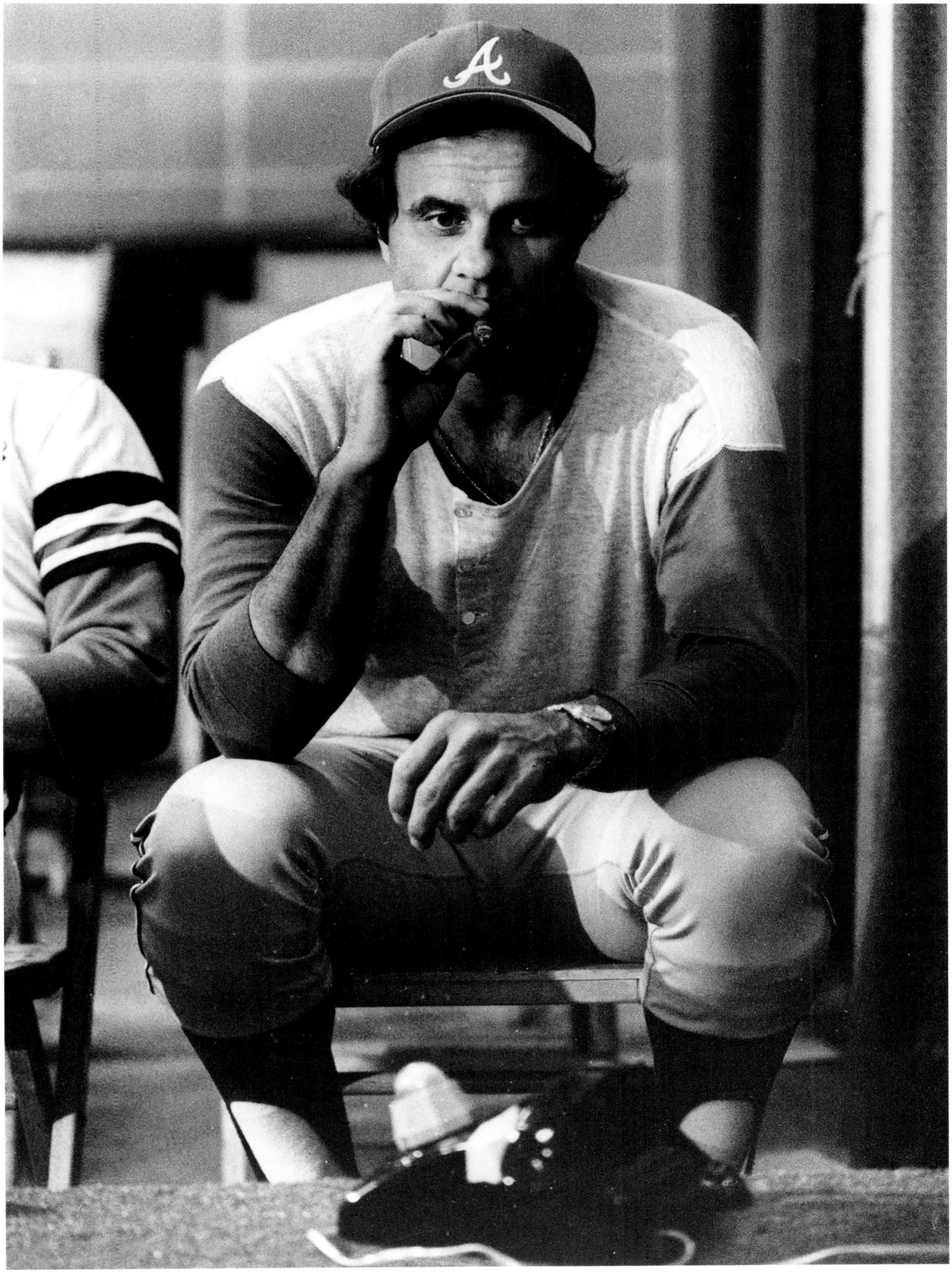

BOLD VISIONARY TO RAW MEDDLER

Old style club owners were a different breed – bold dreamers often operating on a shoestring and dealing in sound business as well as sporting legend. Today's magnates tend to confuse private toys with the public trust.

Most of the old-style club owners would undoubtedly have agreed with Connie Mack that baseball was first and foremost a business venture, one that had to be run by the soundest of economic practices. You had to turn a profit or you were out of business; and as Mack himself once observed, it was usually more profitable to have a team that was in contention for most of the year but in the end finished about third or fourth. That way fan interest was kept high, and you didn't have to give raises to players who didn't win. Charles Ebbets (**OPPOSITE**, with Commissioner Landis, who holds the hat) was one such owner, a sly businessman who joined the Brooklyn club in 1883 as a bookkeeper and bought up shares secretly until he could establish himself as club president in 1898. Harry Frazee (**OPPOSITE BOTTOM RIGHT**) earned lasting infamy for placing business interest above pennant races when he sold Babe Ruth to the Yankees for $100,000, plus a $300,000 loan. Frazee was a shrewd theatrical producer who bought the World Champion Red Sox in 1917 for $400,000, then sold the last-place ballclub in 1923 for $1.5 million. While Frazee often sold his best players to cover sour theatrical investments, Clark Griffith (**ABOVE**, on dugout steps with his 1924 league champion Senators) peddled his stars merely to keep his struggling franchise afloat through the Depression years. Griffith – always a skilled baseball man, both as star player and crack manager – first imported Cuban players as a cost-saving device.

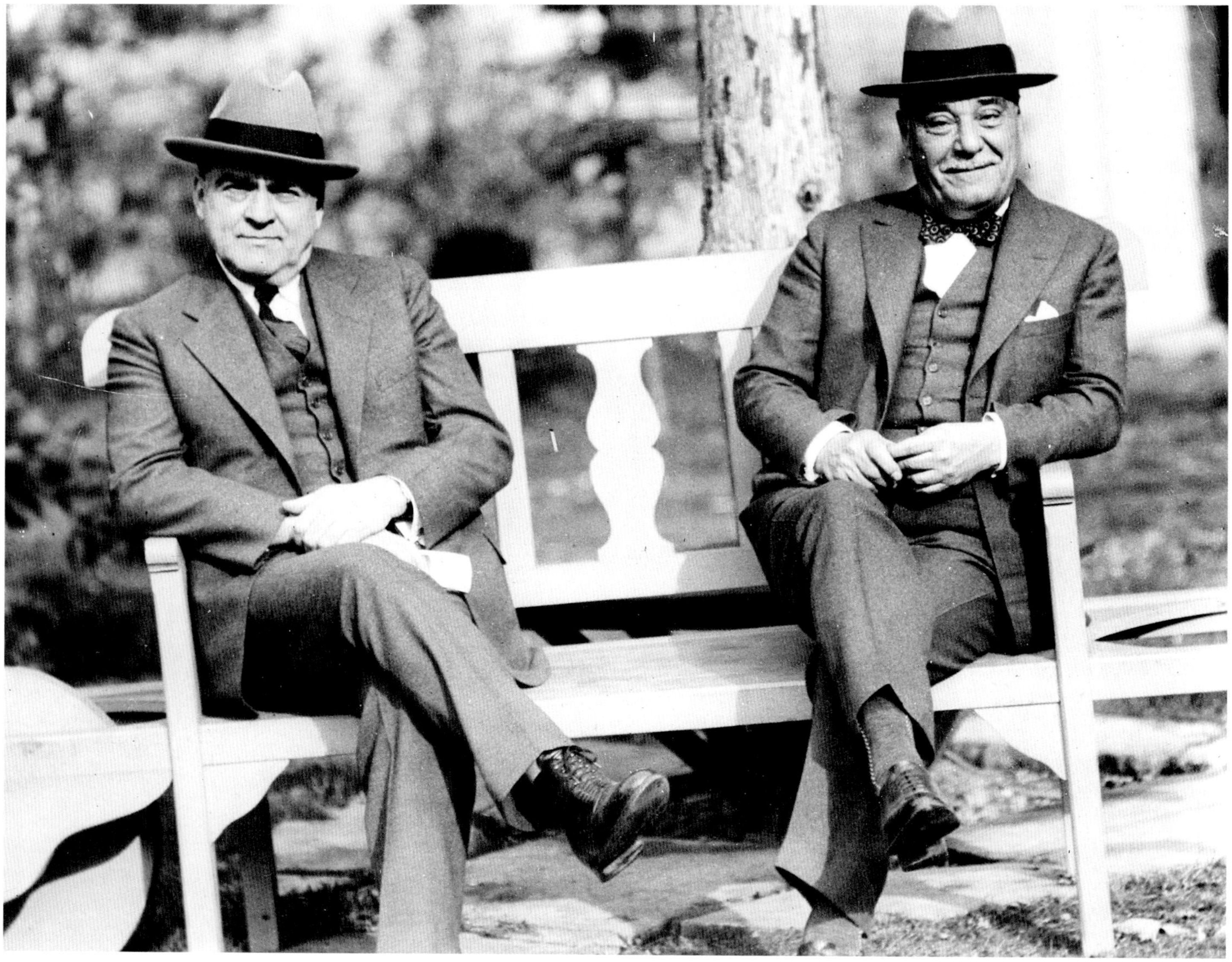

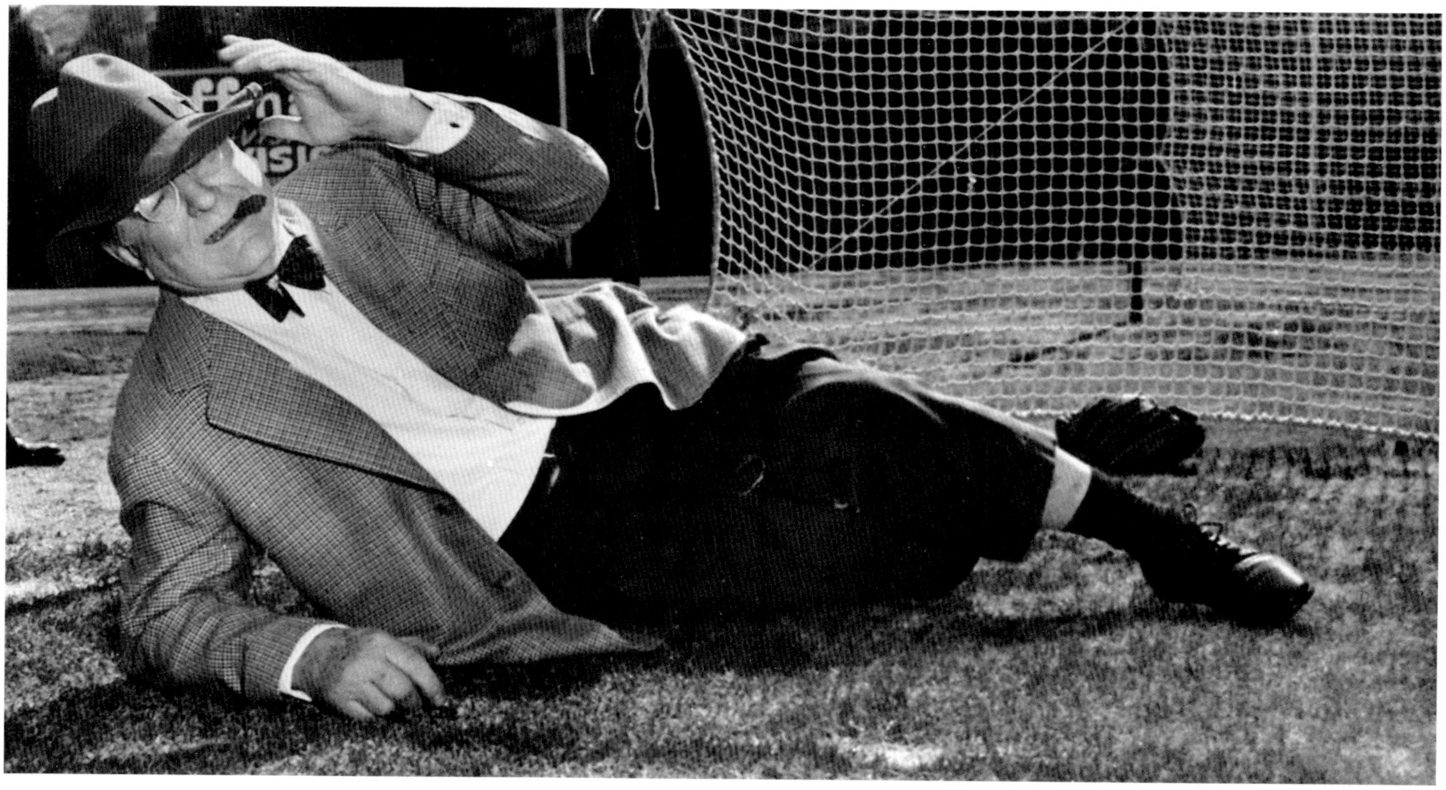

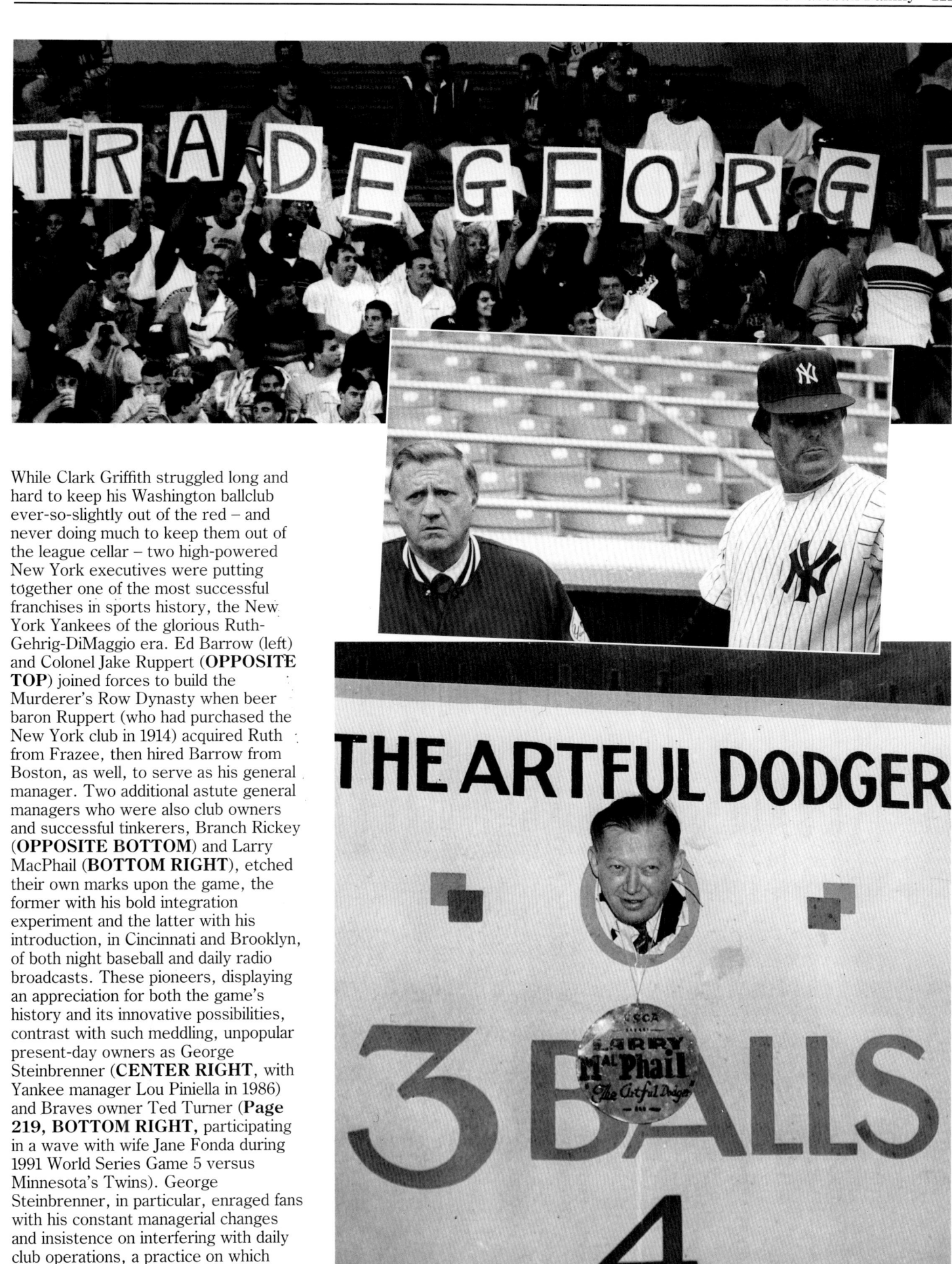

The Baseball Family

While Clark Griffith struggled long and hard to keep his Washington ballclub ever-so-slightly out of the red – and never doing much to keep them out of the league cellar – two high-powered New York executives were putting together one of the most successful franchises in sports history, the New York Yankees of the glorious Ruth-Gehrig-DiMaggio era. Ed Barrow (left) and Colonel Jake Ruppert (**OPPOSITE TOP**) joined forces to build the Murderer's Row Dynasty when beer baron Ruppert (who had purchased the New York club in 1914) acquired Ruth from Frazee, then hired Barrow from Boston, as well, to serve as his general manager. Two additional astute general managers who were also club owners and successful tinkerers, Branch Rickey (**OPPOSITE BOTTOM**) and Larry MacPhail (**BOTTOM RIGHT**), etched their own marks upon the game, the former with his bold integration experiment and the latter with his introduction, in Cincinnati and Brooklyn, of both night baseball and daily radio broadcasts. These pioneers, displaying an appreciation for both the game's history and its innovative possibilities, contrast with such meddling, unpopular present-day owners as George Steinbrenner (**CENTER RIGHT**, with Yankee manager Lou Piniella in 1986) and Braves owner Ted Turner (**Page 219, BOTTOM RIGHT,** participating in a wave with wife Jane Fonda during 1991 World Series Game 5 versus Minnesota's Twins). George Steinbrenner, in particular, enraged fans with his constant managerial changes and insistence on interfering with daily club operations, a practice on which New York fans often loudly voiced their opinion (**ABOVE**).

VOICES OF THE NATIONAL PASTIME

Baseball is a uniquely literary game – a sport that lends itself to words. Without its bards – its reporters, historians, novelists, poets and, perhaps above all, its breathless sportscasters – it just wouldn't be the same.

For much of its first half-century baseball's story was spread through the land by those first crude poets and chroniclers of the game – the newspaper sports reporters. It was the daily press, exclusively, which carried box scores and detailed descriptions of big league ballgames from around the nation in an age when baseball's map spread no further than from northeastern port cities to the edge of the Mississippi. The working press thus kept alive interest in the local nine and its diamond heroes. Baseball lore and legend in these early days before wireless and moving pictures came alive only through daily newsprint accounts, and it was journalists like Chicago *Tribune* reporter Ring Lardner (**RIGHT**) who enchanted readers with vivid descriptions of the game and its colorful personalities. Ring Lardner recognized early the vast literary potential in baseball's varied and fascinating character types and soon expanded his game coverage to include delightful stories about fictional Chicago pitcher Jack Keefe, the quintessence of all eccentric big league rookies. Lardner covered the 1919 Chicago-Cincinnati World Series from a press box vantage point much like the one illustrated here (**OPPOSITE TOP**), actually a scene of press row activity during the 1911 World Series featuring Mack's Athletics and McGraw's Giants. This photo is reputed to have been taken during a rain delay, and the reporter with the light jacket in the second row is the legendary Damon Runyon himself. By the 1930s, however, radio was beginning to emerge as the hot new medium for following the game, and it was a smooth-talking southerner, Red Barber (**OPPOSITE BOTTOM**), who pioneered daily broadcasts of league games from Cincinnati (1934-1938) and later from Brooklyn. When innovative executive Larry MacPhail moved his act from Cincinnati to Brooklyn in 1938, he took Barber with him, thus ending a long-standing gentleman's agreement among the Dodgers, Giants and Yankees not to broadcast daily home contests. Unable to foresee the vast surge of fan interest that radio would create, the three New York ballclubs had previously been suspicious of the medium, fearing that to give games away free to their ticket-buying public would only hurt attendance at the ballpark gate. Barber himself would later pioneer again as baseball's inaugural television voice, announcing the first commercially televised big league game, between the Dodgers and Reds, from Brooklyn's Ebbets Field on August 26, 1939.

The Baseball Family 223

224 THE BASEBALL SCRAPBOOK

Nowadays the voices which bring the game alive to us flow from our television or radio receivers. But in an earlier time the voices came from quite a different source – the megaphone of the ever-present field announcer who barked line-up changes and scorer's decisions to grandstand patrons during the days before public address systems and press-box electronics. This baseball tradition was carried on in some cities well after megaphones were replaced by blaring ballpark loudspeakers, and in Chicago's Wrigley Field "Pat" Pieper (**TOP RIGHT**) was one such on-field fixture from 1916 until the time of his death in 1974. Pieper was also an unwitting participant in one of the strangest events ever witnessed in that venerable northside ballpark, a bizarre turn of events that saw two balls in play at the same time during a Cubs-Cardinals match on June 30, 1959. A wild pitch to Stan Musial was retrieved by Pieper from his field spot behind the plate and handed to Cubs' third sacker Alvin Dark. At exactly the same time umpire Vic Delmore gave another ball to hurler Bob Anderson. When Musial broke toward first on the errant ball-four toss and then shot toward second, both Dark and Anderson gunned their balls at Cubs shortstop Ernie Banks. The resulting confusion is more than can be detailed fully here – like all else in baseball, you could look it up! Today's play-by-play announcers and color commentators are increasingly ex-diamond stars who have moved from dugout to press box after their retirement as active players. One of the earliest to pave the way in this transition was 1940s New York Yankee infield legend Phil Rizzuto (**OPPOSITE**), here practicing his golf stroke in the radio booth on the occasion of his 63rd birthday. Rizzuto is currently completing his fourth full decade of broadcasting from his press box perch in Yankee Stadium. Another, less successful pioneer in the ex-player-turned-sports-commentator club was Dodgers pitching legend Sandy Koufax (**OPPOSITE TOP RIGHT**), here seen interviewing an ex-teammate, Los Angeles mound ace Don Drysdale, immediately following Drysdale's 1968 record 58⅔ scoreless innings. Two additional broadcast legends share a private moment in the Wrigley Field booth as popular Cubs play-by-play man Harry Caray gives a brief refresher course to a visiting Ronald Reagan (**BOTTOM RIGHT**). Reagan received his own media start as a Cubs announcer (doing game recreations) on Iowa station WOC in the mid-1930s.

DON'T CARE IF I NEVER GET BACK

Fans have seldom been known to shed a tear over the demise of a basketball arena or to wax poetic over the beauty of an empty gridiron. But baseball is different. Just mention Wrigley Field!

The Baseball Family

The big-league ballpark is all things to all fans: a shrine, an arena of combat ideal for the display of incomparable athletic talent and unmatched sporting excitement, a stage for the enactment of gripping human drama and the unfolding of colorful pageantry. It is, as well, a movable feast of hot dogs, watered-down beer, soda pop and stale peanuts. It is an American landmark, unrivaled for its symphony of sounds, sights and smells – changeless from season to season and from generation to generation. This sameness of ballpark spectacle seems to remain intact despite the passing of such traditional venues as Ebbets Field, Forbes Field, Shibe Park, Braves Field and, most recently, Chicago's Comiskey Park. The sameness persists despite the intrusions of plastic grass, covered sky and luxury air-conditioned skybox seats. Sixteen-year-old ballpark vendor Patrick Giblin (**OPPOSITE**) might well have been hawking his treats in Yankee Stadium in 1989 instead of the actual 1949 Opening Day scene which is captured here although scorecard and peanut prices on the young vendor's cap suggest that some things have indeed been lost forever. Yankee Stadium concession-stand workers (**CENTER RIGHT**), here busy preparing miles of hot dogs for that same Opening Day in 1949, would not have been a bit out of place in any big league ballpark four decades later. And the pre-game pageantry surrounding any Opening Day of a new season has been a ballpark fixture for as many generations of fans as have bleacher seats and pennant races themselves. Here the ceremony of Opening Day is observed 60 long seasons ago (April 14, 1931) in Washington's Griffith Stadium (**BOTTOM RIGHT**), as players and military color guard salute the flags of various North and South American nations, providing special honor for Pan American Day as well as for the opening of a new diamond season. A still earlier scene of Opening Day pageantry (**TOP RIGHT**) finds a proud Mrs. Ed McKeever, wife of the vice-president of the Brooklyn Baseball Club, raising a new flag for the first game ever played in Ebbets Field (April 9, 1913). From the hour of its birth Brooklyn's Ebbets Field would be scene for some of baseball's daffiest moments: this very flag-raising ceremony was delayed for more than an hour because ballclub aids forgot to bring along the one indispensable ingredient, the American flag.

228 THE BASEBALL SCRAPBOOK

Despite great advances in scoreboard technology, spectator comfort and all-weather playing traditions, today's multipurpose stadia probably have lost some of the character and intimacy of the first-generation ballparks that served the national pastime during the four decades between the dead-ball era and the television age. Two of the most noble of these parks took their final bows very recently. When Comiskey Park (**RIGHT**) closed its gates for the final time on September 30, 1990 – after 80 seasons of uninterrupted major league play – the nation lost one of its most storied relics of baseball's "real-grass" era. Drawing 72,801,381 fans over its proud eight-decade lifespan, this spacious ballpark was ideally suited for dead-ball-era play and was quickly dubbed the "Baseball Capital of the World" after its July 1, 1910 opening. In subsequent decades it was home to baseball's first All-Star Game in 1933, to the infamous World Series of 1919 and to Bill Veeck's revolutionary "Exploding Scoreboard" in 1960. And no ballpark ever celebrated a more memorable octogenarian birthday, as the one on July 1, 1990, which witnessed Andy Hawkins" unparalleled losing no-hit effort against the hometown Sox. The 1991 season will mark the swan song performance as well for venerable Memorial Stadium in Baltimore (**BELOW**), a mammoth park nearly as rich in memory, if not as long in summers, as its erstwhile midwestern counterpart. Built in 1949 as a 30,000-seat minor league facility designed to replace Oriole Park, itself destroyed by fire five years earlier, the expanded Memorial Stadium became a big league venue when the lowly St. Louis Browns moved eastward in 1954 to become high-flying American League Orioles. For 35 seasons since, Memorial Stadium concession stands have served the only crab cakes in big league baseball.

The Baseball Family 229

The passing of the old ballparks is not solely the result of the ravages of time or of the ambitions of club owners to have plush new locations that allow for income-enhancing luxury skyboxes and all the other amenities of the present-day baseball palace. Sometimes it is merely a question of the rise and fall of franchises. Such was the case in 1958, when the odd-shaped and history-drenched Polo Grounds – nestled between Coogan's Bluff and the Harlem River – said goodbye to the westward-bound Giants of New York. The Polo Grounds (**OPPOSITE BOTTOM**) had opened in June 1911 as New York's first steel-and-concrete stadium, had hosted numerous World Series for both the Giants and Yankees, had witnessed the pitching mastery of Christy Mathewson and the miraculous over-the-shoulder World Series catch of Willie Mays and is etched forever in fan memory as the site of Bobby Thomson's 1951 "shot heard round the world" home run. The park is seen here packed with the Giant and Dodgers fans for a crucial late-season game approximately one year after Thomson's famous heroics. Such charming and legendary parks as the old Polo Grounds are now inspiring a fresh nostalgia-based movement in late 20th-century ballpark design. New arenas like Baltimore's popular Camden Yards (**OPPOSITE TOP**) seek to recreate the classic early-century ballpark look so peculiar to the first steel and concrete urban structures.

A few among the nation's shrinking number of vintage ballparks have managed to hold out against the ravages of time and the changing economic conditions of major league play, and one of these, Tiger Stadium in Detroit, has done so only through repeated time-buying renovations and repairs. One such face-lifting (**BOTTOM LEFT**) took place between the 1982 and 1983 seasons and consisted of exterior painting and scraping that cost an estimated $3.6 million. Ballpark beautification of a less noticeable and less necessary type is seen in New York's Shea Stadium (**TOP LEFT**) as Mets' pitcher Craig Swan (r) and coach Joe Pignatano (l) tend their vegetable garden in the ballpark's right field bullpen area. This is a July 1980 scene, and Swan tends the tomato patch while a healthy crop of cabbage grows in the foreground.

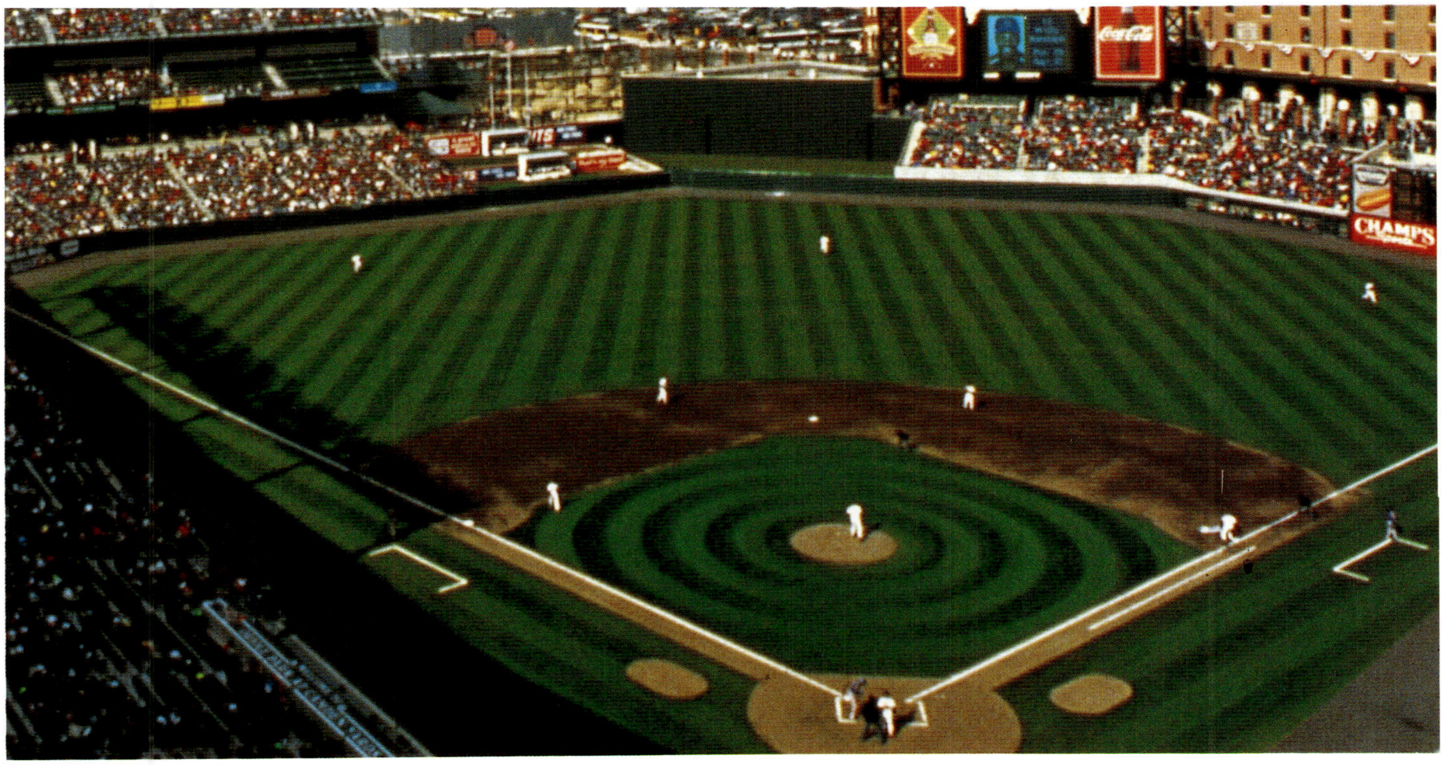
Coca-Cola
CHAMPS

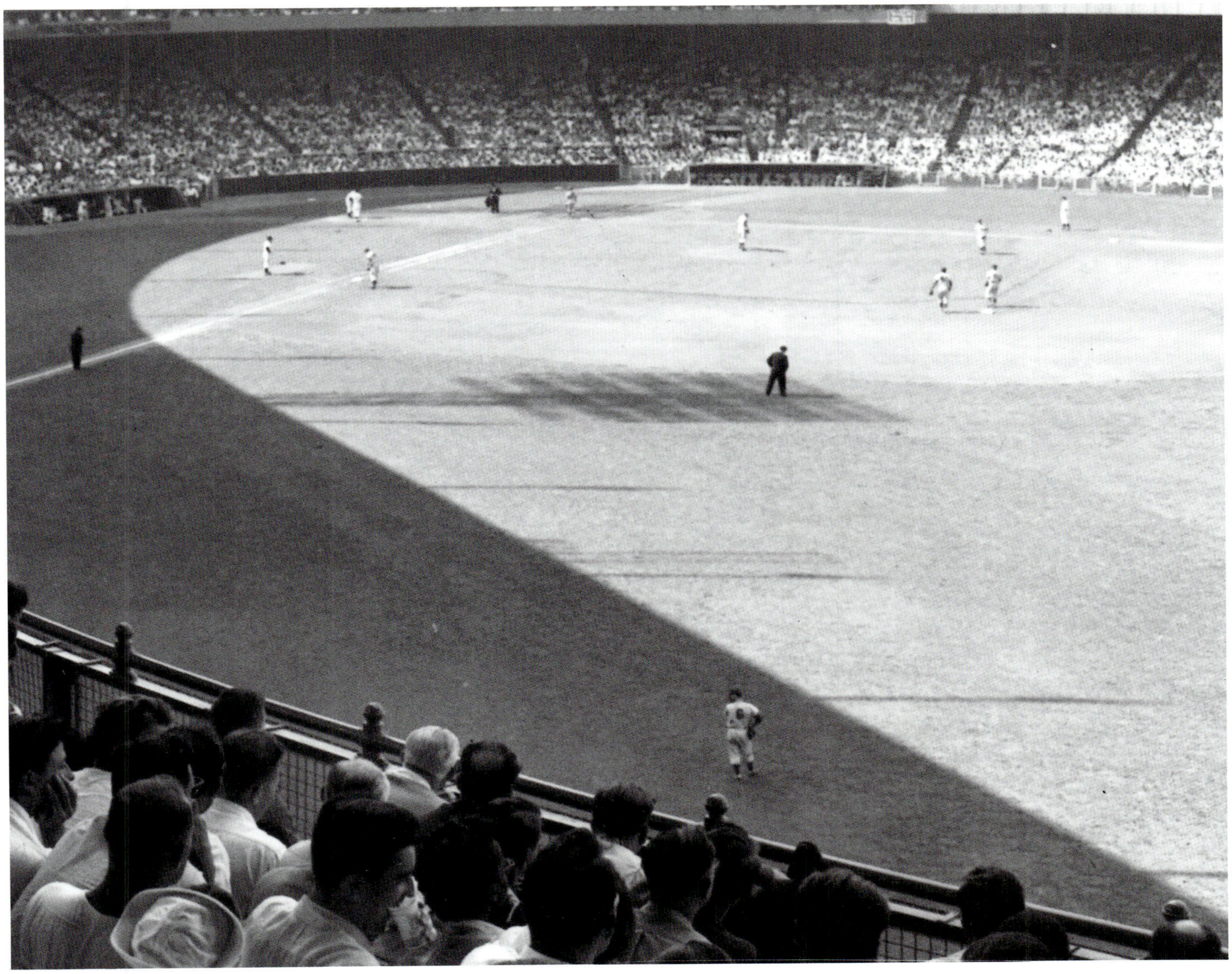

FIELD OF DREAMS

It is a holdover from an era of blue skies, latticed wooden seats and real grass. Its ivy-covered walls and arc-like hand-operated scoreboard are national treasures.

Few ballparks have stirred as much passion and nostalgia as has America's oldest National League fortress, Wrigley Field. The park has earned a reputation as being one of the country's most beautiful, based largely on its intimate confines, its ivy-covered walls, its longtime lack of artificial lighting (which required daytime play only) and its friendly neighborhood surroundings. Only a handful of World Series games have ever been played here (none since 1945), yet this is the site of perhaps the most famous of all World Series moments. It occurred on October 1, 1932, when Babe Ruth is reported to have "called his shot" before homering off Cub hurler Charlie Root. This ballpark's long resistance to nighttime play was famous, yet the absence of lights until August 1988 was as much a wartime accident as a moral commitment. Cubs management had lights all ready to be installed in the park in December 1941, but the bombing of Pearl Harbor caused the suspension of these plans as a gesture of wartime energy conservation. The park has always been venerated as a true baseball garden spot, yet it is neither as noble nor as glamorous as its southside neighbor in the same city: Comiskey Park has always outdistanced its northside rival both in splendor and in important baseball events. Finally, Wrigley Field has always been reputed as a hitters' park, yet it was home as well to what may have been the finest single pitching display in the history of the national pastime: on May 2, 1917, Chicago's Hippo Vaughn and Cincinnati's Fred Toney hooked up here to produce the only double no-hit game that major league baseball ever witnessed. When 91-year-old Cub fan Harry Grossman (**OPPOSITE BOTTOM RIGHT**) hit the switch to light Chicago's first National League night game on August 8, 1988 (the game was then rained out, and night play did not officially take place until the next evening), one long-standing Wrigley Field tradition came to a ceremonious ending. Another remains, however, as legions of fans (**OPPOSITE BOTTOM LEFT**) still crowd the famed outfield bleachers to enjoy bright summer sunshine and cheer loudly for the local Cubbies, one of the diamond sport's most lovable and legendary year-in-and-year-out summertime losers.

THE HOME OF THE BUMS

It was the place where Jackie Robinson played, the Boys of Summer captured our hearts and the Daffiness Boys charged into their basepath misadventures.

"Cramped and colorful" is perhaps the only way to describe Ebbets Field, a ballpark that lives on vividly in the mind's eye of a generation of fans who grew up with Willie, Mickey and the Duke, to say nothing of Erskine, Pee Wee, Jackie, Furillo and Newcombe. The Baseball Gods must have smiled that April Day back in 1913 when Charles Ebbets threw open the gates of his proud baseball grounds (but only after some delay, while an assistant returned home to search for the misplaced keys to the main gate). That was also the day when a rain-diminished crowd of 12,000 arrived to see the Dodgers lose 1-0 to the Phillies, when the ceremonial flag was misplaced and when a horrified press corps entered the new facility only to discover that no one had thought to construct a press box. This was merely a foretaste of highlights and lowjinks that would soon follow and would continue all through the more than four decades that the beloved Dodgers played in their friendly bandbox ballpark. Jackie Robinson (**OPPOSITE BOTTOM RIGHT**, leaving the park during his first week of play in April 1947) broke baseball's odious racial barrier here; Duke Snider blasted tremendous home runs into Bedford Avenue, over the famed slanting right field scoreboard (**TOP RIGHT**), while Carl Furillo played caroms off that same wall as though it were a fine-tuned instrument. Carl Erskine (**OPPOSITE BOTTOM LEFT**, posing with a baseball-decorated wrecking ball for demolition ceremonies which saw the old ballpark razed), along with other "Boys of Summer," worked their magic here, for most of the full decade when the Dodgers were the most dominant team in senior circuit history. And in the 1920s and 30s such "daffiness boys" as Babe Herman, Dazzy Vance, Rube Bressler, Jigger Statz, Max Carey and manager Casey Stengel established a reputation for baseball mayhem here as well, later to be rivaled only by the Dizzy Dean-led Gashouse Gang Cardinals. One truly memorable, if quite apocryphal, tale has a Brooklyn cab driver passing the park in the 1930s, shouting to fans at the top of the grandstand for a report on the score. "The Dodgers have three men on base!" comes the response. "Which base?" is the wide-eyed driver's next question.

MORE THAN JUST A GREEN MONSTER

It was the stage for the league's only two one-game playoffs and for the greatest game in World Series history. A folk hero homered here in his very last at-bat, and a seagull once dropped a three-pound fish in the middle of the mound.

The Baseball Family 237

Fenway Park has changed little since its extensive renovations in 1934. It still features a single-decked grandstand (though some roof seats and luxury boxes have been added, as seen already during the 1946 All-Star Game, **OPPOSITE BOTTOM**). A permanent fixture is the massive bleacher section in right and center fields (**OPPOSITE TOP**). There is almost no foul territory deep in the outfield corner (where the foul pole here receives fresh paint in 1960, **ABOVE**). Steel girders supporting the overhang roof create some of the most obstructed views any ballpark has ever known, the seating capacity (34,000) is small and absence of neighborhood parking facilities is a trial for fans. Yet these drawbacks have not been enough to keep the popular Red Sox from attracting two million excited fans for almost every recent season. About the only external element of this scenic park that has changed significantly in its appearance over the past six decades has been the face of the ballpark's true signature piece, the famed "Green Monster" left field wall. One of baseball's most distinctive ballpark features, this 37-foot-high barrier extends straight from the left field corner (315 feet from the plate) to dead center field, and it is topped with a 23-foot net which runs along Landsdowne Street and hangs over the sidewalk to protect pedestrians below from falling baseballs (**BOTTOM RIGHT**). The "Green Monster" has been green only since 1947, however, the year it received a complete coat of grass-colored paint covering all but the familiar hand-operated scoreboard at ground level in left-center field. Previous to its 1947 painting, the monster – credited with converting high flies into cheap homers and certain line-drive homers into sliding doubles as they carom off its surface – was for years covered with huge and colorful advertisements (**TOP RIGHT**).

BABE LIVED HERE

It may not compare with Fenway Park or Wrigley Field for scenery; it may not have the seniority of Comiskey Park or Tiger Stadium; and it never had the off-beat charm and intimacy of Ebbets Field; but no ballpark offers a bigger piece of baseball history.

The Baseball Family 239

From its construction in the winter of 1923 (**OPPOSITE TOP LEFT**) and its grand opening on April 18, 1923 (**OPPOSITE BOTTOM**), through the years of Murderer's Row and Babe Ruth's dramatic revolution of the hitting game, through the World-War II era of DiMaggio and Rizzuto, through the glorious 1950s decade of Mantle, Berra and Ford, down to its complete renovation and reopening in 1976 and the subsequent Steinbrenner Years, this splendid "House that Ruth Built" has served as the scene for more championship play that any other American sports arena. Crowds such as the one packed in shoulder-to-shoulder for Series Game Two in 1937 (**LEFT**) and the one arriving for Game One in 1961 (**ABOVE**) have jammed the stadium for 31 different Fall Classics, witnessing such heroics as Don Larsen's perfect game, Brooklyn's only World Title party and Reggie Jackson's three homers on three consecutive pitches. And outside of Series play, Ruth smashed his legendary 60th roundtripper here, and Roger Maris collected his 61st precisely 34 years later. There have been some of the game's most touching moments enacted here as well – Lou Gehrig's "Luckiest man on the face of the earth" farewell speech on July 4, 1939, and Babe Ruth's final on-field appearance a decade later. And of course there was that day in August 1948 when the Babe's body was carried to the palace (**OPPOSITE TOP RIGHT**) to lie in state for viewing by thousands of his adoring fans.

LET'S PLAY BALL

There is only one 'Opening Day' with capital letters, and baseball has it. Other first days, like those of the fishing season or the football season, just don't merit a capital.

President William Howard Taft was the first to throw a ceremonial pitch in 1910, at Griffith Stadium in the nation's capital, thus beginning a tradition as honored as the seventh-inning stretch and stale peanuts at the ballpark. The unique and colorful ceremony of first-ball tossing was the brainchild of Senators owner Clark Griffith, and it was soon a standby of the season's Opening Day. The tradition has now become so firmly implanted in the soil of baseball that all manner of dignitaries are invited to participate, and the Opening Day ritual has been extended to launch the World Series, the All-Star Game and all manner of other local occasions meriting special ceremony at the ballpark. Taft's first toss (**ABOVE**) was caught by Washington pitcher Walter Johnson, inaugurating a tradition in the capital city that eventually extended through nine presidents (Taft, Coolidge, Hoover, Harding, Wilson, FDR, Truman, Eisenhower, Kennedy). The last of these original presidential hurlers was John Kennedy, seen here (**ABOVE RIGHT**) tossing out a ceremonial first ball at the 1962 All-Star game in spanking new D.C. Stadium, later to carry his own brother's name.

The Baseball Family   241

With baseball's initial departure from the nation's capital in 1961, and then its second and final leave-taking in 1971, the traditional home base of the season's inaugural Opening Day Game shifted to another longstanding baseball capital, Cincinnati, home of the first professional team in 1869 and a pioneer city in the diamond sport since the earliest years of organized play. The city of Cincinnati has grown so proud of its status as home of the season's first ceremonial pitch that in recent seasons when American League play in Boston or Toronto has actually begun a full hour earlier than the scheduled start of the season's first game in the Queen City, city fathers have decreed a new "Baseball Time Zone" in Riverfront Stadium and set the clock back two hours, thus symbolically preceding the first East Coast pitch. Presidents have also visited the traditional National League opener in Ohio, as Gerald Ford does here (**LEFT**) on Opening Day in 1974. Baseball's commissioners have also filled this ceremonial role from the game's earliest years; in this instance Kenesaw Mountain Landis (**P.240, BOTTOM**) launches an opening toss with rare good form to start the 1922 World Series.

BLEACHER BUMS TO TRUE FANATICS

In the 1880s they were known everywhere as "cranks," referring to the strange pessimism with which locals discussed their hometown nine. Now they are usually just called "fanatics." Both terms aptly describe the true fan.

The Baseball Family 243

They come in all sizes, shapes and ages. What distinguishes them from non-fans is their unbounded enthusiasm for the game and for the ballclub of their choice. That enthusiasm is typically in evidence – despite the miserable rainy weather – in this group of stoic Gotham bleacherites, cheerfully awaiting the opening of ballpark ticket windows and a chance to grab prized ducats for the first game of the 1955 World Series in Yankee Stadium (**OPPOSITE**). Sometimes such fan enthusiasm has little to do with the ballgame in progress, as demonstrated by an eager pack of Shibe Park youngsters who scramble up the backstop net in pursuit of a foul ball during 1948 game action between the hometown Athletics and visiting Indians (**OPPOSITE BOTTOM LEFT**). At least one veteran Detroit Tigers rooter pictured here (**ABOVE**) wears a look of eternal optimism, as well as a hand-lettered sign of undying faith in the local heroes that seem to belie the pessimism often attributed to the game's original "cranks" of the past century. Another veteran booster from Ohio appears far more vocal in his unwavering support for his hometown favorites during pre-game activities before a Cincinnati-Yankees 1939 World Series contest in Yankee Stadium (**TOP RIGHT**). And a final hardy senior citizen displays proud trophies of past World Series visits on the eve of a 1970 Fall Classic opener in the Queen City of Cincinnati (**BOTTOM RIGHT**). Cornelius Blackman of Chicago is, in fact, about to attend Series play for an incredible 36th time over the course of his 74 years. Only a true 'fanatic' would dedicate his life to such an unbroken string of annual fall pilgrimages to baseball's finest show.

From the mythical "Fans' Hall of Fame" come a few of the more extreme and bizarre instances of unbridled boosterism.

(**TOP LEFT**) There was standing room only for this group of spectators and their row of "dead soldiers" during Series opening game action at Sportsman's Park in St. Louis on October 7, 1946. What they were viewing from the precarious perch in the grandstand section was a dramatic 3-2 triumph by the visiting Red Sox, earned on the strength of a heart-wrenching 10th-inning Rudy York home run. Open another round, boys!

(**BOTTOM LEFT**) A moment of lighthearted fan-player interaction transpires in Dodger Stadium as a surprise "mystery girl" chases down Los Angeles batter Wes Parker (playfully being restrained by Houston Astros infielder Doug Rader) in order to plant a kiss on the cheek of her special favorite before escaping back to the safety of the grandstand.

(**OPPOSITE TOP LEFT**) A free World Series seat is the prize for this inventive New York fan, who checks out the action from afar with his trusty artillery spotters. Unable to find a ballpark ticket, he had instead exclusive claim to this rooftop perch in a building across the street from Yankee Stadium. The setting is Game One of the 1947 World Series, and the year's combatants are the Yankees and the crosstown rival Brooklyn Dodgers.

(**OPPOSITE TOP RIGHT**) While today's fans jam phone lines attempting to place ticket orders for Series and playoff games, yesterday's rooters were forced to wait in long stadium lines or try their luck with snail-paced mail orders. Here workers in the office of Connie Mack's Athletics empty sacks of ticket requests for upcoming 1929 Series action between the American League champion Mackmen and Chicago's National League Cubs.

(**OPPOSITE BOTTOM**) A sleepy yet high-spirited contingent of optimistic New York faithful camp overnight outside Yankee Stadium ticket windows, awaiting the morning's sale of precious passes to a 1941 World Series opener between the heavily favored Yanks and surprise National League Champion Brooklyn Dodgers. Here's hoping there were some Dodger fans in the lot.

The Baseball Family 245

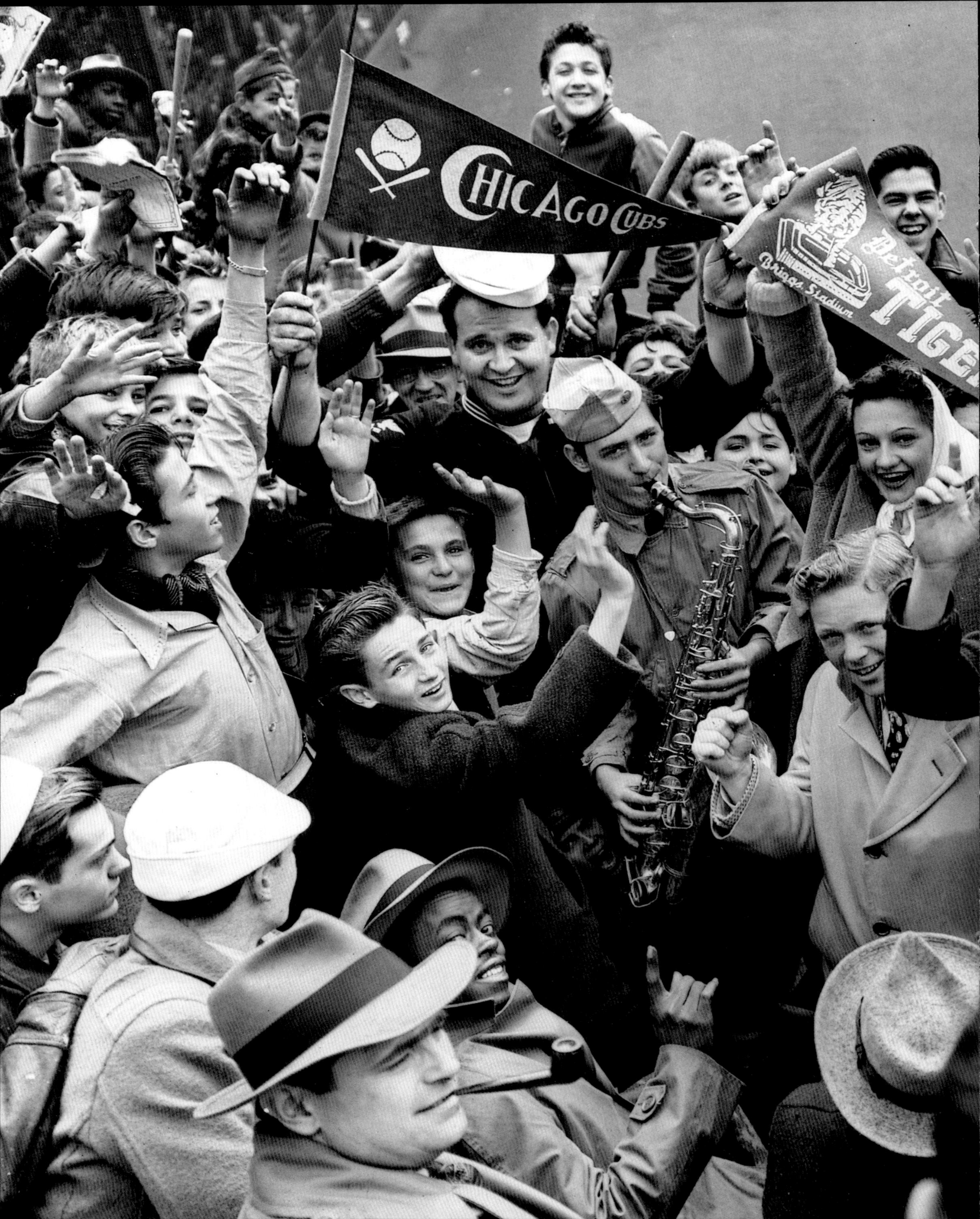
CHICAGO CUBS
Detroit
Briggs Stadium
TIGE

The Baseball Family 247

While we fans have little influence over the outcome of games featuring our favorite ballclubs, it is a prerogative of fandom to always act as though we did in fact possess such power. Filling the Briggs Stadium bleachers before the third game of the 1945 World Series, a younger generation of Chicago and Detroit fans enjoys a grand time boosting personal favorites, as demonstrated here by the cheerful sailor plugging the visiting Cubs and the young lady showing similar enthusiasm for the hometown Tigers (**LEFT**). Fans of either city could hardly know at the time how long it would be before their favorites would again experience Series play: Detroit boosters were destined to wait another 23 long seasons, and Cubs backers are still lusting for Series action. It is almost as though these two proud baseball cities and their fans have been jinxed by Series play, a fate that still another "fanatic" (**ABOVE**) actually tried to bring down upon the highly successful Yankees and their pitcher Eddie Lopat during a June 1951 game in Cleveland's Municipal Stadium. Duly impressed, Lopat seems to keep strictly behind the path of this black kitten, which was placed on the mound by intrepid Cleveland supporter Andrew Jackson Antal. When the Indians rose up to beat Lopat that day for the first time in two seasons, Antal's bar-room buddies quickly took up a cash collection to send the successful "spellbinder" all the way to New York in order to again administer his "medicine" at the next meeting between Lopat and the hometown favored Tribe.

IMMORTALS ALL!

It is the moment of which all ballplayers dream – the moment when a diamond career reaches its pinnacle with announcement of the highest honor the game can bestow, admittance to the halls of Cooperstown, where the game's greatest heroes are enshrined. To be placed alongside them is to be immortalized.

"TO THE PIONEERS WHO WERE THE MOVING SPIRITS OF THE GAME IN ITS INFANCY AND TO THE PLAYERS WHO HAVE BEEN ELECTED TO THE HALL OF FAME..... WE PAY JUST TRIBUTE. BUT I SHOULD LIKE TO DEDICATE THIS MUSEUM TO ALL AMERICA....."

KENESAW M. LANDIS
Commissioner of Baseball
1920–1944

Cooperstown has always been far more than just a museum for preserving the great artifacts of the national game. This charming village also provides a yearly site for baseball's greatest ceremony. This tradition dates from the time of the grand celebration of baseball's centennial year more than a half-century ago (**ABOVE**). On that august occasion ten of the game's greatest living legends (**BELOW**) gathered to honor the bright memories of all who had once played the game. The immortal gallery on that occasion included (standing, from l to r) Honus Wagner, Grover Alexander, Tris Speaker, Nap Lajoie, George Sisler and Walter "Big Train" Johnson, alongside (seated, from l to r) Eddie Collins, Babe Ruth, Connie Mack and Cy Young. During the festivities a troupe of actors marched on to Doubleday Field for the re-enactment of a nineteenth-century game of "town ball" in fitting celebration of the game's misty origins (**LEFT**).

The Baseball Family 249

The highlight of each summer's Hall-of-Fame season is the admittance of new Cooperstown inductees, a late-summer ritual that today draws thousands of spectators to the mecca of the baseball world. The 1984 ceremony is pictured here (**BELOW**), with incoming immortals and past inductees Rick Ferrell, Pee Wee Reese, Don Drysdale, Luis Aparicio, Roy Campanella and Harmon Killebrew among the dignitaries visible upon the dais. Even for those larger-than-life baseball legends who have so often stood fearless in the batter's box or upon the pitcher's mound, the emotions surrounding this most special of baseball occasions are often overpowering, as was the case for "Say Hey" Willie Mays (**LEFT**) when he first stepped before a microphone after the announcement of his own Cooperstown election in January 1979.

TAKE ME OUT TO THE BALLGAME

The game of baseball – with its rich historical fabric and vivid fan appeal – is largely a matter of memory and nostalgia. For some, it is all summed up in the memory of a catch by Willie Mays of a towering Vic Wertz blast into deepest center field of the phantom Polo Grounds. For others, perhaps, it is the home run trot which made Bobby Thomson a legend, or the indelible image of Jackie Robinson stealing home, or Roberto Clemente rifling a throw from the outfield recesses of old Forbes Field. It may be memories as time-worn as a faded daguerreotype of Honus Wagner or as recent as Andy Hawkins' incredible no-hitter loss which opened a new decade, the latter performed on the exact day in 1990 when Chicago's venerable Comiskey Park celebrated its 80th anniversary of major league action. Baseball is also how we feel about our favorite big-league nine, how we pin our hopes on them, how even our personalities are affected by them. Chicago Cubs fans seem always to be both unassailably cheerful and resigned. (The old bleacherite version of the Cubs fan from the Ernie Banks era, at least, if not the yuppiefied hordes who now crowd a renovated Wrigley Field.) New York Yankee rooters have, again recently, appeared to take victories as their personal due. By contrast, Red Sox and Tigers faithful are subdued, prepared to be victims of the outrageous.

The stuff of baseball memories is, however, woven as much from the fine web of folklore as from the stout thread of reality. With no other sport is the line between myth and history so indistinguishable. We baseball fans admittedly like to take our history with a strong dose of palatable fiction, thank you!

It begins at the very beginning with baseball's sanctified but wholly unsubstantial creation myth. This is the tale, at every schoolboy's command, that Abner Doubleday invented this marvelous game on a cow pasture in Cooperstown, New York. Ever since Robert W. Henderson exploded this fiction in the 1940s there has been absolutely no credence paid by any reputable sports historian to the fable that General Doubleday had anything to do with the invention of our national game. Doubleday never saw baseball, never mentioned it in his voluminous diaries, never was anywhere near Cooperstown (he was a cadet at West Point that year) at the supposed time of the game's conception. American baseball was never 'born', it slowly evolved from European bat and ball games known as 'rounders', 'stoolball', 'base-ball' and a host of other names. It was Albert Spalding who fostered the Doubleday myth, and for the noblest of American entrepreneurial purposes – to sell his lucrative sporting goods. Why then has the myth held fast in the popular imagination? Harvard biologist and baseball fan Stephen Jay Gould says that we Americans seem to need our creation myths, prefer them, indeed, to any less colorful account that we know to be true.

If baseball's birth is shrouded in myth, many of its most famous moments are also so tainted. There is the matter of the most memorable moment in World Series history, for example. Everyone has heard the story of Babe Ruth dramatically calling his home run shot in his last Series appearance, at Chicago's Wrigley Field. For years controversy has surrounded the incident, but the bottom line seems to be that most fans and qualified sports historians simply do not wish to know what really happened, especially since the best evidence suggests that the event is pure legend.

There are plenty of other examples. It is common knowledge, for instance, that Jackie Robinson was the first black man to play in the big leagues. The trouble is that this just isn't accurate. Catcher Moses Fleetwood Walker was a black man who played in the American Association (very much a "major" league) in 1884, before being hurriedly drummed out of the circuit by white players and owners. It is also a fact that a dark-skinned Cuban pitcher, Tommie de la Cruz, hurled several games (9-9, 3.23 ERA) with the Cincinnati Reds in 1944, before it was decided that his skin was a bit too dark and he was conveniently dropped from the Cincinnati roster. Robinson's achievement in integrating modern baseball is enormous; why diminish it by festooning it with irrelevant untruths?

The other spectacular event of that decade, Joe DiMaggio's unmatchable 56-game hitting streak, also warrants some scrutiny. This was a truly remarkable achievement, yet it might equally be seen as a series of short streaks rather than one long one. One hit came on a highly questionable scorer's decision at Comiskey Park in Game 25; another was a bad hop off Luke Appling's shoulder in Game 30; a third was a weakly-topped roller in Game 54. Also, DiMaggio was stopped altogether in an exhibition game by a minor league pitcher (Jimmy Halperin of the Norfolk Tars) along the way on May 26th (between Games 11 and 12). By the same token, and to Joe's further credit, he continued on another streak of 17 games after the famous skein had ended. Thus a spectacular series of three streaks (strung out over a full half season of 74 games) might be closer to the truth, though the record book doesn't show it that way.

The infamous Black Sox World Series scandal – so much in the popular imagination after a recent series of hit films and novels exploiting its timely themes – is yet another case of baseball history coated over with legend. There is little evidence that Shoeless Joe Jackson actually threw any ballgames to the opposition (he was the leading batsman in the Series, with a .375 average), and there is less evidence still to implicate Buck Weaver (who was at his career best with 11 hits and flawless fielding). The eight accused ballplayers were guilty, certainly, of conspiring with gamblers, but they changed their minds in midstream and the deed was never executed as imagined. It was convenient for baseball's ownership to use them as scapegoats, and much show was made of their 1920 trial (at which they were acquitted) and subsequent banning by Commissioner Landis; yet the man who masterminded the entire plot, New York gangster Arnold Rothstein, went scot-free. This is not to exonerate the behavior of the unethical eight, yet it does suggest that Joe Jackson was a victim as well as a beneficiary of baseball legend. Without the scandal Jackson might well have earned his rightful place in Cooperstown, although it is doubtful he would have ever enjoyed an equal role in American folklore.

When we hold up baseball myths to the facts we are not always engaged in debunking. Few but the most ardent historians-fans are aware of how often the miraculous in baseball history outstrips even the best of baseball-inspired fiction and fantasy. Baseball's best novel (and its best movie as well), *The Natural* by Bernard Malamud, is filled with miraculous events that seem to challenge our credulity. Roy Hobbs returns from a lost youth to set the baseball world afire as a slugging 38-year-old rookie. He smacks titanic homers that break a scoreboard clock, knock the cover off a ball and resurrect a last-place team in to a pennant winner in half a season.

Yet it is the strength and achievement of Malamud's novel that all its events have their real-life parallels. Hobbs' near assassination is based on the story of Cubs' first baseman Eddie Waitkus. The clock-breaking and cover-knocking stories have their big-league parallels in events at Washington's Griffith Stadium. Dozens of the events and characters of the novel are drawn straight from the baseball record – Joe Jackson (Roy Hobbs), Wilbert Robinson and Rabbit Maranville (Pop Fisher), the Whammer (Babe Ruth) and countless more. As Casey Stengel would have said, you could look it up!

All this is to suggest that we baseball fans are blessed with having our history and our mythology as well. In the pages that follow some of the game's most memorable moments of myth and history again intertwine. First comes the catalogue of unforgettable moments which are so vivid in outline and yet so fuzzy in detail – from Bobby Thomson's timely homer to untimely boots by Mickey Owen and Phil Rizzuto, and from the pitching mastery of Don Larsen to the defensive wizardry of Willie Mays. Then there are the legendary World Series moments, black pioneers, colorful flakes and unexpected heroes that so enrich our memories.

Finally, on the lighter side of the national pastime, there are the expansion deadbeats, the shameless publicity stunts, the joyous celebrations and the surreal events of wartime baseball. All blend together in a collage, part myth and part reality, part living history and part musty legend, that is the woof and warp of the national game.

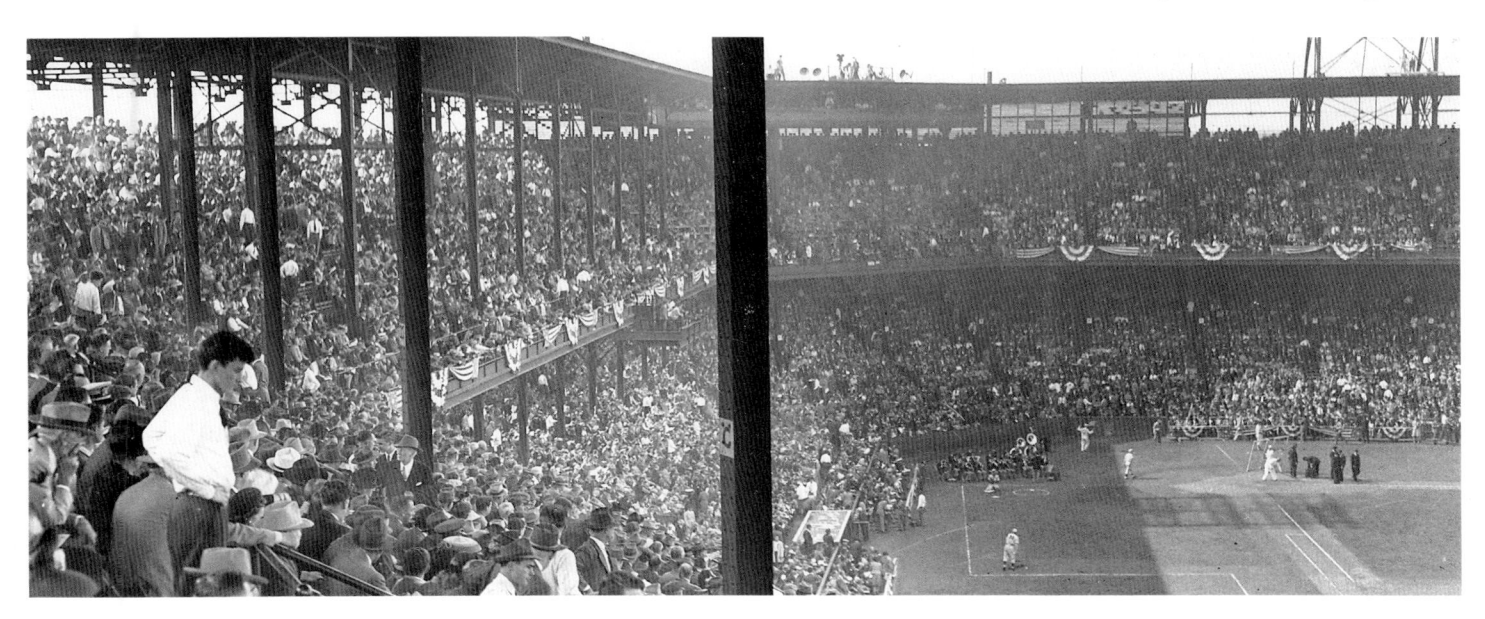

"THE GIANTS WIN THE PENNANT!"

They are moments like no others, burned into our memories with lasting clarity, monuments to a game that buoyed our youth and is there to cheer us once again when life's defeats crowd in upon our adult lives.

Ruth Calls His Shot

Take Me Out to the Ballgame

Baseball's great moments are enshrined in its lore, but one of the most "memorable" of these may never have happened. For years Ruthologists have argued the events surrounding the most famous home run in diamond history, the Babe's "called shot" in the 1932 World Series. Photographic evidence from that renowned Wrigley Field game seems to verify that Ruth did indeed gesture toward center field. But was he truly indicating the spot where he would park the next pitch (as suggested in a famed artist's rendition, **OPPOSITE**)? Or was he reminding hurler Charlie Root of the count, or merely suggesting he was prepared to rip the next offering through the box? Was the feat a fiction propagated by Ruth himself and by sportswriters who had hooked on to a great story? Certainly the best witness, pitcher Root himself, maintained until his dying day that had he thought for a moment Ruth was signaling a homer he would have knocked the Babe onto his very large posterior on the very next pitch! So Ruth's most touted feat remains a mystery, a fitting place to begin a gallery of great moments in a sport whose history is almost indistinguishable from its mythology. Of course there was nothing of mystery surrounding baseball's second most famous roundtripper, only the stuff of pure magic. When Bobby Thomson smacked his season-ending 1951 blow against the Dodgers at the Polo Grounds in October 1951, Brooklyn faithful were all too painfully aware of what had just transpired before their eyes. In the brief moment of the ball's dramatic flight (**CENTER RIGHT**) a pennant was snatched away by the hated rivals, and a nation of radio and television fans sat stunned as announcer Russ Hodges delivered what has become the most famous call in big league history: "The Giants win the pennant! The Giants win the pennant!" Such moments as Ruth's questionable call and Thomson's unforgettable clutch blow remain the common heritage of baseball fans of all generations – those who saw them and those who have only heard the often-retold accounts. From the first World Series, which drew huge throngs to the Huntington Avenue Field in Boston in 1903 (**TOP RIGHT**), the Series has been a special repository of such moments, and none was more incredible than Mickey Owen's dropped third strike (**BOTTOM RIGHT**) in the fourth game of the 1941 classic; it allowed Tommy Henrich to reach first and the Yankees to rally for a Series title.

If the World Series is an unrivaled stage for baseball memories, no single events are more often relived or more deeply cherished by fans of the baseball capital of New York than Eddie Stanky's slide in 1951 (**ABOVE**), Billy Martin's desperate game-saving snatch in 1952 (**RIGHT**) or Willie Mays' most famous of all Series catches in 1954 (**OPPOSITE BOTTOM**). Always noted for his rough and spunky style, the Giants' Eddie Stanky earned Series immortality when he stole second and ignited a well-timed rally by kicking loose a throw from the waiting glove of New York Yankee shortstop Phil Rizzuto. Martin, who always rose to the peak of his talents during the October Classic, streaked across the infield for a breath-taking and game-saving grab of a towering pop by Jackie Robinson, with the bases crammed full of Dodgers in the 7th frame of the 7th contest. Mays made perhaps the finest defensive play in Series history in the opening 1954 contest, racing deep in center field to snatch (over his shoulder and with his back to the plate) a 400-foot drive by Vic Wertz, with the game tied and two men on base. Mays then whirled to throw a frozen rope to second, preventing Cleveland runners from advancing and killing a sure Indian rally. While such Series heroics became regular fare in New York during the 1950s, fans in cities like Washington had to find their mythic moments buried in less significant games played out in the heat of midsummer, like the titanic homer by Mickey Mantle that sailed out of Griffith Stadium (**OPPOSITE TOP**) on April 17, 1953, landing in a backyard some 562 feet from home plate.

Take Me Out to the Ballgame   255

Reggie Jackson's three consecutive 1977 homers, Sandy Amoros' clutch 1955 catch of Yogi Berra's sinking liner, Billy Martin's Series-saving nab of Jackie Robinson's towering pop fly, Tommy Henrich's rally-starting third strike, which skipped past Mickey Owen, and Cookie Lavagetto's pinch-hit heroics, which ruined Floyd Bevens' bid for an unprecedented Series no-hitter. New York has relished an unmatched string of unforgettable World Series moments. And the majority of these have surprisingly featured one-time heroes, men recalled from obscurity by a single clutch moment of Series achievement. Yet no such thrilling Series moment quite matches one that occurred in Yankee Stadium on October 8, 1956 – either for raw excitement or sheer achievement. For on that incredible afternoon, journeyman Don Larsen of the New York Yankees did what no hurler has done before or since; Larsen set down 27 Dodgers in a row for the only perfect game (and only no-hitter) in Series history (**ABOVE** and **RIGHT**). All fans remember in graphic detail this supreme pitching performance of Larsen's otherwise mediocre career. What few remember is that Larsen had been rather lackluster that same season (11-5, 3.26 ERA) and had been knocked from the box on his previous Series start in Game Two. Larsen threw but 97 pitches that day, and the last was a called third strike to pinch-hitter Dale Mitchell. Although the pitch appeared outside to many press box observers, before Mitchell could turn to argue with plate umpire Babe Pinelli (calling the last pitch of his career), mayhem had erupted in Yankee Stadium and Berra had leaped into Larsen's arms in one of baseball's most memorable celebrations.

Don Pitches Perfect Series Game!

Not all of baseball's most celebrated and spectacular events during the glorious decade of the "Golden Fifties" occurred in New York City – it just seemed that way. There were indeed other venues of spectacular achievement which featured heroes donning uniforms of teams other than the Giants, Dodgers or Yankees. Even such a lost and barren big league outpost as Pittsburgh knew its brief moments of glory and its occasional encounter with the spectacular. And like all precious baseball moments, Pittsburgh's scant portion blended the joys of victory with the taste of defeat. No pitcher ever suffered more from the irony of the gods, for example, than did Pirate lefty Harvey Haddix on May 26, 1959 (**LEFT**) in Milwaukee's County Stadium. Haddix was supreme in retiring 36 consecutive batters over 12 innings (the longest perfect game ever hurled in the big leagues), yet the crafty southpaw was pitching that night for the stumblebum Pirates, who picked that occasion not to score even a scratch run of their own. Unflinching, Haddix labored boldly on. But Braves batter Felix Mantilla reached base on an error by Pittsburgh third sacker Don Hoak to open the home 13th (there went the perfect game!). The tired Haddix intentionally passed the feared Hank Aaron (there went the web of total domination Haddix had spun!). And what happened next bordered on the truly surreal, as Joe Adcock smashed a Haddix delivery over the left field wall (there went everything!), then passed Aaron on the basepaths in the ensuing bedlam and was called out, providing a final 1-0 score in favor of Milwaukee. Haddix appeared stunned as he left the mound and was greeted by manager Danny Murtaugh – the victim of perhaps the cruelest joke ever played by Lady Luck upon a diamond hero. Shocked disbelief was again in order for these same Pirates and their fans little more than a year later, yet with a far different aftertaste the second time around. On the afternoon of October 13, 1960, Bill Mazeroski circled the bases (**OPPOSITE**) in the midst of excitement and chaos after smacking the first (and still only) Series-ending homer in the annals of Fall Classic play. Maz's famous blow in the ninth-inning of Game Seven off Yankees hurler Ralph Terry brought the long-feeble Pirates their first World Title since the distant autumn of 1925. It was a far nobler date with destiny for Mazeroski than the one experienced by teammate Haddix, and a fitting career climax for a man many consider the best defensive second sacker ever to play the game.

Take Me Out to the Ballgame 259

262 THE BASEBALL SCRAPBOOK

Often a ballplayer's entire career seems to be encapsulated in the public imagination by a single event. For Fred Merkle of the Giants it was a single World Series blunder that would all but obliterate all his other career achievements. All informed fans past 40 vividly recall Bill Mazeroski's trot around the bases in the autumn of 1960, while at the same time seemingly forgetting almost everything else about Maz's true Hall-of-Fame credentials. Willie Mays' robbery of Vic Wertz, or Brooks Robinson's diving third base stops during the 1970 World Series seem in retrospect only metaphors for entire careers composed of such slick-gloved heroics. Bobby Thomson lived the shortest career in baseball history – at least in the hazy glow of memory – a single swing on October 3, 1951. And into this category as well falls the reckless abandon that marked the playing style of "Charlie Hustle" Pete Rose, inspirational leader for Cincinnati's Big Red Machine clubs of the 1970s. Whenever one thinks of Rose, no image comes more quickly to mind than that of the shattering collision between Rose and Cleveland catcher Ray Fosse at home plate during the 1970 All-Star Game in Riverfront Stadium. It was a single to center by Chicago's Jim Hickman that brought Rose streaking home with the winning run in the 12th inning (**ABOVE** and **ABOVE RIGHT**). Rose entered national folklore forever by blasting into Fosse as the hapless backstop attempted in vain to block the plate (**RIGHT**). Rose would achieve Cooperstown status as the all-time hits leader, then spoil his proud reputation and dishearten his legions of fans with a lifetime suspension and prison term brought on by a gambling addiction and income tax fraud. But in the mind's eye he is still "Charlie Hustle" – running bases with abandon and smashing down all obstacles to victory on the big league diamond.

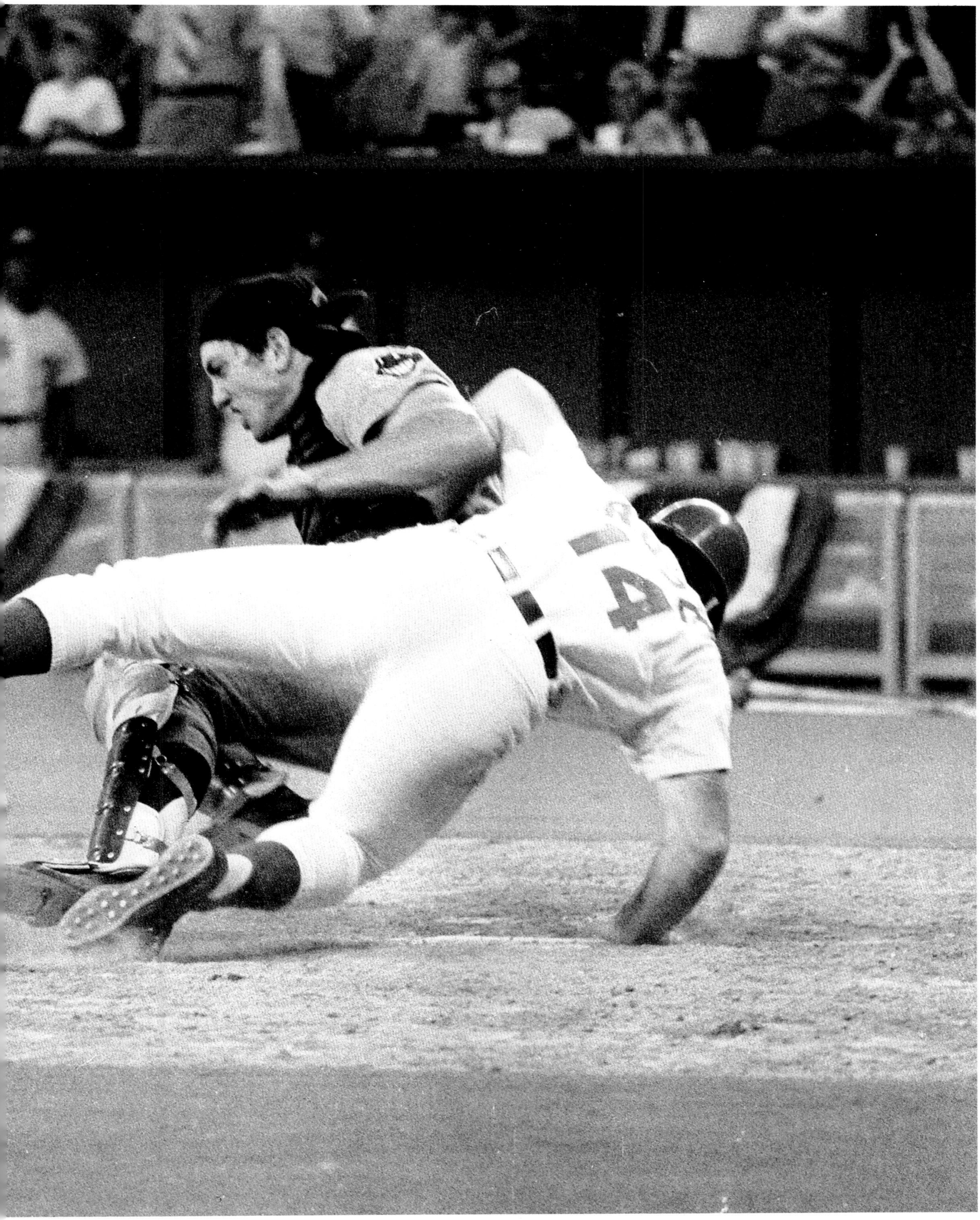

264 THE BASEBALL SCRAPBOOK

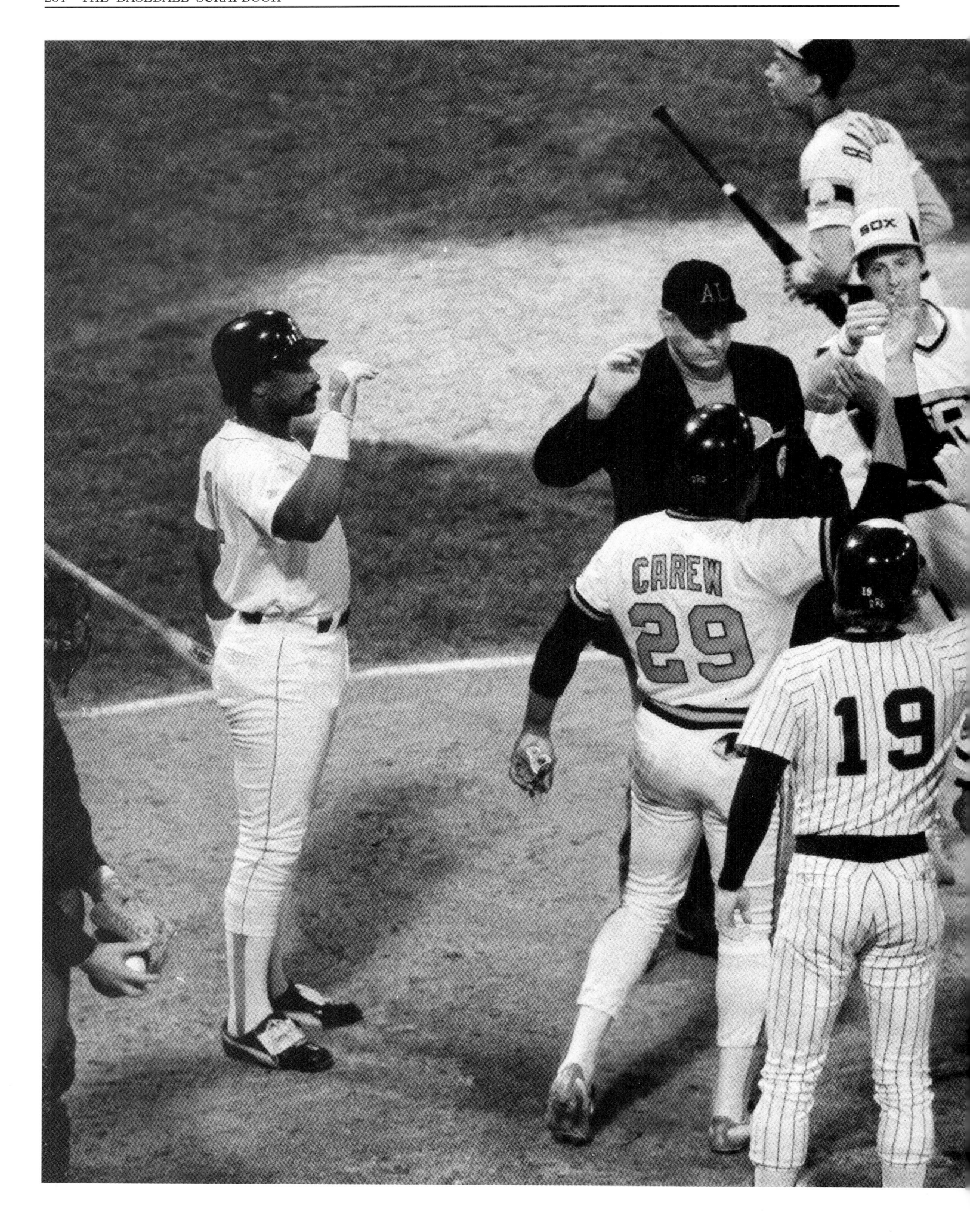

Take Me Out to the Ballgame 265

During its century of national popularity the diamond sport has spawned a large contingent of folk heroes – Anson, Mathewson, Ruth, Gehrig, Greenberg, DiMaggio, Williams, Ryan and a great many more. Yet baseball is ultimately a team game, and it is the thrill of a heated pennant race – city against city – or the final showdown of a well-matched World Series which most rivets our attention. The prospect of team victory alone provides the rationale for individual heroics. For this reason alone the World Series is usually more fertile territory for memorable individual performance than is that other mid-summer showcase of individual skills known as the All-Star Game. And yet it is indisputable that baseball's Mid-Summer Classic has had its own set of legends as well. There was Carl Hubbell of the Giants striking out five future Hall-of-Famers in a row in 1934. There was Ted Williams winning a 1941 All-Star matchup with the most dramatic hit of his storied career – a clutch ninth-inning homer off Claude Passeau in Detroit's Briggs Stadium. There was Williams again, providing another memorable circuit clout in 1946 off the famed "eephus" delivery of Rip Sewell in Fenway Park. Unforgettable, too, were Pete Rose's reckless charge to the plate and Red Schoendienst's moment of triumph in 1950 with a dramatic 14th-inning game-winning clout. There was even Babe Ruth winning the first Classic with a home run in 1933, and DiMaggio doing the same in 1939. And ranking high on the list of cherished All-Star Game heroics was Fred Lynn (**LEFT**), smashing the first and only All-Star Game grand slam homer, a feat achieved on the same evening the Mid-Summer Classic returned to Chicago's Comiskey Park for its ceremonial 50th anniversary year. Sixty-one All-Star Games have now been played, yet only Fred Lynn – quite incredibly – has succeeded in smacking a circuit blow with the bases crammed full of runners.

266 THE BASEBALL SCRAPBOOK

Take Me Out to the Ballgame 267

Sometimes it is a single player's relentless pursuit of a celebrated record that provides the nation's fans with incomparable memories of diamond action. On other occasions it is a last-second heroic effort by an altogether unlikely star, performed under the extreme pressure of championship play. The latter scenario was precisely the one enacted by Bill Mazeroski of the Pirates in 1960 and by Bobby Thomson of the Giants in 1951, and it was the one again played out when Bucky Dent's dramatic homer clinched yet another pennant for New York in 1978. The normally light-hitting Dent (here being greeted at the plate by Roy White and Chris Chambliss, **BOTTOM RIGHT**) became an unlikely hero when his short-fly-ball seventh-inning homer off reliever Mike Torrez into the Green Monster screen at Fenway Park gave the Yankees a playoff victory and World Series berth over the ill-fated Bosox. In contrast with Dent's sudden and quite unexpected date with destiny, Roger Maris' 1961 chase after Babe Ruth's record was more clearly the classic kind of legend-in-the-making. It has been the case as well with the seemingly endless string of record-besting strikeout performances by Nolan Ryan, as the ageless right-hander climbs one record-book mountain peak after another. Recently there have been Ryan's overhauling of Walter Johnson's career standard and his toppling of the apparently insurmountable 5000 strikeout barrier. But first came the memorable September 1973 effort which surpassed Sandy Koufax's single-season standard of 382, a season-ending performance in which the young Ryan wiffed 16 Minnesota batters over 10 innings to surpass Koufax by the narrowest margin of one (**OPPOSITE**). Pete Rose's pursuit of Ty Cobb (which ended with career base hit number 4192 on September 11, 1985, **TOP RIGHT**) also paralleled Maris' chase of Ruth, yet there were some important differences that separated Rose's countdown from that of the Yankee slugger. An unpopular Maris, hounded by the press and jeered by fans, was chasing after a sanctified legend, and few in press box or grandstand seemed to be in his corner. In Rose's case, however, an unpopular Ty Cobb was finally being ousted from hitting pre-eminence by an immensely popular and colorful contemporary hero. Maris' pursuit was an affair of a single season, but Rose's benefited from the full head of steam generated over several dramatic countdown summers.

THE OCTOBER CLASSIC

It is still America's greatest sports event. Each year's brief seven-game Series is a miniature season in itself, somehow condensing all the drama of the longer campaign that preceded it.

Long-suffering Red Sox fans speak mournfully of the "Curse of the Bambino", a seemingly relentless string of pennant-race disasters which has befallen the favorite local nine ever since penny-pinching Boston owner Harry Frazee sold away Babe Ruth to the hated Yankees for $100,000, thus seemingly mortgaging a proud city's entire baseball future. Some veteran Bosox watchers speak even more heatedly of the "Curse of Johnny Pesky" – some momentary hesitation in which all is lost, a big play not made which foils a championship bid. Surely there were ghosts of Pesky on the field when Mookie Wilson's seeing-eye grounder dribbled between usually sure-handed Bill Buckner's legs at Shea Stadium in 1986. Or again when Denny Doyle threw a routine double play ball into the first base dugout to open the flood gates for Cincinnati in the final game of 1975. The "Pesky Curse" dates from 1946, when the Red Sox had all but sealed a seventh-game World Series triumph – just as irreversibly as they apparently had in 1975 and then again in 1986 – only to see it all unravel on a single fateful play. It was the final game of a nip-and-tuck Fall Classic with St. Louis, the score tied at three, and the Cardinals had Enos Slaughter on first, with two retired and no apparent threat in the offing. Then Harry "The Hat" Walker lined a solid hit to right field. With Slaughter running on the pitch, Sox second baseman Pesky held the relay throw in an inexplicable moment's hesitation, allowing Slaughter to slide across the plate uncontested with the World Series' winning run (**OPPOSITE BOTTOM**). The St. Louis clubhouse was soon a scene of jubilation (**BOTTOM RIGHT**, with Slaughter celebrating with teammates Harry Brecheen, Terry Moore and Harry Walker). For Boston owner Tom Yawkey (**OPPOSITE TOP**, at the Series opener with Mr. and Mrs. Eddie Collins and his wife, Jean) it was perhaps the worst moment in all the four decades a World Championship had eluded his ballclub. For Red Sox supporters it was the World Title that had somehow slipped away. All had started so brightly for Boston that fall when the Series had returned to Beantown for the first time in 28 seasons. There had been an especially satisfying 4-0 victory in Game Three, behind ace pitcher Boo Ferriss (**TOP RIGHT**, pursuing St. Louis slugger Stan Musial in a rundown with third sacker Pinky Higgins). In the end, however, only another depressing Boston legend was born.

Between 1947 and 1956 it seemed that the World Series was merely an annual autumn exhibition put on by teams representing the city of New York. Six times in that 10-year span it was the Yankees and Dodgers who shuttled between Yankee Stadium and Ebbets Field in what soon became popularly known as the "Subway" Series. And none of these inter-borough clashes would bring more drama and last-minute heroics than the first of the string, played out over seven games in 1947. There was unprecedented excitement surrounding the Brooklyn club that year, as Jackie Robinson broke the modern-era color barrier and blazed across the senior circuit on his way to landslide choice as the National League's first-ever Rookie-of-the-Year. Though manager Leo Durocher was serving a year's suspension for consorting with gamblers, the Dodgers seemed to be inspired by Robinson's on-field heroics and fortitude, and the Brooklyns had raced to a five-game final spread over the defending World Champion Cardinals. Brooklyn fans wildly celebrated their club's pennant triumph (**BOTTOM LEFT**), then were buoyed by their team's charge back from a two-game deficit to knot the Series at two apiece. Game Four provided one of the gems of Series history, as Brooklyn pinch-hitter Cookie Lavagetto (**TOP LEFT**) doubled home two runs with two out in the ninth frame to end Floyd Bevens' dream of a first-ever Series no-hitter. The usually undistinguished Lavagetto was carried to the Dodgers dressing room like a true conquering hero (**OPPOSITE**), having wrested both the no-hitter and the game from the disappointed Bevens with a single swipe of his bat. Robinson played boldly in his first Series and stole two bases, including one pictured here in Game Two (**CENTER LEFT**), and veteran hurler Hugh Casey won two straight in relief for the Brooklyn team of substitute manager Barney Shotton. Yet in the end the Yankees prevailed – as they would five straight times over their Brooklyn rivals – when Joe Page checked the Dodgers with five brilliant relief innings during Game Seven. The Bronx Bombers had emerged victorious largely on the strength of Tommy Henrich's clutch RBI hitting and the equally potent bat of current American League President Bobby Brown, who made Series history with two doubles, a single and a base on balls in four pinch-hitting appearances.

Take Me Out to the Ballgame 273

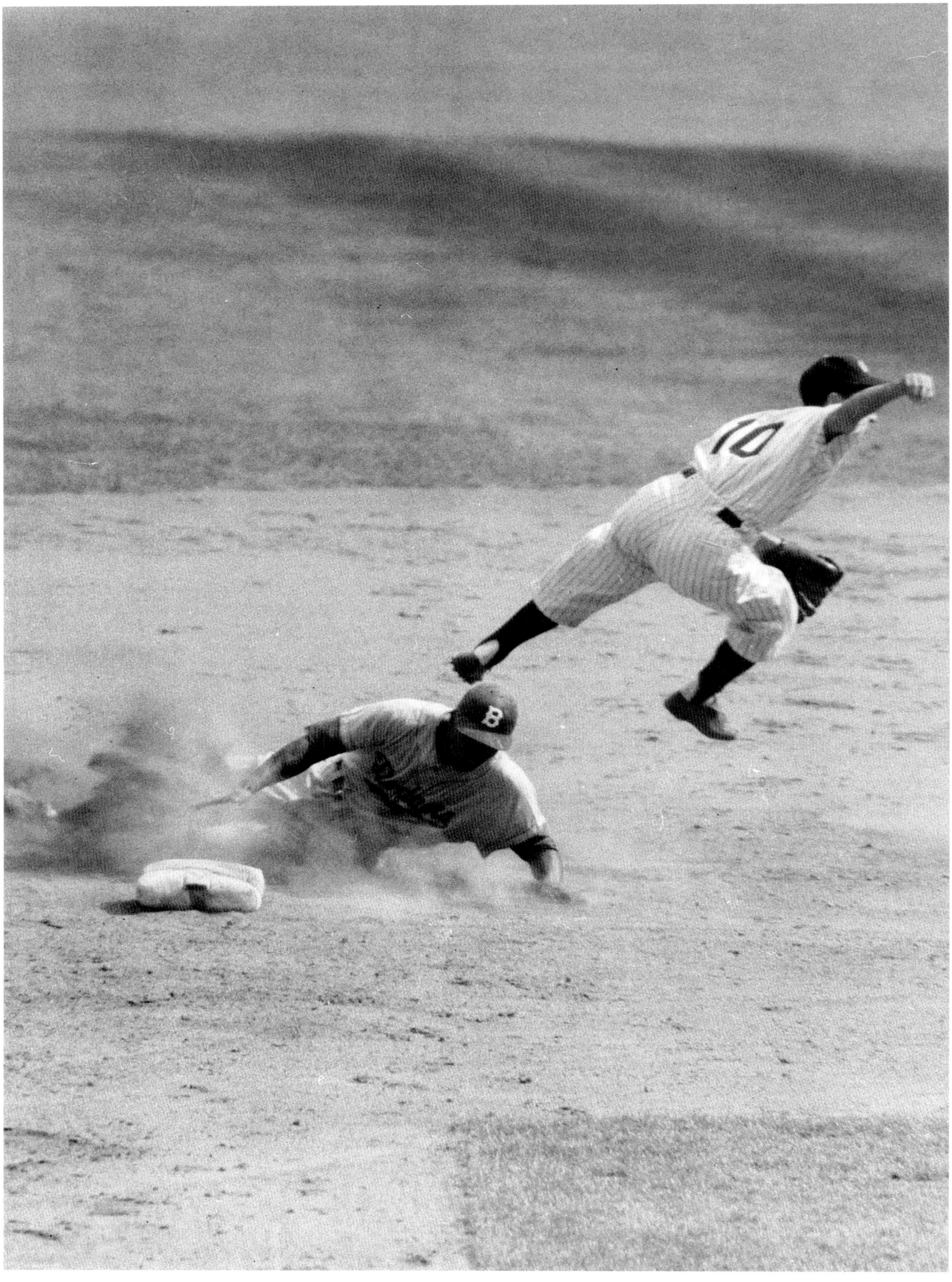

The "Boys of Summer" Dodgers were indeed the most dominant teams in National League history. Between 1946 and 1956 there were six pennants won at Ebbets Field, with three more lost by the narrowest of margins. A third-place 1948 campaign (seven-and-a-half games behind Boston) represents the only summer in eleven that the Dodgers were not serious contenders at least until the season's final week. In ten years in contention, one five-game deficit behind the Giants during the second-place finish of 1954 represents the only season when a pennant was not either won or, at worst, lost on the season's final day. Victories on the final day of the campaign in 1946, 1950 and 1951 would, in fact, have given Brooklyn an unprecedented nine of 11 pennants. Only the Yankees ever accomplished quite that kind of league domination. Yet for all their prowess, all their National League pennants and October near-glories, this was a team fated by history to be branded as hopeless losers. In October, when the World Series rolled around, it was always the Bronx Bombers who somehow prevailed; it was the Yankees who appeared in every World Series but two between 1949 and 1962, winning an unprecedented five World Titles in succession. The Dodgers might have been the second best club in baseball, but it was also the second best team in the City of New York. Then came the magical autumn of 1955 and the unforgettable clutch catch by reserve outfielder Sandy Amoros of a sinking Yogi Berra line drive (**TOP RIGHT**). The 1955 World Series had started out once again in anything but spectacular fashion for Brooklyn, as the Casey Stengel Yankees, led by the slick fielding of veteran shortstop Phil Rizzuto and ace second sacker Billy Martin, cruised to two straight (albeit tight) victories at Yankee Stadium. Rizzuto (**OPPOSITE**, turning a double play over the sliding Junior Gilliam) was making his ninth and final Series appearance. But the Dodgers clawed back for three straight wins of their own, and only the brilliant pitching of Whitey Ford in Game Six could force a seventh game. When 23-year-old Johnny Podres became a permanent Brooklyn immortal by shutting down the Yankees in the finale, and then rushed off the mound to celebrate with third baseman Don Hoak and catcher Roy Campanella (**BOTTOM RIGHT**), none among the delirious Dodgers faithful could possibly have known that Brooklyn was experiencing not only its very first – but also its last World Title.

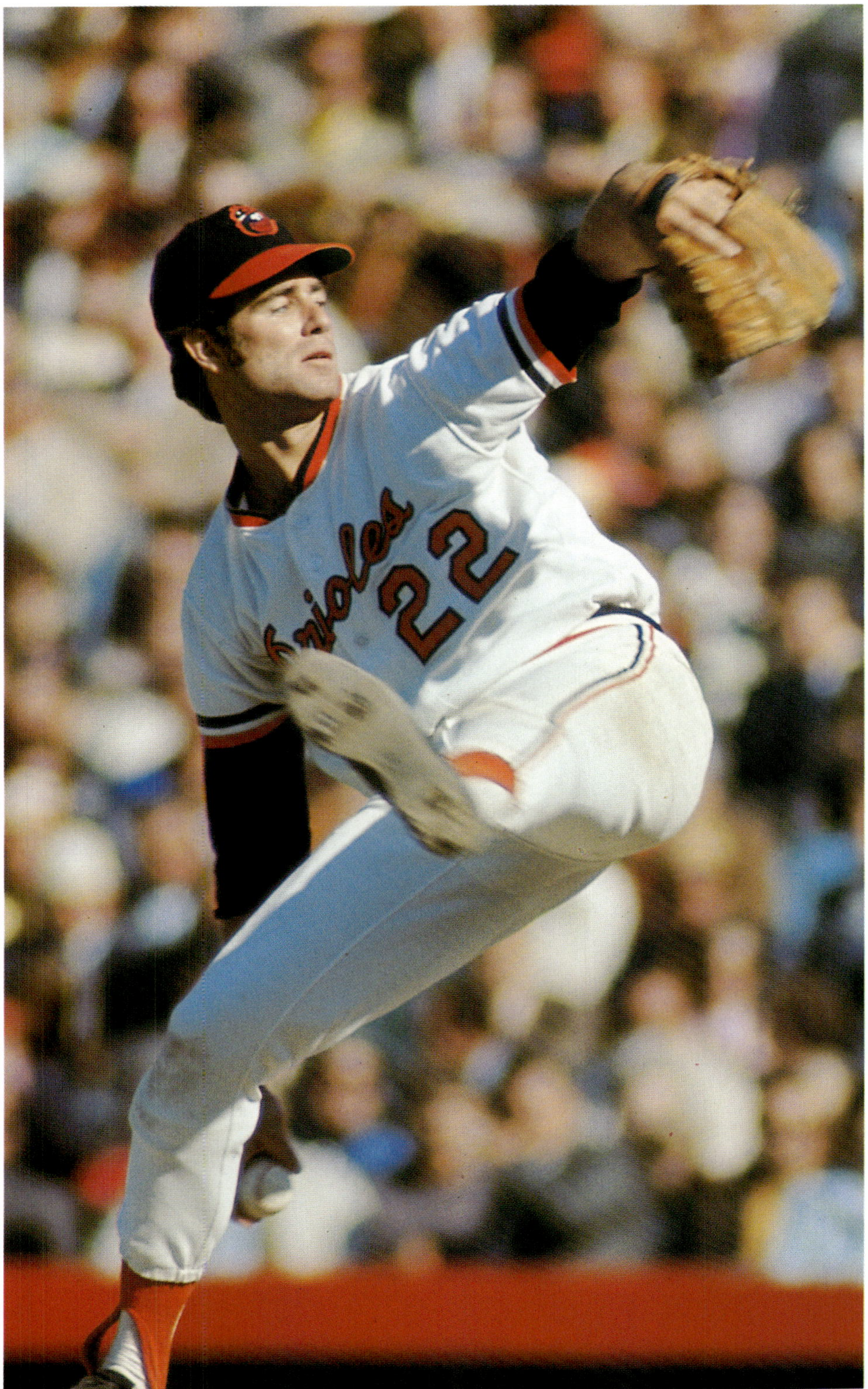
22

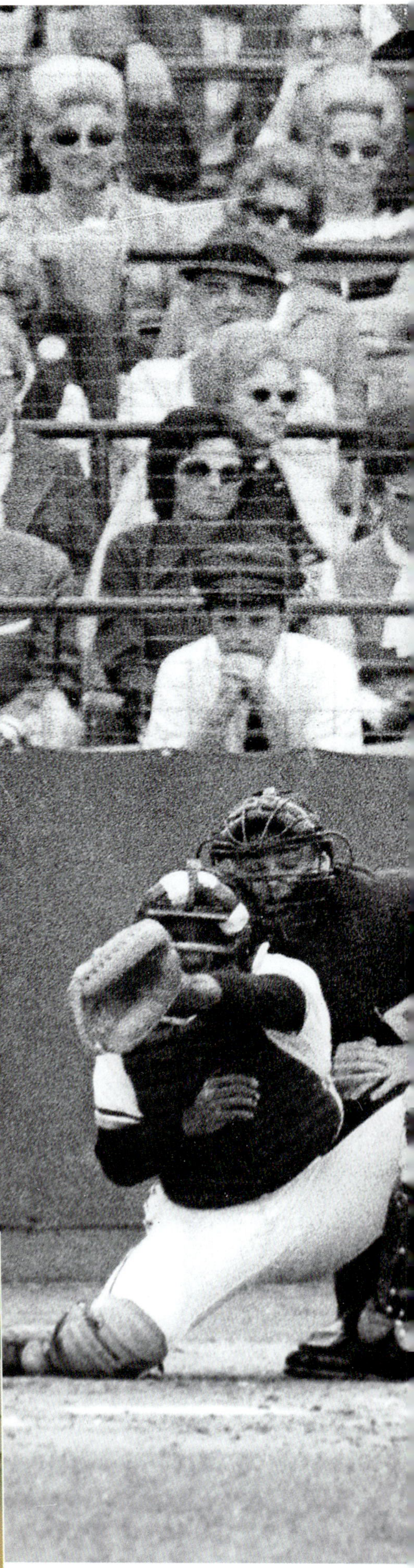

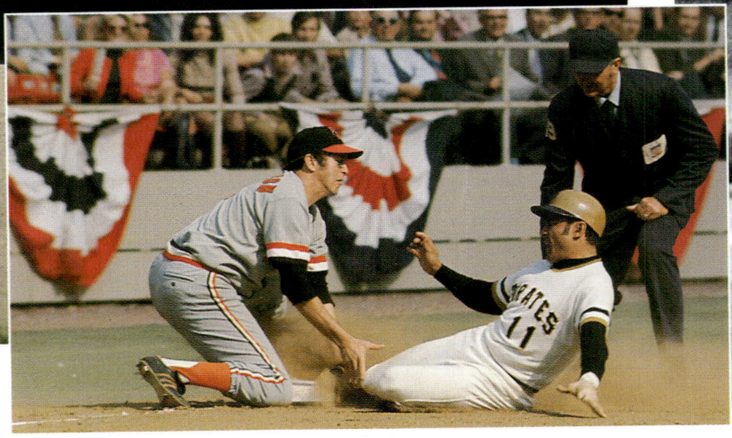
11

Take Me Out to the Ballgame

There cannot have been many World Series that left more indelible images in our memories than did the 1971 Fall Classic. Jim Palmer of Baltimore (**OPPOSITE FAR LEFT**), kicking his leg high and delivering another aspirin tablet plateward. The O's incomparable Brooks Robinson (**OPPOSITE BOTTOM LEFT**) sprawled in the dirt at third base as he redefined the meaning of fielding excellence. Puerto Rico's batting wizard, Roberto Clemente of Pittsburgh (**LEFT**), lunging at another fastball and slashing base hits to all fields. Never has a single batter so dominated a Series with his lumber than did Bob Clemente in 1971, driving out 12 base hits, socking two home runs, scoring three vital runs, driving home four more and batting at a stratospheric .414 clip across seven games. And never has a fielder been more spectacular than Brooks Robinson, continuing the sparkling defensive work that had earned him the label "Hoover" in the 1970 Series with Cincinnati. Along with his sparkling performance in the field, Robbie would also tie a Series record in Game Two by reaching base in five consecutive at-bats, on two walks and three hits. Fresh off the second of four consecutive 20-win seasons, future Hall-of-Famer Jim Palmer also flashed his customary wizardry with a Game Two victory and a nine-inning masterwork in Game Six (before leaving with the score still tied). Palmer's frustration in the 1971 Series – which saw him hurl brilliantly for 17 innings and yet win only once – reflected that of his entire Baltimore team, surprise seven-game victims of an inspired Pittsburgh ballclub that would win its fourth seven-game World Series in only as many tries.

278　THE BASEBALL SCRAPBOOK

If each World Series stands in our collective memory as a collage of images - Sandy Amoros spearing Yogi Berra's line drive in 1955, Berra leaping into Don Larsen's waiting arms in 1956, Clemente spraying hits across the diamond in 1971 – then most of the images of the 1975 Series are of Carlton Fisk. And seldom have two photographs better captured the ebb and flow of an unpredictable Series than those shown here. In the tenth frame of Game Three it was Fisk who collided with Cincinnati batter Ed Armbrister while pursuing a bunt in front of home plate (**RIGHT**), then threw wildly to second trying to gun down Reds runner Cesar Geronimo; when the umpire ruled that no interference had occurred, Armbrister wound up on second and Geronimo on third. Seconds later Geronimo would score the game-winning run, and Cincinnati would take the early Series lead. Yet Fisk was not quite through with the spotlight, and in Game Six the popular catcher enshrined his name forever in Sox history with a 12th-inning, game-winning blast of his own, one which many consider the most dramatic home run in World Series history. Fisk's twisting and leaping gyrations as he pranced down the first base line, urging the ball far (**ABOVE**), were captured for millions by the magic of television, and this scene alone etched the term "reaction shot" forever into the working vocabulary of television sports production.

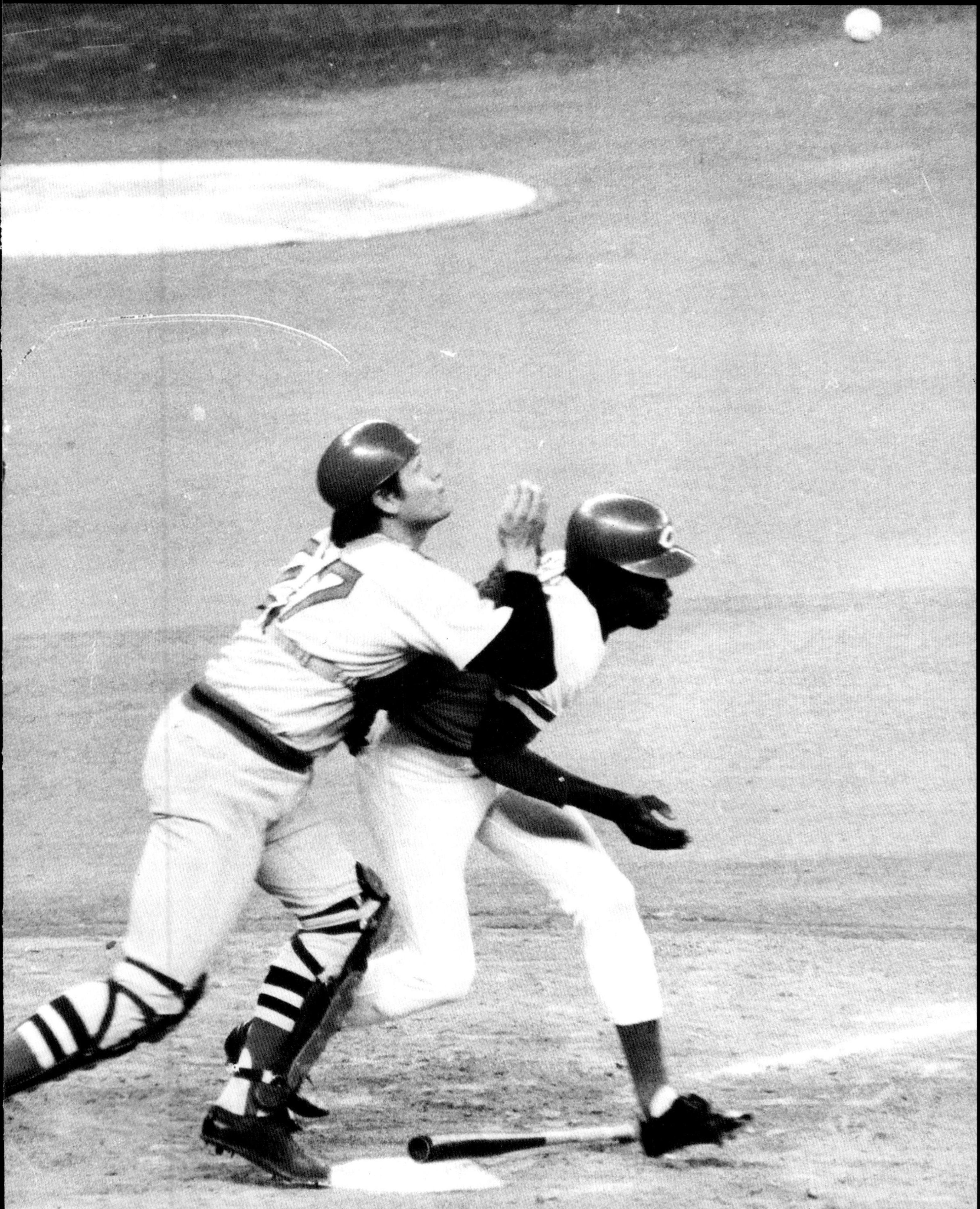

BREAK OUT THE CHAMPAGNE, BOYS!

The taste of victory is as sweet on the diamond as it is in all other walks of life, and for ballplayers, club owners and fans alike victory celebrations are as stylized as any other aspect of our most traditional game.

Take Me Out to the Ballgame 283

Fans rushing the field in explosive hordes to celebrate a pennant victory with destructive abandon (**OPPOSITE**) and prankish ballplayers dowsing staid club owners with freshly uncorked champagne (**BOTTOM RIGHT**) – these are now familiar scenes at seasons end in a baseball era made for television. Yet victory celebrations have a lengthy history and have always been wonderfully colorful. No ballplayer, for example, had a more uniquely personal brand of victory dance than did Chicago Cubs' third baseman Ron Santo (**BOTTOM LEFT**), who performed his post-game heel-kicking "jump for joy" after each Cubbies' victory in the late 1960s. And in Brooklyn, where pennant victories became a norm in the decade following World War II, the fine art of celebration reached new inventive heights. For 20 years between their pennant runs of 1920 and 1941 the Flatbush partisans had little indeed to cheer about. There were tens of thousands of serious-minded and sober folks in New York City between the two great wars who no doubt feared a Dodger pennant victory, realizing that the reaction of the frenetic Brooklyn fans would likely be like nothing ever seen before. How right they were is evident in this joyous scene (**TOP RIGHT**) in a bar on Withers Street, where Brooklyn faithful have gathered to toast their first of three pennants in the 1940s.

284 THE BASEBALL SCRAPBOOK

A few more memorable scenes of unrestrained joy, as ballplayers take to the field, and fans to the streets, to release pent-up emotions after a long and successful pennant-race summer.

(**TOP LEFT**) The conquerors seem to have taken a cue from their victims in this 1960 scene, as Pittsburghers stage their own version of the famed New York ticker-tape parade. An early autumn blizzard of paper cascades on downtown Pittsburgh streets as Bucs fans celebrate the surprise 1960 World Series triumph over the American League New York Yankees, the city's first title flag in 35 seasons.

(**LEFT CENTER**) The real thing, New York style, is seen here as Manhattan turns out in force to greet its conquering heroes. The usually strife-ridden New York Yankees are paraded through the nation's baseball capital on the heels of their second consecutive six-game World Series triumph over the Los Angeles Dodgers in October 1978. The men of George Steinbrenner seem to be loving every minute of the adulation, waving back, blowing kisses and wagging their fingers to proclaim "We're Number One!" Mayor Ed Koch and Governor Hugh Carey proclaimed it "New York Yankees Day" and presented their heroes with the traditional keys to the City of New York.

(**BOTTOM LEFT**) Before the staged public celebrations with fans come the private and spontaneous celebrations with teammates. Here Red Sox players storm the field on September 29, 1986 to whoop it up at the conclusion of a 12-3 Fenway Park division-clinching victory over Toronto's Blue Jays.

(**OPPOSITE**) Two of the sport's memorable moments of unrestrained joy followed the World Series game-winning home run blasts of Kirk Gibson and Joe Carter. Gibson's 1988 clout (**TOP**) in a pinch hit role launched the Dodgers' charge to a world title versus Oakland. Joe Carter (**CENTER** and **BOTTOM**) became only the second player in history to end a Series on a dramatic homer when his 1993 ninth-inning smash at SkyDome against the Phillies clinched a second straight title for Toronto's Blue Jays. Both homers set off on-field celebrations burned forever into public record by the magic of the television camera. And one 1990 poll of sportscasters tabbed Kirk Gibson's roundtripper as one of the most dramatic moments in all of sports history.

Take Me Out to the Ballgame 285

They started out as one of baseball's great dynasties and ended as one of its most infamous legends. The 1919 Chicago White Sox (**TOP LEFT**), a dominant team under manager Kid Gleason (**BOTTOM LEFT**), had cruised to a second American League flag in three seasons and seemed an odds-on favorite in the upcoming Fall Classic. An illiterate product of a cotton-mill town and unsophisticated in city ways, Shoeless Joe Jackson (**BELOW**) was nonetheless a hitter Ty Cobb called the best he had ever seen. Yet when his limitations outstripped his gifts, Jackson became a symbol of tragedy both in baseball and in American life.

SAY IT AIN'T SO

"Say it ain't so, Joe!" was the melancholy plea of the young fan who greeted Joe Jackson on the steps of a Chicago courtroom in 1920. The story – like all of baseball's best tales – is certainly apocryphal.

Indicted for throwing the 1919 World Series in return for payoffs from gamblers, the eight 'Black Sox' were cleared of wrong-doing by a Chicago grand jury (**LEFT**) yet were nevertheless banned from the sport for life by newly appointed Commissioner Kenesaw Mountain Landis (seated at far left). Only a handful of the accused had apparently received any payment, and Joe Jackson had hit .375 in the Series to lead both teams. Heavily penalized also was slick-fielding third sacker Buck Weaver (**BELOW**, in 1919 Series action), who was at his best in the 1919 Series, with 11 hits, a .324 BA and flawless infield play. Weaver's crime was that he knew of his teammates' shady dealings and never breathed a word. For his stoic silence Weaver paid the price of a lifetime ban and the loss of Cooperstown immortality almost as sure as Jackson's.

THEY CALL THIS STUFF BASEBALL?

For five decades the baseball map was as changeless as the taste of ballpark franks. Then suddenly the Dodgers were gone from Brooklyn and overnight you could hardly tell where the teams were without an Atlas.

Take Me Out to the Ballgame 289

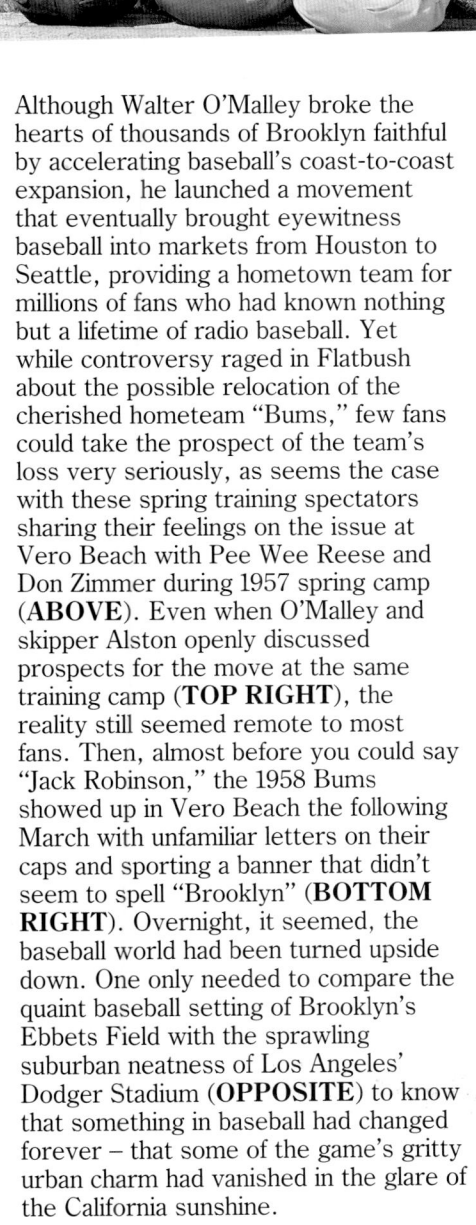

Although Walter O'Malley broke the hearts of thousands of Brooklyn faithful by accelerating baseball's coast-to-coast expansion, he launched a movement that eventually brought eyewitness baseball into markets from Houston to Seattle, providing a hometown team for millions of fans who had known nothing but a lifetime of radio baseball. Yet while controversy raged in Flatbush about the possible relocation of the cherished hometeam "Bums," few fans could take the prospect of the team's loss very seriously, as seems the case with these spring training spectators sharing their feelings on the issue at Vero Beach with Pee Wee Reese and Don Zimmer during 1957 spring camp (**ABOVE**). Even when O'Malley and skipper Alston openly discussed prospects for the move at the same training camp (**TOP RIGHT**), the reality still seemed remote to most fans. Then, almost before you could say "Jack Robinson," the 1958 Bums showed up in Vero Beach the following March with unfamiliar letters on their caps and sporting a banner that didn't seem to spell "Brooklyn" (**BOTTOM RIGHT**). Overnight, it seemed, the baseball world had been turned upside down. One only needed to compare the quaint baseball setting of Brooklyn's Ebbets Field with the sprawling suburban neatness of Los Angeles' Dodger Stadium (**OPPOSITE**) to know that something in baseball had changed forever – that some of the game's gritty urban charm had vanished in the glare of the California sunshine.

290 THE BASEBALL SCRAPBOOK

Take Me Out to the Ballgame

Between 1903 (date of the first World Series play between the fledgling American League and its more venerable National League rival) and 1953 (the year the Braves changed their address from Beantown to Beertown), there were exactly two leagues, 16 teams and only an occasional change in uniform design or the replacement of a crumbling wooden ballpark with a new steel-and-concrete structure to convince the nation's hardball fans that anything in the baseball world ever varied. Once O'Malley took the Dodgers west, however, with Horace Stoneham and the Giants dragged along in tow for good measure, it was as though the landscape of baseball transformed. Soon fans in San Francisco were cheering for a team called "Giants" (but hardly resembling Polo Grounders), as well as for one called "49ers" (**OPPOSITE TOP**). And not too far down the road a team with a space-age name and space-age uniforms was circling the bases indoors, under a protective bubble, in as remote a baseball outpost as Houston (**OPPOSITE BOTTOM**). By the time these storms of change had finally subsided baseball was well into an age of expansion that would see the American League with two more teams than its counterpart, with ballclubs strutting their stuff in Canada and in multipurpose stadia (like the Toronto Skydome, **LEFT**) which seemed more like self-contained space stations than the familiar notion of a ballpark. One wonder of this expansion saga has been a team called the Seattle Mariners (**ABOVE**, represented here by hard-throwing Mark Langston, the only legitimate superstar in the team's decade and a half of life), which has now completed 14 seasons of history without a single winning campaign. At least the St. Louis Browns had the Murderer's Row Yankees, one-armed Pete Gray and the misadventures of Bill Veeck for an excuse.

292 THE BASEBALL SCRAPBOOK

Of course expansion-era baseball has had its memorable moments and glorious, even legendary, teams; it also has built some breath-taking ballparks. Talk about unique in a modern-age stadium and "The Big A" comes foremost to mind (**BELOW**). Home of the California Angels since its opening in 1966, Anaheim Stadium drew its famous sobriquet from the massive left field scoreboard supported by a 230-foot-high Angels logo, a letter "A" topped by a halo. But that rare piece of ballpark uniqueness was soon transformed into a parking lot once double-decked outfield grandstand seating was added in 1980 – for the purpose of accommodating an NFL franchise, of course. Not to be outdone by Houston or Canadian rival Toronto, the proud city of Montreal boasts its own entrant in the field of space-station ballparks (**RIGHT**), the new retractable-roofed Olympic Stadium, a venue where one can sit more than a hundred feet from home plate and yet still occupy a prime first baseline box seat! An overflow crowd of 57,592 (rarely duplicated or even approximated in baseball's French-speaking capital since) is seen here in Montreal for the inaugural game of the new Olympic Stadium on April 15, 1977. (**OPPOSITE TOP**). An old Milwaukee hero, former Braves catcher Del Crandall, greets a new Milwaukee ballclub after taking over as Brewers manager in May 1972. In two decades' time Milwaukee loved and lost one expansion franchise, then gleefully greeted another. Of all baseball's expansion sagas, however, none provides more fairy-tale plot lines than that of the New York s Mets. In but eight summers this charming collection of no-names, hoary veterans, and implacable stumblebums rose from the worst doormat outfit ever to the "Amazin' Mets" World Champions of 1969. Hollywood scriptwriters could hardly have done a better job than the geniuses who put together this first Polo Ground outfit in 1962 (**OPPOSITE BOTTOM**).

Take Me Out to the Ballgame 293

BLACK LEAGUES

We usually talk about baseball history in terms of the two major leagues, but of course there were four major leagues – two white and two black. While one America cheered on Babe Ruth and Lou Gehrig, another marveled at the home run feats of Josh Gibson. For every Tris Speaker there was an Oscar Charleston, for every Pie Traynor there was a Judy Johnson, and Walter Johnson and Lefty Grove had their match in Smokey Joe Williams and Bullet Joe Rogan.

Take Me Out to the Ballgame   295

Today we take the presence of black players on major league teams for granted. Yet for decades they had to work their ballpark magic in a tenebrous world all but unknown to white men. Fun-loving Josh Gibson (**OPPOSITE LEFT**) was a robust catcher whom many historians now consider the greatest Negro League player of all-time, and perhaps the best hitter of his era (1930-1946) in any of the four major leagues. It is Josh Gibson who is now credited by *The Sporting News* with hitting the longest homer ever seen in Yankee Stadium, a ball traveling 580 feet from home plate. William "Judy" Johnson (**OPPOSITE TOP RIGHT**) was a premier third sacker of black league play in the 1920s and 1930s whom Connie Mack once told: "If you were a white boy you could name your own price." John Henry "Pop" Lloyd (**OPPOSITE BOTTOM RIGHT**) was a baseball nomad who performed spectacularly enough at shortstop for at least a dozen teams in his 26-year career to be widely promoted as "The Black Wagner." Leroy "Satchel" Paige (**LEFT**) flashed only a shadow of his former blackball greatness once he finally arrived as a 42-year-old big league rookie in 1948. And James "Cool Papa" Bell (**BELOW**) blazed the bases with such speed that only one thing kept him from burying Ty Cobb's baserunning legend; he simply couldn't run through the iron doors that excluded his race from big league play.

With the historic signing of Jackie Robinson in 1946 (**LEFT**), Branch Rickey blazed a bold and unpopular path by bringing black ballplayers back into the major leagues for the first time in over half a century. It was to be Rickey's Dodgers who also continued to lead the integration movement – to the dismay of several other club owners, as well as to the obvious on-field good of the Dodger ballclub itself. Robinson was soon joined by Roy Campanella and Don Newcombe (**OPPOSITE BOTTOM**), and by 1952 Rookie-of-the-Year hurler Joe Black (**BOTTOM RIGHT**). It was this contingent of black stars as much as anything else that soon propelled the Brooklyn club into its position as the premier National League power of the decade between 1947 and 1957. Campanella probably did as much for the acceptance of blacks with his soft-spoken style and workhorse efficiency at the catcher's position as Robinson had done with his flamboyant baserunning and combative spirit.

JACK BE NIMBLE

While superstars like Josh Gibson, Pop Lloyd and Oscar Charleston were destined by fate and the inhumanity of the times to work far from the big league limelight, a handful of post-World War II stars who inherited their legacy suddenly found themselves the subjects of Branch Rickey's "noble experiment."

Take Me Out to the Ballgame 297

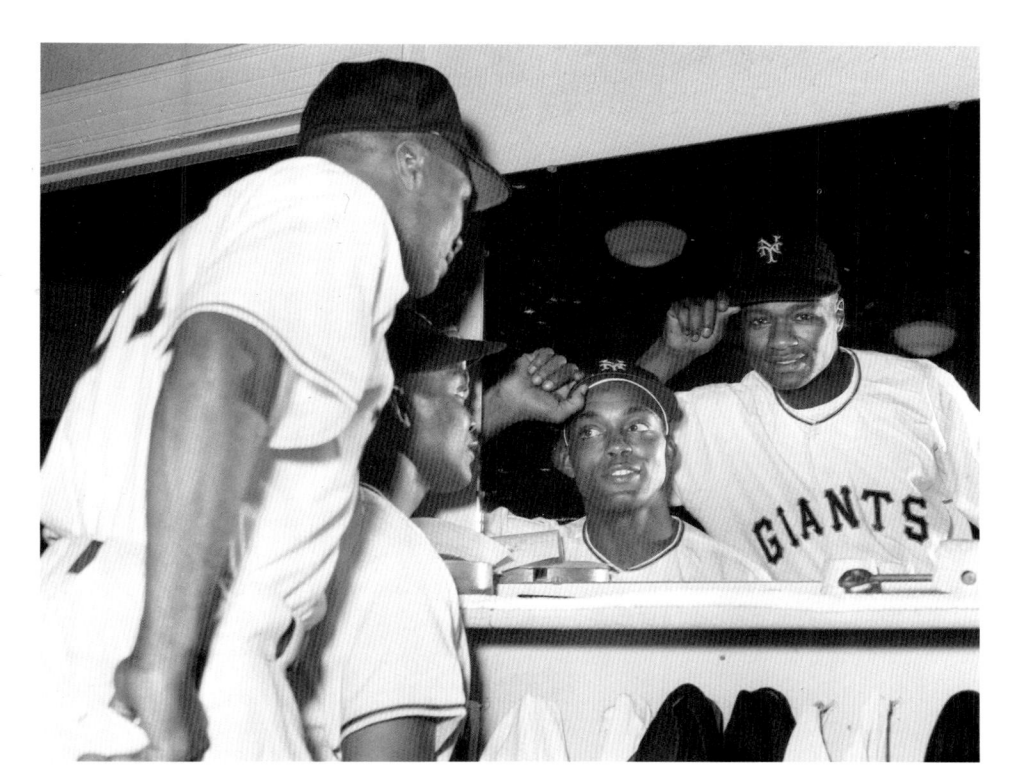

While the new influx of black players keyed the success of Rickey's teams in Brooklyn, they had almost equal impact in another quarter of New York, the Polo Grounds. There the first Giants black stars were Monte Irvin and Hank Thompson (**LEFT** before their debut game in 1949), and they were soon followed by the incomparable Willie Mays. While the Dodgers and the Giants owed much of their successes in the 1950s to their willingness to throw down the inexcusable racial barrier, another franchise rich in history may well have had to attribute its lackluster showings to a failure to do the same. Boston owner Tom Yawkey would have nothing of the trend, once turning down the chance to sign both Willie Mays and Hank Aaron after those two sterling black prospects were given token tryouts by the Beantowners. Boston finally became the last big league club to integrate by promoting journeyman infielder Pumpsie Green (**OPPOSITE BOTTOM LEFT**) in July 1959.

BASEBALL GOES TO WAR

War can affect baseball in strange ways. Sometimes old-timers and one-season wonders have to man the leagues while other players, in different uniforms, go forth to play an infinitely more lethal game on distant fields.

While the continuation of big-league play in the nation's ballparks during America's wars may have buoyed the nation's spirits on the homefront, many illustrious diamond stars fought those wars in earnest far from the dugouts and dressing rooms of Fenway Park and Ebbets Field. Red Sox star Ted Williams, posing alongside his Panther jet in Korea during a second tour of combat duty in 1953 (**OPPOSITE**) hardly seems to resent the several lost diamond seasons which robbed him of even more batting records (he most assuredly would have hit 600 homers) than those he now possesses. Yankee shortstop whiz and 1941 World Series hero Phil Rizzuto strikes an equally proud and cheerful pose (**LEFT**) during 1942 training at Norfolk Naval Training Station, as does Tigers slugger Hank Greenberg (**BELOW**), while he demonstrates his famed batting stance to the boys of the Army Air Force Pursuit Squadron at Bolling Field in Washington, DC, in another 1942 wartime publicity shot. One of the first major leaguers inducted into military service in 1941, Greenburg was discharged from the army after a first duty tour in December 1941. He volunteered for re-enlistment as an officer candidate immediately upon hearing the news of Pearl Harbor.

HEADLINE HOGGERS

P.T. Barnum never owned a ballclub, but Bill Veeck and Charlie Finley did, and the result was flamboyant reminders that there are more ways than winning games to bring fans into the ballpark.

No one holds a candle – or should it be a magic wand – to Bill Veeck when it comes to the title of baseball's most outrageous and inventive promoter. In Cleveland he pioneered Ladies' Day and handed out free nylons to women entering the park. In Chicago, two decades later, he unveiled an exploding scoreboard. But the stunt for which Veeck will always be remembered best was the surprise insertion into the Brown's lineup of 3'7" 65-pound midget Eddie Gaedel before a house of 18,369 in Sportsman's Park on August 18, 1951. Sporting number 1/8 on his uniform back and wearing slippers turned up at the end like elf's shoes, Gaedel strode to the plate and (after St. Louis manager Zack Taylor presented a valid contract to umpire Ed Hurley) took four straight balls from unglued Detroit pitcher Bob Cain (**TOP RIGHT**). Despite Gaedel's "instant offense," the Browns succumbed that day 6-2, and a furious AL President Will Harridge wasted no time striking Gaedel's name from the record books and from the St. Louis roster. Yet never before or since did a less talented and less likely "major leaguer" ever so entertain a big league crowd. Harridge may have gotten rid of Gaedel, but that didn't stop the ingenious Veeck, who later that same month demonstrated that he had more tricks up his sleeve to promote his lackluster ballclub. Charles Hughes (**left**) and Clark Mitze (**right**), both attired in Browns uniforms, were two fans selected from the grandstand on August 31, 1951 to take over manager Zack Taylor's duties for the night (**OPPOSITE TOP LEFT**). The remainder of the fans in attendance were assigned to help the amateur skippers run the ballclub by voting "yes" or "no" (**OPPOSITE**) to strategy choices held aloft by Circuit Court Judge James E. McLaughlin. It was the judge's august duty to determine the fans' preference and relay the popular choice to acting managers Hughes and Mitze. To everyone's amazement, the Browns registered one of their season's 52 victories that night, not exactly a confidence builder for manager Zack Taylor or the visiting Washington Senators. What Bill Veeck pioneered in the big leagues, other club owners had long practiced in the more promotion-minded minor leagues. A case in point is the short-pants uniforms unveiled by the Pacific Coast League Hollywood Stars during the 1950 season (**BOTTOM RIGHT**), a sure drawing card in fashion-minded Tinsel Town.

302 THE BASEBALL SCRAPBOOK

And now, ladies and gentlemen, its time for an encore! Performing in the second ring – located behind first base – is the marvelous feathered Fredbird, four Martian midgets and the incomparable St. Louis Browns Blues Band. You say you want more? Stick around, then, for the old ballgame!

(**TOP LEFT**) St. Louis Cardinals' mascot "Fredbird" does a little dance for San Diego coach Bobby Tolan and ballpark fans between innings of a June 1981 game in St. Louis. Tolan attempted to ignore the Busch Stadium fixture, but Fredbird finally managed (here) to get Tolan's attention. Or was the feathered mascot simply inquiring about the whereabouts of the San Diego Chicken?

(**BOTTOM LEFT**) Just to prove that he was still around and kicking, and that anything worth doing once was likely worth doing twice, Bill Veeck pulled out his midget routine one more time in Chicago's Comiskey Park on June 1, 1959. This time the inventive owner – now signing paychecks for the Chicago White Sox – staged a pre-game raid by "little men" from outer space, arriving (to the crowd's delight) by helicopter to visit their compatriots, equally tiny White Sox keystone partners Luis Aparicio and Nellie Fox.

(**OPPOSITE TOP**) Veeck was at it once again in his favorite arena for high jinks – Sportsman's Park, St. Louis – when he had several Browns perform a passable between-games imitation of a St. Louis jazz band. Performing here are (l to r) Coach Ed Redys, Satchel Paige, Johnny Berardino and Al Widmar. Just let some wiseguy say that as ballplayers the Brownies make better musicians!

(**OPPOSITE BOTTOM**) Hardly a match for today's fuzzy giant mascots – those plastic and cloth behemoths cut in the mold of the Phillie Phanatic or San Diego Chicken – the New York Giants secret weapon, "Queenie," attentively guards bats and players' equipment during 1950 spring training drills at the Polo Grounders' camp in Phoenix, Arizona.

Take Me Out to the Ballgame   303

FLAKY FAVORITES

Phil Linz, Bill Lee, Jackie Brandt, Doug Rader, Pepper Martin, Ross Grimsley, Jim Piersall and the archduke of mayhem, Lefty Gomez. Not a crew fit for Cooperstown, perhaps, but one ripe for a lengthy lunar expedition.

He's been around since the first covered grandstand and ballpark beer vendors; he's been an integral part of the game at least as long as fungo bat, bleacher bums and the first spring training trips into the sunshine belt. He's the "baseball flake," that wacky eccentric whose antics are as unpredictable as a Carl Hubbell screwball and as lovable as a Sunday doubleheader. The term was reputedly first used on the diamond in the 1950s with specific reference to Giants outfielder Jackie Brandt, but the breed is a good deal older than that. They were "daffiness boys" in the days of the Gashouse Gang St. Louis Cardinals, and that rare bunch of manager Frankie Frisch's clowns became role models for all aspiring to the art of diamond mayhem. No two ballplayers ever packed more tomfoolery or shenanigans into shorter careers than did Gashouse charter members Dizzy Dean and Pepper Martin (**OPPOSITE TOP LEFT**), with Martin here providing Dean with a "close shave" at the Cardinals' 1933 spring training camp in Bradenton, Florida. Dean was an outrageous self-promoter who often delighted in "blowing his own horn" and did so literally in more than one on-field prank while wearing a Cardinals uniform (**OPPOSITE**). Even such staid teams of the Gashouse era as the Ruth-led Yanks had their occasional clown prince of comedy – in this case "El Goofo" Vernon "Lefty" Gomez, a pitcher of Hall-of-Fame credentials.(**TOP LEFT**). "Goofy" here feigns erudition at the Braves' wartime Choate School spring camp in Wallingford, Connecticut, near the end of his illustrious career. When it comes to modern-era ballplayers, try topping Jimmy Piersall (**BOTTOM LEFT**). No, fans, you're not looking in a mirror here, and the editor didn't print the negative backwards. That's just crazy Jimmy circling the basepaths backwards on the occasion of smacking his 100th career major league dinger. The year is 1963, and (you guessed it!) that's a Mets uniform that the intrepid Piersall is wearing for the occasion.

ORIGINALS

Unlike their football and basketball counterparts, baseball players don't conform to any particular physical type. Indeed, some have had physiques that were extraordinary by any standards.

Some otherwise totally undistinguished ballplayers remain memorable for some oddity in their appearance or some unique physical trait that served to set them apart. Don Mossi of the Tigers and Indians, for instance, had ears so large that, as one wag has noted, they seemed to have been borrowed from a much larger species and then surgically attached without the proper procedures or supervision. If nothing else, Mossi has earned the starting lefthander's spot on the all-time ugly team. Carmen Hill of the World War I Pirates – the first man to wear glasses in the major leagues in 1915 – had the term "bespectacled" attached so frequently to his name that you would have thought it was found on his birth certificate. Garland Buckeye was a 260-pound southpaw laboring for the Cleveland Indians in the 1920s who would be remembered for absolutely nothing at all if he weighed about 80 pounds less; as it is, Buckeye (who simultaneously played pro football, almost a full three quarters of a century before Bo Jackson) remains illustrious only as baseball's fattest pitcher, with the appropriate nickname of "Gob." No baseball fan fails to recognize the name Pete Gray (**OPPOSITE**). How could you play 77 big league games, collect 51 hits, bat .218, never hit a big league homer and yet still be remembered a half-century later? By having only one arm! Gray (whose real name was Pete Wyshner and who was apparently highly unpopular with teammates who blamed him for the 1945 failure to repeat as league champs) is today no longer baseball's only one-armed player, since southpaw hurler Jim Abbott has burst on the scene as a pitcher of sufficient skill to obliterate his handicap. Abbott (technically missing a hand and not a complete arm) would achieve every pitcher's dream in late 1993 by hurling a no-hit game for the Yankees against Cleveland (**BOTTOM RIGHT**, being congratulated by teammates Matt Nokes and Wade Boggs). While we're at it, who is baseball's tallest pitcher? No-hit ace Randy Johnson of the Seattle Mariners at 6'10" (**OPPOSITE INSET**). The shortest moundsman? Five-foot six-inch Bobby Shantz (**TOP RIGHT**), who once won 24 games in a single season for Jimmy Dykes' Athletics. A couple of pretty fair hurlers who will likely both be remembered for things more substantial than their suit sizes.

INTERNATIONAL BASEBALL

A tired myth that baseball is exclusively America's national pastime has finally been put to rest. Not only are big league rosters today bursting with Latin and Asian imports, but baseball enjoys numerous homes outside North American borders—where fans are equally impassioned and games are equally enthralling.

Take Me Out to the Ball Game 309

The national pastime is alive and well today in many parts of the world as a new baseball century dawns, and that national pastime is the one claimed as *besuburo* by the Japanese, *pelota* by the Cubans, and *béisbol* by the Dominicans, Venezuelans, and other Caribbean baseball epicenters. Baseball has thrived in these distant outposts for most of the past century—before their infamous 1959 revolution the Cubans boasted a professional league which traced its roots back to 1878, a mere two years after the founding of the august National League; Japan's professional circuit has thrilled millions since before World War II; and Winter League play has provided an alternative baseball universe for decades in Mexico, Puerto Rico, Venezuela, and the Dominican Republic. Even the Russians have gotten into the act and the University of Moscow already boasted its own "nine" before the collapse of the former Soviet Union (**OPPOSITE BOTTOM**). Each distant baseball outpost has fostered its own legendary heroes, such as all-time home run king Sadaharu Oh (**TOP RIGHT**) and Russian-born mound ace Victor Starffin (**TOP LEFT**) of Japan. Major league baseball today relies heavily on Caribbean and Japanese talent to round out big league rosters, and has also begun seizing upon new markets for televised big league action among fanatical fans in Japan, Mexico, Puerto Rico, Venezuela, and other Caribbean outposts. Regular-season big league contests have been staged in Tokyo (Mets vs. Cubs in 2000) and in Monterrey (Padres vs. Mets in 1998). Spring training match-ups have of late occurred in Mexico (**OPPOSITE TOP**), Puerto Rico, and Venezuela (where the Devil Rays met the Braves in March 2000 (**BOTTOM**). During the 2003 season MLB launched its boldest international experiment to date when the beleaguered Montreal Expos booked a significant portion of their home schedule for Hiram Bithorn Stadium in San Juan, Puerto Rico. Of course such international connections are not entirely new, with spring training visits to Havana having been a regular staple of the 1940s and 1950s, before Cuba's communist takeover. Havana once even boasted minor league teams, with the Class A International League Sugar Kings of the late 1950s and the Class B Florida International League Havana Cubans of the 1940s (**MIDDLE**). And organized professional baseball U.S.-style does not hold an exclusive franchise on international diamond play. Amateur world championships (either annual or spaced several years apart) have matched Caribbean, European, Asian, and U.S. national teams in heated competitions since the early forties, while Olympic play has flowered after 1992, and such popular competitions have long been dominated by the powerhouse national teams representing Fidel Castro's Communist Cuba.

DÉTENTE

Highly publicized showdown matches between the big league Orioles and Cuban National Team in Havana and Baltimore broke the ice of 40 years of baseball "cold war" between the neighboring ballplaying nations and demonstrated in the end that Castro's Cuba is still a rich source of untapped diamond talent.

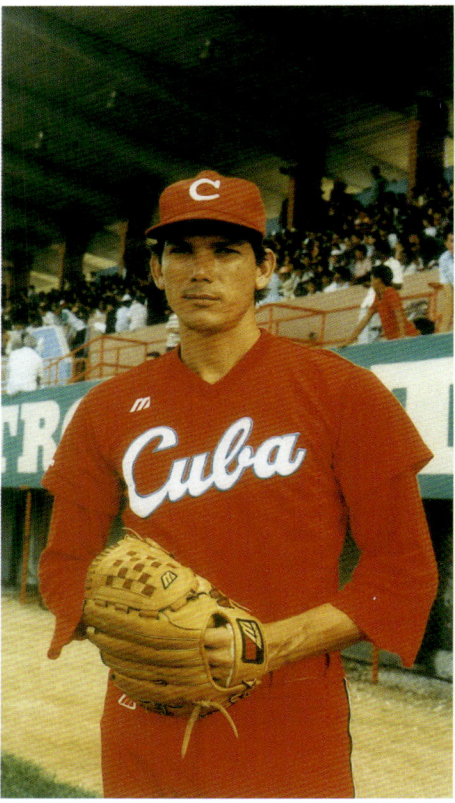

Take Me Out to the Ballgame 311

It was a special moment and one to be savored by all fans who hanker for a more innocent version of North America's national pastime. DH Andy Morales had just blasted a titanic homer into the center field bleachers at Camden Yards, thus capping a game-clinching five-run ninth-inning outburst against the Orioles' touted big-league pitching by the underdog Cuban national team. With unrestrained joy at his accomplishment the Cuban slugger next provided a scene that remains the single lasting image of a highly publicized Cuba–Orioles showdown: Morales tiptoed over three bases with his arms lifted toward the heavens, hugged the sky as he rounded second, and gleefully jumped atop home plate as he finally reached a mob of his waiting teammates (**OPPOSITE BOTTOM LEFT**). Orioles veteran B.J. Surhoff later expressed typical big league sourness when he quipped in a post-game interview that "no one appreciates the guy running around like an idiot!" For big leaguers, Morales's display of spontaneous joy was sadly out of place. Morales's timely circuit blast not only added an exclamation point to Cuba's resounding 12–6 drubbing of the Orioles in Baltimore, but also capsulized the stark difference in flavor between international amateur baseball and the troubled big-league professional version of the game. While Cuban ballplayers danced in the dugout and around home plate after both Danel Castro's rally-inspiring triple in the second frame and Morales's power blast in the ninth, Baltimore's nine sleepwalked through the contest with little enthusiasm. With the lackluster big leaguers there was no evidence of playing for national pride, no displays of competitive sporting spirit, no battling for personal honor or even any apparent appreciation of the pure joys of top-flight ballplaying. Thus the contrast couldn't have been any more obvious or any more compelling between the two opposing baseball systems. Current Cuban stars are most visible in the U.S. because of big-league defectors like Rolando Arroyo (**OPPOSITE TOP RIGHT**), but back home heroes Omar Linares (**OPPOSITE TOP LEFT** with Cal Ripkin, Jr., and **LOWER RIGHT**) and .400-hitter Yobal Dueñas (**TOP**) remain hidden baseball treasures. And if Fidel Castro (**CENTER** and **BOTTOM**) was never a true big-league pitching prospect as time-worn myth still has it, he was nonetheless a star attraction when the Orioles and Cubans kicked off their exhibition series in Havana.

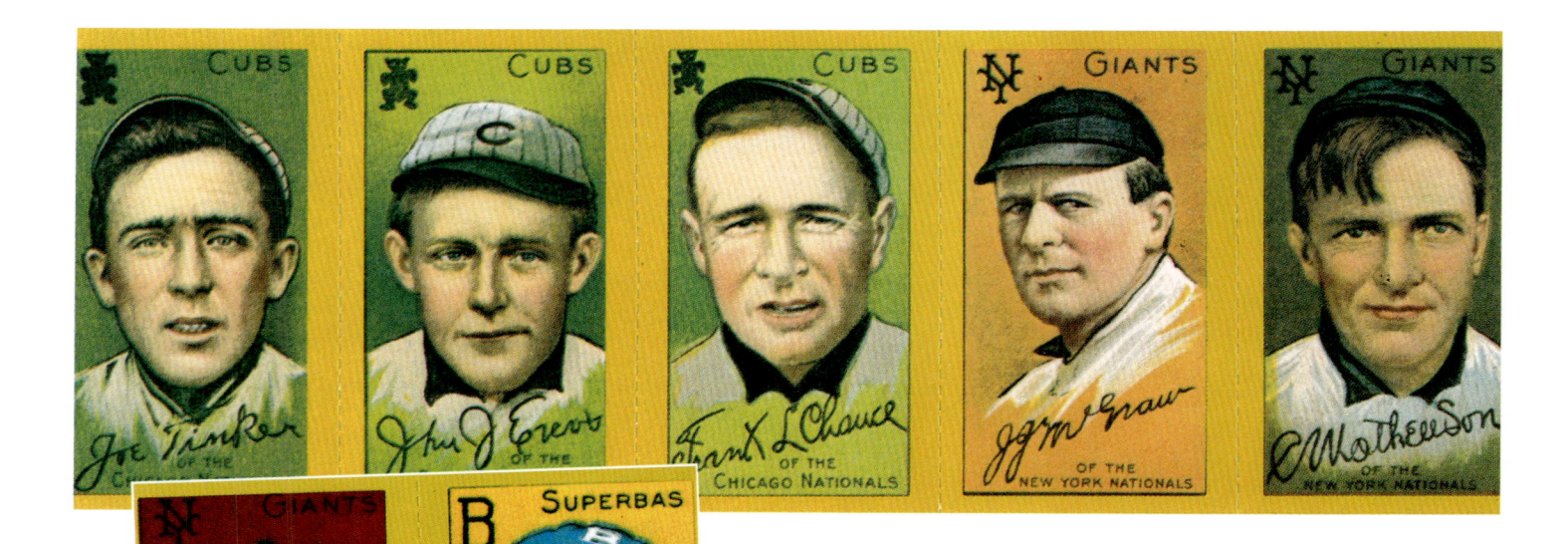

I GOT A REGGIE!

A multi-million-dollar business in collectibles forms the cornerstone of today's baseball popular culture movement; indeed, bubble gum cards are now as much an adult passion as a childhood diversion.

Take Me Out to the Ballgame

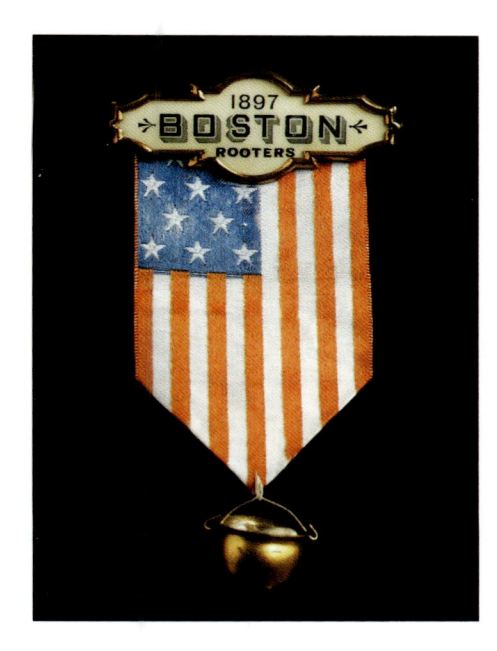

Like the national pastime itself, the hobby of baseball collectibles has its roots in the nineteenth century. By the late 1880s tobacco companies had seized upon the promotional value of this popular new game, using cards bearing the likenesses of ballplayers as premiums to be given away with their products. These tiny cardboard icons would serve to boost tobacco sales, promote interest in baseball and give birth to a hobby whose present-day popularity is at an all-time high. Obviously the collectors of these earliest versions of today's bubblegum cards were for the most part drawn from an adult male population who used tobacco products. Some of these colorful forerunners of the modern-day baseball card are here illustrated (**OPPOSITE TOP** and **CENTER**) from the popular T205 Gold Border set issued in 1911 and containing such pre-World-War-One heroes as John McGraw, Christy Mathewson and the Cubs' famed keystone trio of Tinkers, Evers and Chance (**OPPOSITE TOP**). Originals of these cards are now traded at a market value of about $30 apiece, just about the same price as a complete set of newly issued big-league bubblegum cards (**OPPOSITE BOTTOM**). Tobacco and bubblegum cards are the favorites of the modern baseball collector, though lively interest now exists in all manner of antiques featuring images of the national game, including old sheet music covers (**BOTTOM RIGHT**), old-style press pins and rooters' badges (**ABOVE**) and early film strips with baseball motifs as well (**TOP RIGHT**).

BOSTON RED SOX
TED WILLIAMS
U.S. BASEBALL SERIES I
30¢
GRENADA
Mets
DARRYL STRAWBERRY
U.S. BASEBALL SERIES I
30¢
GRENADA
Atlanta Braves
DALE MURPHY
U.S. BASEBALL SERIES I
30¢
GRENADA
DETROIT Tigers
JACK MORRIS
U.S. BASEBALL SERIES I
Dodgers
FERNANDO VALENZUELA
U.S. BASEBALL SERIES
OAKLAND ATHLETICS
LEFTY GROVE
U.S. BASEBALL SERIES I
CHICAGO CUBS
ERNIE BANKS
U.S. BASEBALL SERIES I
30¢
GRENADA
SINCE 1876 NATIONAL LEAGUE OF PROFESSIONAL BASEBALL CLUBS
U.S. BASEBALL SERIES I
30¢
GRENADA
CLEVELAND INDIANS
JULIO FRANCO
U.S. BASEBALL SERIES I
30¢
GRENADA
JUNE 11, 1989
BRONX, NY 10451
LOU GEHRIG STAMP
SECOND DAY OF ISSUE
Lou Gehrig
USA 25

For the serious collectors of baseball memorabilia the present marketplace provides a cornucopia of treasures, some of the strangest of which are illustrated here. Stamp collectors can delight in the recent issues of a full set of baseball postage stamps by the island nation of Grenada, featuring past and present heroes of the American national game (**OPPOSITE TOP** and **CENTER**). Another delight of stamp collectors and baseball enthusiasts are "first day covers" and special cancellations. An example in this June 1989 Lou Gehrig U.S. postage stamp, here attached to a picture postcard of Yankee Stadium (**OPPOSITE BOTTOM**). Less popular and less abundant, yet with their appeal for collectors of the arcane, are baseball cartoons, such as these 1882 lithographs (**RIGHT**) and this 1890 magazine cartoon strip illustrating positions and actions of the national game (**ABOVE**).

Down through the decades of the past and present century, as the previous pages have no doubt illustrated, the American game of baseball has remained an endless source of excitement, folklore and pure entertainment for millions of fans who have spent countless hours of joyous rooting in big league ballparks. It is for just such fans as these that this book has been compiled – no matter what teams they follow or which stars hold their special loyalties. Like the young 1942 World Series rooters found on the following page, we all maintain that special place in our hearts for the ballpark. Like them, we really mean it when we sing that sweet refrain, "I don't care if I never get back!"

RED SOX NATION

Boston Red Sox rooters spread across the six New England states boast a reputation—alongside diehard Chicago Cubs and Detroit Tigers boosters—for relentless devotion to clubs more often colorful than potent. But the 2000s brought championship glories and a new phenomenon known as Red Sox Nation.

Take Me Out to the Ballgame

It may seem like pure provincialism in other quarters, but Boston fans of the 21st century have become a truly passionate fraternity distinguished by their zealous devotions to their beloved two-time world champions. October 2004 marked the first Red Sox World Series title since 1918, an 86-year span of futility highlighted by memorable last-minute collapses in both the 1946 and 1986 fall classics. And the Bosox won in grand style, cruising past the Cardinals in only the 18th sweep in World Series history—this after posting a miraculous comeback from a 3-0 deficit in the American League Championship Series with the hated-rival Yankees. Boston's long-awaited breakthrough also saw them become the first team in MLB history to win eight straight in the same post-season, and also the fourth team never to trail in a World Series match-up. Big guns of 2004 were Series MVP Manny Ramirez, slugger David Ortiz (**ABOVE**), and veteran hurler Curt Schilling (**RIGHT**). Schilling provided special television drama when he hurled six innings of Game Two on a sutured right ankle, his bloodied stocking the focus of numerous camera close-ups throughout the contest. And Boston's storybook rise to the top of the baseball world proved to be no passing fluke, with the Bosox—paced by MVP Mike Lowell (**BOTTOM RIGHT**)—returning to center stage three seasons later for another near-effortless sweep of the NL-champ Colorado Rockies during the 2007 Series. A second fall classic sweep underscored the Red Sox Nation's boasts that their ball club was indeed "America's Team" of a dawning new baseball century.

WORLD BASEBALL CLASSIC

Baseball's acknowledged international appeal was never more visible than with the MLB-sponsored World Baseball Classic, staged in San Juan and Tokyo as well as on American soil. When the dust settled in the March 2006 showcase, favored Team USA sat on the sidelines while the sport's other two acknowledged hotbeds—Cuba and Japan—battled for the title of true "world's champion."

Take Me Out to the Ballgame

For half a century Cuba has dominated such international venues as Olympic competitions and the IBAF amateur world series. In 49 major international-level tournaments since 1959, Cuba has either won or at least reached the finals in every single event. Skeptics have questioned the legitimacy of this dominance by reminding that these victories were earned against amateurs and collegians and not versus top American pros or big league stars. The first World Baseball Classic, however, was enough to erase any doubts, as the talented Cuban League all-stars—without a single big leaguer on their roster—swept aside Dominican, Venezuelan, and Puerto Rican professionals to square off in the title match with another set of outsiders representing the Japanese professional league. It was the clearest signal possible that the era of baseball as a world sport had truly arrived, and that the American big league version was no longer the only game in town.

A single big leaguer—Ichiro Suzuki, hoisting the trophy (**OPPOSITE TOP**)—took the field when Japan edged Cuba 10-6 at the showcase finale in San Diego's PETCO Park. Japan showed early and late offense from stars like Tsuyoshi Nishioka (**OPPOSITE LEFT**). A wild victory party saw legendary manager Sadaharu Oh hoisted skyward by his triumphant ball club (**OPPOSITE RIGHT**). Yet the most exciting WBC venue was a play-down round in San Juan, billed as a long awaited "true Caribbean series" between skilled Latino big leaguers. Cuba celebrated surprise triumphs over both Venezuela and Puerto Rico (**RIGHT**) before advancing to upset the Dominicans (**ABOVE**) in the hard-fought San Diego semifinals.

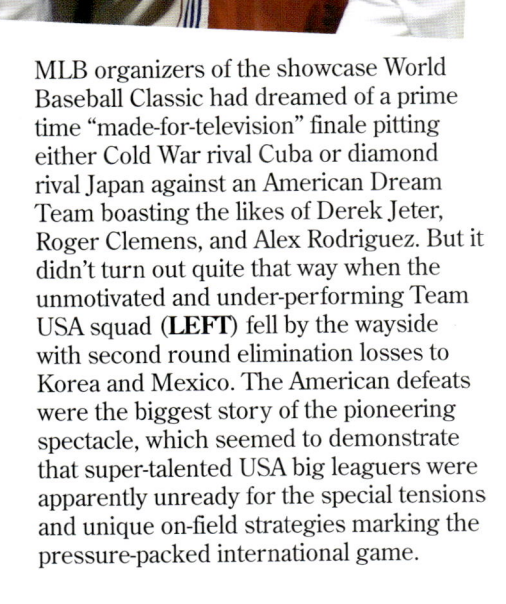

MLB organizers of the showcase World Baseball Classic had dreamed of a prime time "made-for-television" finale pitting either Cold War rival Cuba or diamond rival Japan against an American Dream Team boasting the likes of Derek Jeter, Roger Clemens, and Alex Rodriguez. But it didn't turn out quite that way when the unmotivated and under-performing Team USA squad (**LEFT**) fell by the wayside with second round elimination losses to Korea and Mexico. The American defeats were the biggest story of the pioneering spectacle, which seemed to demonstrate that super-talented USA big leaguers were apparently unready for the special tensions and unique on-field strategies marking the pressure-packed international game.

320 THE BASEBALL SCRAPBOOK

INDEX

Aaron, Henry 13, 17, *17*, 74, 137, 139, 258, 297
Abbott, Jim 307 *307*
Adams, Franklin P 114, 115
Adcock, Joe 258
Alexander, Grover 8, 248
Alexander, 'Pete' 124, 130
Ali, Muhammad 40
All Star Games 2, 4, 60, 79, 89, 103, 105, 118, 122, 127, 166, 228, 240, 265, *265*
Allen, Mel 41, 197
Alomar, Roberto 202
Alomar, Sandy 194, 202
Alomar, Sandy Jr. 202
Alou, Felipe 194, 195, 199, *199*
Alou, Jesus 194, 195, 199, *199*
Alou, Matty 194, 195, 199, *199*
Alston, Walter 56, 214, 215, 216
American League 255; 50th anniversary 127
Amoros, Sandy 256, 275
Anaheim Stadium 292, *292*
Anderson, Sparky 11, 20
Anson, 'Cap' 133, 136, *136*
Aparicio, Louis 134, 249, 302
Arizona Diamondbacks 205
Armbrister, Ed 278
Arroyo, Rolando 310, 311
Atlanta Braves 53, 161, 216

Baker, Frank 12
Baltimore Orioles 79, 103, 166, 173, 184, 185, 189, 213, 215, 261, 276, 310-11
Bankhead, Dan 184
Banks, Ben 201, *201*
Banks, Ernie 18, 19, *19*, 107, 127, 139, *139*, 225
Barber, Red 222, 223
Barrow, Ed 220, 221
baserunning 143, 177-78, 181; classic bungle 9; records 31, 75, 295. See also slides; squeeze play
baseball: attendance 7, 239, 293; centennial 248; collectibles see memorabilia below; comparison with other sports 124; dead balls versus lively 141 (see also strategy); expansion teams 60, 255, 289, 292; greatest moments 11, 253-68; history/lore 7; innovations 221, 223, 228; media coverage 41, 49, 50, 101, 115, 222, 223, *223*, 225, 235; memorabilia 5, 312-15, *312-15*; as national pastime 7; night games 232, 233; origins 250; publicity/promotion 2, 4, 300-02, *300*, *301*, *302*, 303; rules 177; as spectator sport 124-25, 195; stadiums 227-28, 230, 233, 235, 292 and Opening Day ceremonies 227 (see also individual ballparks); statistics 7; strategy 142, 145, 173, 213

(defensive 159, 166) (offensive 148); team dynasties 11, 77; victory celebrations 282, 283-84, *283*, *284*. See also equipment; fans; managers; owners; players
batters 38-9, 94, 141, 143, 145, 147; base hits, record 135, 136-37, 143, 221; lefthanded 79, 145; records 74, 92, 121, 250; style 37, 41, 97, 147; switch hitters 63; title holders 29, 30, 31, 47, 50, 63, 89, 105, 122, 199
batting averages: records 21, 31, 55, 63, 79, 118, 136, 173, 209; career 89, 108, 109, 199, 213
Bauer, Hank 63
Baylor, Don 147
Bell, Buddy 194
Bell, Gary 194
Bell, James 295, *295*
Bench, Johnny 11, 20, 21, *21*, 74
Bender, Chief 151
Bernardino, John 303
Berra, Dale 194
Berra, Yogi 11, 63, 149, 186, *186*
Bevans, Floyd 256, 272
Black, Joe 296
'Black Sox' See Chicago White Sox
Blackman, Cornelius 243
Blair, Paul 177
Blyleven, Burt 154, 155
Boggs, Wade 137, 143
Bonds, Barry 22, *22*, 23, *23*, 142-43, 194
Bonds, Bobby 23, *23*, *138*, 139, 194
Boone, Bob 194
Boone, Ray 194
Bordagary, Stanley 169
Boston Braves 9, 177, 201, 209, 213; relocation 255
Boston Red Sox 3, 9, 35, 46, 76, 77, 94, 108, 109, 118, 121, 133, 164, 166, 216, 219, 270, 271, 275, 280, 284, 297; and World Series 'curses' 271, 280
Boudreau, Lou 42
Bouton, Jim 7
Boyd, Oil Can 3
Boyer, Clete 175
Boyer, Ken 194
Boys of Summer See Brooklyn Dodgers
Brandt, Jackie 304, 305
Brantley, Jeff 180
Brecheen, Harry 271
Brock, Lou 53, *137*, 173, *173*
Brocklander, Fred 206
Brooklyn Dodgers 9, 11, 13, 14-15, 27, 45, 89, 110, *110*, 113, 149, 175, 182, 183, 187, 215, 219, 272, 274, 282; as 'daffiness boys' 9, 235; and integration 296; multiple pennants 275; relocation 289

Brown, Bobby 272
Brown, Jim 124
Buckeye, Garland 307
Buckner, Bill 271, 280
Bunning, Jim 157
bunting 148-49, 175
Burkett, Jesse 173
Burrus, Dick 177
Butler, Dick 269

Cain, Bob 300
California Angels 55, 101, 166
Camden Yards 103, 231, 311
Campanella, Roy 26, 27, *27*, 149, 175, 249, 274, 297
Candlestick Park (San Francisco) 268
Cannon, Jimmy 126
Caray, Harry 225
Carew, Rod 137, 203
Caribbean leagues 28, 311
Carlton, Steve 24, *24*, 25, 131
Carrigan, Bill 209, 210-11
Carter, Joe 53, 285
Casanova, Paul 260
Casey, Hugh 272
Castro, Daniel 311
Castro, Fidel 310, 311, *311*
catchers 20-1, 27, 151, 160, 177, 199, 278, 295; awards 27; equipment 192
Cedeno, Andujar 194
Cedeno, Cesar 194
centerfielders 63, 73, 109, 136
Chambliss, Chris 267
Chance, Frank 115, *115*, 312
Chandler, 'Happy' 119
Chapman, Ray 158, 159
Charboneau, Joe 45
Chase, Hal 71
Chicago Cubs 9, 11, 17, 53, 69, 77, 107, 115, 163, 182, 209, 213, 233, 250, 282
Chicago White Sox 9, 10, 11, 43, 107, 159, 164, 228, 302, *302*; and 'Black Sox' scandal 250-51, 286-87, *287*
Cicotte, Ed 160, 161
Cincinnati Reds 8, 11, *11*, 20, 21, 45, 62, 71, 209, 250, 262
'circus' catches 162, 163, *163*, 165-66
Clark, Will 181
Clarke, Fred 176
Clemens, Roger 3, 34, 35, *35*, 127, 132, 134, 280
Clemente, Roberto 28, 29, *29*, 107, 137, *137*, 194, 277
Cleveland Indians 43, 109, 179, 254, 307
coaches 23, 108, 160, 206, 213, 302, 303
Cobb, Ty 30, 31, *31*, 33, 90, 109, 136, 172, *172*, 196, 197
Cochrane, Mickey 176, 183, *183*
Colavito, Rocky 50
Coleman, Joe 194
Coleman, Ray 178
Collins, Eddie 133, 136, 248, 270

Collins, Joe 11, 170, 183
Colorado Rockies 205
Comiskey Park (Chicago) 178, 228, *228*, 233, 250, 265, 302
Conigliaro, Billy 201, *201*
Conigliaro, Tony 201, *201*
Cooper, Mort 200, 201
Cooper, Sam 200, 201
Cooper, Walker 200, 201
Cooperstown 248, *248*. See also Hall of Fame
Craig, Roger 186
Crandall, Del 293
Crawford, Sam 141
Cronin, Joe 116, 117, 127, 214
Crosley Field 62
Cuban National Team 310-11
Cuellar, Mike 81, 133, 134
curveballs 154-55
Cy Young Award 35, 53, 57, 81, 130, 133, 134

Davis, Mark 135
D C Stadium (Washington, D.C.) 117, 240, 260
Dean, Dizzy 9, 12, 170, 199, 304, 305
Dean, Paul 'Daffy' 12, 199, 201
Delahanty brothers 194
Dent, Bucky 267, *267*
Detroit Tigers 81, 157, 183, 213
Dickey, Bill 23
DiMaggio, Dom 199, *199*
DiMaggio, Joe 36, 37, *37*, 38-9, 40, 41, *41*, 42, 63, 76, 77, 116, 118, 196, 197, 199, *199*, 265; hitting streak 250
DiMaggio, Vince 199, *199*, 201
Dodger Stadium (Los Angeles) 74, 75, 85, 244, 288
Doubleday, Abner 250
Doubleday Field 248
Doyle, Denny 271, 280
Dressen, Charlie 187, *187*
Drysdale, Don 159, 224, 249
Duenos, Yobal 311
dugout: view from 190, 191
Dunston, Shawon 180
Duren, Ryne 124
Durocher, Leo 12, 87, 170, 207, 214, 215, 272
Dykes, Jimmy 190

Earnshaw, George 8
Ebbets, Charles 218, 235
Ebbets Field (Brooklyn) 227, 234, 235, *235*
Ennis, Del 13
equipment 21, 31; bats 193; facemasks 192; gloves 192; pitching machine 192
ERA records 81, 134, 151, 154
Erskine, Carl 149, 234
Evers, John 114, 115, 312
Exhibition Stadium (Toronto) 147

fans 2, 9, 36, 65, 75, 117, 121, 122, 145, 162, 219, 221, 231,

Sylvester, Johnny 95
Taft, William Howard 240, *240*
Tebbets, George 183
televised games 223, 261, 278
Terry, Bill 79
Terry, Ralph 258
Texas Rangers 101
third basemen 79, 163, 166, 295
Tiger Stadium (Detroit) 230, *230*
Tinker, Joe 114, 115, 312
Thomas, Frank 186
Thomson, Bobby 11, 267; famous home run 8, 231, 253, *253*, 262
Thompson, Hank 297
Thorn, John 41
Tolan, Bobby 302
Toney, Fred 233
Toronto Blue Jays 35, 129, 145, 189, 285
Toronto Skydome 255, 285
Torre, Frank 194
Torre, Joe 216, 217
Trillo, Manny 181
Trucks, Virgil 129
Turner, Ted 219

Uecker, Bob 160
umpires 25, 79, 179, 206, 207, *207*, 256, 278

uniforms, for promotion 301

Valenzuela, Fernando 124, 152, 188
Vance, Dazzy 151, *151*
Vander Meer, Johnny 129
Vaughn, 'Hippo' 233
Veeck, Bill 300, 302, *302*
Viola, Frank 133

Wagner, Honus 79, 103, 124, 136, 141, 172, 173, 248
Waitkus, Eddie 251
walk records 87, 121
Walker, Dixie 146, 194
Walker, Harry 194, 271, *271*
Walker, Moses Fleetwood 250
Waner, Lloyd 198
Waner, Paul 136, 198
Wagner, Travis 198
Washington Senators 62, 117, 163, 209, 219, 260, 261
Weaver, Buck 251, 287
Weaver, Earl 215, *215*
Wertz, Vic 250, 254
Westrum, Wes 7
White, Frank 180
White, Roy 267
Whiz Kids See Philadelphia Phillies

Widmar, Al 303
Wilhelm, Hoyt 157, 161, *161*
Williams, Billy 163
Williams, Dick 24
Williams, Ted 37, 41, 47, 63, 116, 116, 117-18, *117*, *118*, 119, 121, 124, 139, *139*, 265, 298
Wills, Maury 172, 173
Wilson, Hack 67, 124, 140, 141
Wilson, Mookie 271, 280
Winfield, Dave 147
Woodling, Gene 47
World Baseball Classic 318, 319
World Series: *1903* 133, 253; *1914* 9; *1916* 113; *1919* 228; *1922* 240; *1926* 8; *1931* 8; *1937* 49, 239; *1939* 243; *1941* 245, 253; *1945* 233, 247; *1946* 271, 280; *1947* 5, 245, 272, 272; *1948* 43; *1949* 149, 174; *1950* 45; *1951* 254; *1952* 254; *1954* 109, 255; *1955* 275, 275, 278; *1956* 278; *1959* 164; *1960* 162; *1961* 239; *1962* 45, 45, 175; *1963* 56; *1964* 146; *1967* 85, 122, 280; *1968* 81; *1969* 9, 261, 261; *1970* 243, 262, 277; *1971* 276, 277, 278; *1973* 73; *1975* 20, 278, 280; *1976* 20; *1978* 165, 267; *1980* 105; *1983* 103; *1985* 180; *1986* 271, 280; *1989* 101; *1999* 35; and earthquake 268, 268; batters' records 63, 272, 277; blunders 280; consecutive winners 8; home run records 11, 258; managers' records 24, 77, 79; MVPs 127; no-hit games 256; players' rankings in 24; subway series 9, 272
Worthington, Craig 166
Wrigley Field (Chicago) 9, 18, 105, 107, 232, 233, *233*

Yankee Stadium 42, 50, 60, 77, 98-9, 110, 191, 197, 226, 238, 239, *239*, 314
Yastrzemski, Carl 120, 121, *121*, 137
Yawkey, Tom 270, 297
Yost, Eddie 163, *163*
Young, Babe 183
Young, Cy 50, 71, 117, 130, 133, 157, 197, 248
Yount, Robin 137

Zimmer, Don 186, 289

ACKNOWLEDGEMENTS

The author and publisher would like to thank the following individuals who helped in the preparation of this book: Rita Longabucco, picture editor; Don Longabucco, designer; John Kirk, Stan Schindler, editors; Cynthia Klein, indexer.

PHOTO CREDITS

All photographs courtesy of UPI/Bettmann Newsphotos except the following:

Agence France Presse/Corbis-Bettmann: 53 (top left), 68, 69 (top), 102 (bottom), 106 (both), 107 (middle).

ALLSPORT: 145 (bottom left); Glenn Cratty: 145 (right center); Jonathan Daniel: 145 (top right); Otto Greule: 142-43; Jim Gund: 145 (top left); Will Hart: 285 (top); Doug Pensinger: 103 (bottom); Janice Rettaliata: 231 (top); Rick Stewart: 285 (bottom left).

Peter C. Bjarkman: 319 (middle).

Courtesy, Boston Red Sox: 236 (top).

Brompton Photo Library: 54 (bottom), 225 (both), 228-29, 240-41 (top).

Corbis/AFP: 34, 35 (bottom).

Corbis/Bettmann-UPI: 69 (middle), 102 (top), 103 (top and middle), 107 (top).

Corbis/Reuters: 35 (middle), 53 (top right), 69 (bottom right).

Chevrolet Division, General Motors Corporation: 252.

Getty Images: 317 (bottom), 318 (bottom right).

Karl Merton Ferron, Baltimore Sun: 310 (bottom left).

Focus on Sports: 154 (top right), 276 (top), 280 (top).

Nanine Hartzenbusch, Baltimore Sun: 311 (bottom).

Nancy Hogue: 131 (bottom right).

Alfred Mainzer, Inc: 314 (bottom).

Major League Baseball: 1999: 23 (top); 2001 Jeff Carlick/MLB: 23 (middle); Jeff Carlick/MLB: 137 (2nd row, left); 1996 David L. Greene/MLB: 77 (bottom); 2002 Kee/MLB: 204 (bottom); 2002 Brad Mangin/MLB: 22 (inset); Rich Pilling/MLB: 137 (3rd row, far right, 4th row, far left); 1997 Rich Pilling/MLB: 205; 1998 Rich Pilling/MLB 138 (bottom); 1999 Rich Pilling/MLB: 137 (top right); 2001 Rich Pilling/MLB: 22, 77 (top right), 87 (top); 2002 Rich Pilling/MLB: 86 (top); 1997 John H. Reid III/MLB: 87 (bottom); 2000 Robert Rogers/MLB: 309 (bottom); 2001 Robbie Roger/MLB: 308 (top); 1999 Bob Rosato/MLB: 77 (top left); Don Smith/MLB: 23 (bottom); 2001 Ron Vesely/MLB: 204 (top); 2002 Michael Zagaris/MLB: 76; 2002 Michael Zagaris/MLB: 138 (top center).

MLB via Getty Images: 316, 317 (top, middle).

Ron Modra: 280 (bottom).

National Baseball Library, Cooperstown, NY: 2 (bottom left), 10 (top), 12 (bottom), 16, 26 (bottom right), 27 (right), 28 (top right), 30 (left), 30-31 (center), 32-33, 52, 61 (top left), 72 (bottom), 73 (bottom), 79 (top), 94 (left), 105 (top), 108 (top), 109 (top), 112 (bottom), 114, 115 (left), 126-27, 129 (top, bottom), 134 (top, bottom), 140 (top right), 141 (bottom), 145 (center left), 148, 158, 159 (top), 168 (top), 170-71, 172 (top left), 176 (both), 196 (top), 198 (both), 200 (top right), 206 (bottom left), 208 (bottom left, bottom right), 212, 214 (top), 222 (both), 227 (top), 232 (top), 240 (top left, bottom), 248 (top), 253 (center), 266, 286 (top left, bottom left), 294 (top right, bottom right), 295 (bottom), 313 (top left, bottom right).

Courtesy, Glenn Peterson: 137 (1st row: center; 2nd row: center, right; 3rd row: left, left center).

Ponzini Photography: 2 (top, left center), 232 (bottom left).

Renata Galasso, Inc: 138 (left center).

John W. Ripley: 313 (top right).

Bruce Schwartzman: 128, 132 (both), 133 (center), 135 (bottom left, bottom right), 145 (bottom right), 228 (bottom left), 306 (bottom left), 312 (bottom).

Southern Stock: Jay Spencer: 184 (top), 185, 189 (top).

Ian Steer: 291 (left).

Gene Sweeney, Jr., Baltimore Sun: 310 (top left).

TOPPS Chewing Gum, Inc: 137 (2nd row: right).

Transcendental Graphics: 308 (bottom), 309 (top left and right), 309 (center).

Transcendental Graphics/Mark Rucker: 310 (top right and bottom right), 311 (top and inset).

UPI/Corbis-Bettmann: 35 (top), 53 (bottom), 69 (bottom left), 107 (bottom).

WireImage: 318 (top, bottom left), 319 (top, bottom).